Teach

Developing as a Reflective
Secondary Teacher

Reflective Teaching and Learning: A guide to professional issues for beginning secondary teachers

Edited by Sue Dymoke and Jennifer Harrison

Reflective practice is at the heart of effective teaching. This core text is an introduction for beginning secondary teachers on developing the art of critical reflective teaching throughout their professional work. Designed as a flexible resource, the book combines theoretical background with practical reflective activities.

Developing as a Reflective Secondary Teacher Series

These subject-specific core texts are for beginning secondary teachers following PGCE, GTP or undergraduate routes into teaching. Each book provides a comprehensive guide to beginning subject teachers, offering practical guidance to support students through their training and beyond. Most importantly, the books are designed to help students develop a more reflective and critical approach to their own practice. Key features of the series are:

- observed lessons, providing both worked examples of good practice and commentaries by the teachers themselves and other observers
- an introduction to national subject frameworks including a critical examination of the role and status of each subject
- support for beginning teachers on all aspects of subject teaching, including planning, assessment, classroom management, differentiation and teaching strategies
- a trainee-focused approach to critical and analytical reflection on practice
- a research-based section demonstrating M-level work
- a comprehensive companion website linking all subjects, featuring video clips of sample lessons, a range of support material and weblinks.

Teaching Mathematics
Paul Chambers

Teaching History
Ian Phillips

Forthcoming:
Teaching Science
Tony Liversidge, Matt Cochrane, Bernie Kerfoot and Judith Thomas

Teaching ICT
Carl Simmons and Claire Hawkins

Teaching English
Alyson Midgley, Peter Woolnough, Lynne Warham and Phil Rigby

Teaching Mathematics

Developing as a Reflective Secondary Teacher

Paul Chambers

Los Angeles | London | New Delhi
Singapore | Washington DC

First published 2008
Reprinted 2009

SAGE Publications Ltd
1 Oliver's Yard
55 City Road
London EC1Y 1SP

SAGE Publications Inc.
2455 Teller Road
Thousand Oaks, California 91320

SAGE Publications India Pvt Ltd
B 1/I 1 Mohan Cooperative Industrial Area
Mathura Road
New Delhi 110 044

SAGE Publications Asia-Pacific Pte Ltd
33 Pekin Street #02-01
Far East Square
Singapore 048763

Library of Congress Control Number: 2007943495

British Library Cataloguing in Publication data

A catalogue record for this book is available from The
British Library

ISBN 978-1-4129-4792-3
ISBN 978-1-4129-4793-0 (pbk)

Typeset by C&M Digitals (P) Ltd, Chennai, India
Printed in Great Britain by Ashford Colour Press Ltd, Gosport, Hampshire
Printed on paper from sustainable resources

CONTENTS

ACKNOWLEDGEMENTS

I wish to thank particularly Gaynor Edwards and Alison McDonald, without whom the book could not have taken its current form. They gave their time to provide me with invaluable video footage and interview material. Both are inspirational teachers. Many thanks also to the many mentors that I have worked with over recent years, whose views and practices I have incorporated into the text as illustrations.

Several people have provided help and advice on individual chapters, and I offer my thanks to colleagues Margaret Chambers, Carol Evans, Gordon Laing and Charles Rawding. Their feedback has been invaluable. Thanks also to mathematics colleagues Steve Feller, Don Pitchers and Julia Phillmore for their support and encouragement. I am indebted to Margaret Wood for her transcription skills, and to Joe Binks for his technical expertise.

Writing this book has enabled me to sum up into one place much of the work that I have done with Postgraduate Certificate of Education (PGCE) and undergraduate students at Edge Hill University over the past 16 years. I am grateful to all these students, who have helped in my own professional development in the role of teacher trainer. I am grateful particularly to recent students Andrew Chambers, Michelle Doyle, Waqas Javed, Ellie Lunney and Natalie Robinson for feedback and/or permission to use extracts from their plans and lesson evaluations.

HOW TO USE THIS BOOK

As you start your training to become a teacher, you will be faced with a bewildering array of information and requests for your personal details. A lot of the information will come from your training provider, and will give details about the course that you are starting. Your personal details will be required in order to compile a CV that can be sent out to your placement schools; they will also be needed so that you can receive clearance from the Criminal Records Bureau (CRB) to work with children. Very early on, you will learn that your success on the training course depends on your ability to demonstrate competence in the Professional Standards for Qualified Teacher Status (QTS) that are laid down by the Training and Development Agency for Schools (TDA).

This book is designed to help you to make a success of your training course. It shows you how to plan lessons, how to make good use of resources and how to assess pupils' progress effectively. But its main aim is to help you learn how to improve your classroom performance. In order to improve, you need to have skills of analysis and self-evaluation, and you need to know what you are try-ing to achieve and why. You also need examples of how experienced teachers deliver successful lessons, and how even the best teachers continually strive to become even better.

The book has a practical focus. It will help you to feel more comfortable about what is expected from you on teaching practice, through demonstrating good practice in mathematics teaching, but also through putting that good practice into a whole-school and a national context. You will, for example, find sugges-tions about how mathematics lessons can contribute to whole-school initiatives such as developing pupils' thinking skills. You will also find examples of how mathematics teachers can contribute to the national Every Child Matters agenda.

A key feature of this book is the accompanying website www.sagepub.co.uk/secondary. The website contains simple links to all of the websites featured in the various chapters, together with additional links to sites that provide use-ful support to trainee teachers of mathematics. The icon shown in the margin will appear throughout the text where additional material is available. The book makes extensive reference to a sample lesson of mathematics. A video file of this lesson appears on the website (divided into eight parts). As you read the book, you will be able to view (in 5-to-10 minute clips) how a successful teacher puts into practice keys aspects of planning, teaching and assessment. The video clips are in Windows media video file format (.wmv), and give the best quality visuals if viewed with Windows Media Player. (Players that support this file type are: Windows Media Player 7, Windows Media Player for Windows XP, Windows Media Player 9 Series, Windows Media Player 10 and Windows Media Player 11.)

Interviews with teachers have been transcribed to give examples of how individual teachers respond to particular issues, such as providing for a range of ability in the classroom. Of particular interest will be the section that deals with teachers' professional development. You will see how the reflective process is in evidence in guiding continuing professional development.

Although the focus throughout is on improving your professional skills, there is no attempt to provide a 'tick list' of how to achieve each of the individual Professional Standards for QTS. I believe that a more holistic approach is better suited to this type of publication. The book addresses professional attributes, professional knowledge and understanding, and professional skills in a more holistic way than they are presented in the Standards. You will, however, find frequent reference to the Standards, and it is hoped that through using the book reflectively, you will acquire the general skills required to gather and present your evidence against each of the Standards statements. A rough guide to where the book addresses individual Standards is given in the chart in Table H.1.

Table H.1   Professional Standards for Qualified Teacher Status

Professional attributes. Those recommended for the award of QTS should:

Standard	**Opportunities to learn more**
Relationships with children and young people	
Q1 Have high expectations of children and young people including a commitment to ensuring that they can achieve their full educational potential and to establishing fair, respectful, trusting, supportive and constructive relationships with them	*Chapter 1 – Professionalism*
Q2 Demonstrate the positive values, attitudes and behaviour they expect from children and young people	*Chapter 1 – Professionalism*
Frameworks	
Q3a Be aware of the professional duties of teachers and the statutory framework within which they work	*Chapter 1 – What is mathematics?* *Chapter 2 – The development of the National curriculum: Progression in mathematics*

(Continued)

(Continued)

	Standard	Opportunities to learn more
Q3b	Be aware of the policies and practices of the workplace and share in collective responsibility for their implementation	*Chapter 1 – Professionalism*
Communicating and working with others		
Q4	Communicate effectively with children, young people, colleagues, parents and carers	*Chapter 6 – Questioning; Record-keeping; Report writing*
Q5	Recognize and respect the contribution that colleagues, parents and carers can make to the development and well-being of children and young people and to raising their levels of attainment	*Not directly addressed*
Q6	Have a commitment to collaboration and co-operative working	*Chapter 1 – Professionalism*
Personal professional development		
Q7a	Reflect on and improve their practice, and take responsibility for identifying and meeting their developing professional needs	*Chapter 10 – Evaluating lessons on teaching practice; professional development within school; career entry and development profile*
Q7b	Identify priorities for their early professional development in the context of induction	*Chapter 10 – Career entry and development profile; the induction year*
Q8	Have a creative and constructively critical approach towards innovation, being prepared to adapt their practice where benefits and improvements are identified	*Chapter 9 Chapter 10 – Evaluating lessons on teaching practice*
Q9	Act upon advice and feedback and be open to coaching and mentoring	*Chapter 10 – Evaluating lessons on teaching practice*

***Professional knowledge and understanding.* Those recommended for the award of QTS should:**

Teaching and learning

Q10	Have a knowledge and understanding of a range of teaching, learning and behaviour management strategies and know how to use and adapt them, including how to personalize learning and provide opportunities for all learners to achieve their potential	*Chapter 5 Chapter 7 Chapter 8*
Assessment and monitoring		
Q11	Know the assessment requirements and arrangements for the subjects/curriculum areas in the age ranges they are trained to teach, including those relating to public examinations and qualifications	*Chapter 6 – National Testing*

	Standard	Opportunities to learn more
Q12	Know a range of approaches to assessment, including the importance of formative assessment	*Chapter 6 – The purposes of assessment; The nature of assessment; Assessment for learning*
Q13	Know how to use local and national statistical information to evaluate the effectiveness of their teaching, to monitor the progress of those they teach and to raise levels of attainment	*Chapter 6 – Use of data*

Subjects and curriculum

Q14	Have a secure knowledge and understanding of their subjects/curriculum areas and related pedagogy to enable them to teach effectively across the age and ability range for which they are trained	*Chapter 2 – Proof in the school curriculum* *Chapter 5* *Chapter 8*
Q15	Know and understand the relevant statutory and non-statutory curricula, frameworks, including those provided through the National Strategies, for their subjects/curriculum areas, and other relevant initiatives applicable to the age and ability range for which they are trained	*Chapter 3* *Chapter 4*

Literacy, numeracy and ICT

Q16	Have passed the professional skills tests in numeracy, literacy and information and communication technology (ICT)	*Not addressed*
Q17	Know how to use skills in literacy, numeracy and ICT to support their teaching and wider professional activities	*Chapter 9*

Achievement and diversity

Q18	Understand how children and young people develop and that the progress and well-being of learners are affected by a range of developmental, social, religious, ethnic, cultural and linguistic influences	*Chapter 7 – Inclusion*
Q19	Know how to make effective personalized provision for those they teach, including those for whom English is an additional language or who have special educational needs or disabilities, and how to take practical account of diversity and promote equality and inclusion in their teaching	*Chapter 7 – Inclusion; Gender; ethnicity; special needs; Gifted and very able pupils; Teaching pupils for whom English is an additional language; evidence from the research*

(Continued)

(Continued)

	Standard	Opportunities to learn more
Q20	Know and understand the roles of colleagues with specific responsibilities, including those with responsibility for learners with special educational needs and disabilities and other individual learning needs	*Chapter 7 – Special needs; Gifted and very able pupils*

Health and well-being

Q21a	Be aware of current legal requirements, national policies and guidance on the safeguarding and promotion of the well-being of children and young people	*Chapter 2 – Staying safe; Being healthy; Safeguarding children*
Q21b	Know how to identify and support children and young people whose progress, development or well-being is affected by changes or difficulties in their personal circumstances, and when to refer them to colleagues for specialist support	*Chapter 2 – Safeguarding children*

Professional skills. Those recommended for the award of QTS should:

Planning

Q22	Plan for progression across the age and ability range for which they are trained, designing effective learning sequences within lessons and across series of lessons and demonstrating secure subject/curriculum knowledge	*Chapter 2 – Progression in mathematics* *Chapter 3*
Q23	Design opportunities for learners to develop their literacy, numeracy and ICT skills	*Chapter 3 – Long term planning*
Q24	Plan homework or other out-of-class work to sustain learners' progress and to extend and consolidate their learning	*Chapter 3 – Homework*

Teaching

Teach lessons and sequences of lessons across the age and ability range for which they are trained in which they:

Q25a	Use a range of teaching strategies and resources, including e-learning, taking practical account of diversity and promoting equality and inclusion	*Chapter 7*
Q25b	Build on prior knowledge, develop concepts and processes, enable learners to apply new knowledge, understanding and skills and meet learning objectives	*Chapter 8*

	Standard	**Opportunities to learn more**
Q25c	Adapt their language to suit the learners they teach, introducing new ideas and concepts clearly, and using explanations, questions, discussions and plenaries effectively	*Chapter 4*
Q25d	Manage the learning of individuals, groups and whole classes, modifying their teaching to suit the stage of the lesson	*Chapter 4*
Assessing, monitoring and giving feedback		
Q26a	Make effective use of a range of assessment, monitoring and recording strategies	*Chapter 6*
Q26b	Assess the learning needs of those they teach in order to set challenging learning objectives	*Chapter 6*
Q27	Provide timely, accurate and constructive feedback on learners' attainment, progress and areas for development	*Chapter 6 – Assessment for learning; report writing*
Q28	Support and guide learners to reflect on their learning, identify the progress they have made and identify their emerging learning needs	*Chapter 6 – Assessment for learning; report writing*
Reviewing teaching and learning		
Q29	Evaluate the impact of their teaching on the progress of all learners, and modify their planning and classroom practice where necessary	*Chapter 10 – Evaluating lessons on teaching practice; evaluating lessons later in your career*
Learning environment		
Q30	Establish a purposeful and safe learning environment conducive to learning and identify opportunities for learners to learn in out of school contexts	*Chapter 2 – Staying safe; Safeguarding Children*
Q31	Establish a clear framework for classroom discipline to manage learners' behaviour constructively and promote their self-control and independence	*Not directly addressed*
Team-Working and collaboration		
Q32	Work as a team member and identify opportunities for working with colleagues, sharing the development of effective practice with them	*Chapter 7 – Special educational needs* *Chapter 10 – Professional development within the school*
Q33	Ensure that colleagues working with them are appropriately involved in supporting learning and understand the roles they are expected to fulfil	*Chapter 3* *Chapter 7 – special educational needs*

As the title of the series suggests, this book aims to help you to develop into a reflective practitioner. Each chapter contains several points for reflection. These encourage you to break off from your reading and consider the issue being discussed. Sometimes you are asked to compare the information in the text with your own experience; sometimes you are asked to complete a small task. It is hoped that you will not be in a hurry to read through the whole book; take your time, reflect on the issues presented and, if possible, discuss the issues with other trainees.

The main focus of the book is on practical advice, but there is another area of your course where I hope that you will find the book useful. If you are undertaking an award-bearing course (for example, leading to a PGCE or a degree with QTS), then you will have to do some assignments. Your assignments will need you to read about research in mathematics education, so that you can argue your point of view. This book aims to provide you with some of that evidence, together with some pointers to where to look for more.

1

WHO ARE MATHEMATICS TEACHERS? WHAT IS MATHEMATICS TEACHING?

This chapter:

- examines the typical motivations and anxieties of mathematics trainee teachers as they begin training
- summarizes the professional demands of training
- discusses different perceptions of the nature of mathematics; whether it is primarily a subject that is interesting in its own right, or whether it is primarily a tool for solving problems
- considers why people think that mathematics is important
- examines the extent to which mathematics is a human construct.

YOUR EARLY DAYS AS A STUDENT TEACHER

Training to be a teacher is a challenging and demanding task, but one that provides enormous rewards. One of the biggest rewards is that moment when a pupil's eyes light up with a sense of understanding, and you know that a small piece of learning is down to you. During your training, you will feel the satisfaction of knowing that your professional skills are developing, and will have the opportunity to work alongside teams of dedicated staff, whose energy you will come to admire.

It is common for people embarking on a teacher-training course to have a number of anxieties. One of these anxieties often concerns subject knowledge. Many people starting training have come straight from university, and many come after a break from study of several years. Whichever background you have, you are likely to be 'rusty' on some elements of school mathematics, either because of the passage of time, or because the mathematical topics you studied at university were very abstract or specialized and did not require the use of topics from school curriculum.

On your first day on the course, you will be relieved to find others like you: maybe other mature students, others whose first degree is not mathematics or others who may never have studied any mechanics. People come from a wide range of backgrounds wanting to become mathematics teachers.

During these early days, you may have some other anxieties: whether you will be able to control the class; whether you will cope with the workload; a worry that you will be placed in a difficult school. Such worries are common, but they can be answered:

- You will get lots of support from other teachers.
- You will not be given the worst class in the school.
- You will learn techniques of class management.
- Workload will be heavy, but it is manageable.
- Trainees who have been in 'difficult' schools are often very positive about their experiences afterwards.

It is important in the early days to get to know other students on the course; they will provide invaluable support as you progress through your training. Not only will they share with you their highs and lows, they will also be able to share ideas and resources that can save you time and effort.

As soon as the course begins, you will be asked to focus on the standards by which you will be judged during, and at the end of, your training. These standards are set nationally and are known as the Professional Standards for Qualified Teacher Status (TDA, 2007), a link to which can be found on the companion website: www.sagepub.co.uk/secondary. There are 33 numbered statements (although some are subdivided, so 40 statements is really a more accurate number) describing your competence as a teacher, and you will have to provide evidence that you meet each of them. A listing of the Standards is given in the 'How to use this book' section of this book, and a link to an electronic listing is provided on the website that accompanies the book. Your training course is designed to help you meet the standards.

One of the best ways to feel your way into the course is to develop your knowledge of the school mathematics curriculum. Whether directed to or not, it is helpful to get hold of a recent GCSE paper and to work through it. The best exercise is for you to work through it as part of a group, discussing the bits that you have forgotten and explaining to others the bits that you can remember. It will not take long for your confidence to return, but make sure you check that the answers that you think are right are indeed the correct ones! Sometimes your confidence may be misplaced, and it is better to discover and correct your own misunderstandings in supportive company than when you are in the classroom.

PROFESSIONALISM

Undertaking a teacher-training course is different from other university study. Because of the professional nature of the course, high standards of attendance, punctuality and commitment are expected, both in university and in schools. Remember that you are a guest in your teaching practice school; the school has volunteered to take a mathematics trainee, it is not obliged to take one.

When you go into school, you need to be aware of the behaviour and standards expected from teachers, and you should exhibit those standards from day one. Although you may not feel like a teacher on your first day, you need to behave like one; the pupils will observe the way that you are and will be forming impressions of you! In addition to the pupils, the teaching staff will be forming impressions of you and, obviously, it is important that you give the right message through the way you work and behave. Here are a few key pointers to acceptable behaviour in school:

- Arrive in plenty of time each morning; be punctual to lessons and meetings.
- Always let the school know if you are going to be absent.
- Treat all members of the school staff with respect. You need to demonstrate that you can work well with others.
- Dress smartly. (Play safe on day one, and after that take your cue from other members of the department.)
- Treat the pupils with respect. Show concern for their learning and welfare, but do not become over-friendly (especially when you are new to the school). Begin to build positive relationships, where pupils see you as someone to be trusted, someone who is fair and someone who can help them to achieve well.
- Set a good example to the pupils. This extends beyond your appearance and behaviour, and includes your values and attitudes; you should demonstrate positive attitudes and encourage the same in your pupils.
- Remain in school during the whole of the normal school day. In general, you should not leave the premises except at lunchtime.
- Use productively any non-contact time that you have. Do not be seen wasting time in the staff room; teachers are busy people, and they will expect to see you working as hard as they are.
- Give positive support to colleagues, especially within the classroom.
- Take care to learn the school rules. Once you are part of the school staff (even as a trainee) you join in the collective responsibility for the implementation of school policies. This professional responsibility supersedes your personal opinion, so you must promote, for example, policies on school uniform, even if you disagree with pupils having to wear a uniform.

You will be assigned a mentor within the mathematics department. Mentors are key people in your training; they provide support and advice, and they also make judgements on you. You need to demonstrate your professionalism to all staff, but particularly to your mentor, throughout your time in school. For example, you can show your commitment to team-working through offering any original work you have done to the rest of the department. (Departments often have facilities for electronic sharing of worksheets, presentations and links.)

 Above all, you need to be aware that during your time in schools, it is not only your skills as a teacher that are being assessed, but also your professional attributes. There are 11 statements in the Professional Standards for QTS that describe the expected professional attributes of a newly qualified teacher (TDA, 2007). Having positive attitudes yourself helps, but you need to go beyond this; you must make it clear to all (pupils, teachers and, on occasions, parents) in all that you say and do, that you have high expectations and are committed to helping pupils to achieve their very best.

MOTIVATIONS

The motivations for wanting to teach are many and varied. My own survey into the reasons for starting a PGCE mathematics course produced some interesting results, with the most common reasons given as:

- to pass on my enthusiasm for the subject
- to make a positive difference
- to do something worthwhile
- it is something that I expect to enjoy/find rewarding
  (Chambers, 2007).

Many respondents mention their enjoyment of doing mathematics. Sometimes they have a fascination for mathematics, and a curiosity that they wish to share with others; in other cases their love of mathematics is based on little more than a personal experience of success in the subject. Examples of trainees' motivations are given in the following quotes:

> I want to turn children on to mathematics, in the same way that I am.
>
> I had one particular mathematics teacher who I really admired, and she made all the difference to me. I would like to be that inspiring teacher to others.
>
> I love mathematics and yet it has such a negative image. I want to help change that image.
>
> I want to show children that mathematics is a fascinating subject.

Many people give their reason for wanting to teach as a desire to do something worthwhile, to feel that their efforts can make a difference to the lives of young people. Sometimes this follows many years spent working in industry, where the main motivation of the workforce is to make money. In comparison with this, teaching is seen as contributing to the common good and to the benefit of society.

Others mention their desire to work with young people. Many cite an experience that has helped confirm their decision. This experience may involve one or more of the following:

- helping out a friend or colleague with their mathematics
- coaching a child in school mathematics (possibly in preparation for an examination)
- working with youth groups (such as scouts, guides, church youth groups)
- observation of school mathematics lessons.

In practice, many training courses expect applicants to have spent some days in a secondary school, observing mathematics lessons. There is little doubt that this gives the best insight into whether mathematics teaching is something that will provide a suitable career.

One question in the survey concerned the trainees' major worries as they started the PGCE course in September. The most common anxiety is 'keeping control of my classes', which is understandable, particularly in view of press stories that tend to emphasize the sensational and the negative aspects of what goes on in schools. More surprisingly, the next biggest worry is coping with the anticipated workload during the training year. This scored considerably more highly than worries about the expected workload of being a teacher in the long term (although this was still the third most widespread anxiety).

Surprisingly, more than a third of the respondents are uncertain at the outset of the course whether teaching is the right career path for them. They start the course expecting to be successful, but they have a niggling worry about whether it is all going to work out. Smaller numbers of respondents mention anxieties about their own subject knowledge, difficult travel problems and whether the school staff would be welcoming.

Sadly, reactions from other people tend to be heavily dominated by negative attitudes to mathematics. When telling other people that they intend to train as a teacher of mathematics, the most common responses are:

- You must be mad.
- I could never do maths.
- You must be clever.
- I used to hate maths.

This gives some indication, if any more were needed, of the widespread fear and/or dislike of mathematics among the adult population.

Point for reflection

Consider your own motivations for wanting to become a mathematics teacher, and whether they fit in with the most common reasons given above. Try to list three things that you think you will enjoy about teaching. Are there any aspects that you think you might not enjoy?

As you talk to people from outside teaching during your training, note how many of them give a negative response to your intended career. Reflect on why they have the negative image that they have. Consider why so many adults feel comfortable with (even proud of) their limited ability in mathematics.

WHAT IS MATHEMATICS?

Anyone thinking of taking up the career of mathematics teacher needs, at some time, to consider this rather big question. In some ways, it is possible for specialist mathematicians in universities and schools to neglect it. Specialist mathematicians are often consumed by a knowledge of, and enthusiasm for, the subject. They take for granted that they understand what mathematics is, and that mathematics as a subject is a valuable area of study. At higher levels of mathematics, the study becomes so specialized that there is often no need for the bigger picture. Even within schools, there are teachers who have a thorough knowledge of the elements of the subject, but whose appreciation of the subject as a whole is weak.

Many people have tried to describe what mathematics is. Most definitions use words like logical ideas, interconnected ideas, relationships, patterns; some include other aspects such as communication, or particular sub-sections like the appreciation of number. Many discussions of the nature of mathematics make distinctions between mathematics as a subject to study in its own right and a subject that is useful. Ernest (1991) characterizes the distinction as deciding which is more important:

- understanding that $5 \times 23 = (4 \times 23) + (1 \times 23)$, or
- understanding that finding the cost of 5 apples at 23p each involves calculating 5×23, and knowing a way of doing it.

This distinction is typical of the different outlooks of pure mathematicians (purist views) and applied mathematicians or engineers (utilitarian views).

The views of the purists can be summarized in the following terms: mathematics is

- objective facts
- a study of reason and logic
- a system of rigour, purity and beauty
- free from societal influences
- self-contained
- interconnected structures.

From the point of view of the extreme purist, applied mathematics is looked down on as being based more on skills than understanding. Applications are inferior to the set of structures that make up pure mathematics, and whether or not a branch of mathematics is useful is an irrelevance. From this point of view, mathematics is a higher-level intellectual exercise, an art form and an example of the creativity of the human mind. Words like aesthetics and elegance are important to the purist (Scopes, 1973).

The description of mathematics as 'what mathematicians do' is sometimes used, but this seems to avoid giving a straight answer. Similarly, to describe the aim of performing mathematical investigations as a means 'to cultivate the art of doing mathematics' (Gardiner, 1987) seems to be insufficient justification. Smith (2004: 11) refers to the value of learning mathematics as being something that 'disciplines the mind, develops logical and critical reasoning, and develops analytical and problem solving skills to a high degree', which is a more helpful articulation of the purist standpoint. 'It must not be imagined', writes Bell (1953: 2), 'that the sole function of mathematics is to serve science … mathematics has a light and wisdom of its own, and it will richly reward any human being to catch a glimpse of what mathematics means to itself.' Similarly, Pedoe (1958: 9) refers to mathematics as not only being of interest to the science student; the subject is also of interest to those with arts backgrounds, and contains 'much which is beautiful and should interest everyone'.

The mathematics curriculum has tended to reflect the spirit of the times. The 1960s was a time of free expression, experimentation and challenges to authority, and it was purist views of mathematics that drove the curriculum changes that took place in UK mathematics classrooms in those years. Topics such as set theory, number bases and matrices were studied for the first time in the 11–16 curriculum. Transformation geometry replaced traditional Euclidean geometry, and there was more emphasis on probability and statistics. The philosophy behind these changes was that pupils needed the opportunity to see the rich structures in mathematics, whereas the existing curriculum had too much focus on routines and techniques. Many mathematics teachers embraced the changes with enthusiasm, but found it difficult to transfer this enthusiasm to parents, who regarded 'new maths' with suspicion.

In the 1980s, this view of mathematics gradually became replaced by a much more utilitarian view of the subject. The spirit of the times was much more geared towards economic success, and this was reflected in mathematics classrooms. Certainly by the end of the decade, education in general was being heavily influenced by the perceived needs of industry. Thus, applications became the most important part of mathematics, and it was from this point of view that the National Curriculum was first developed. In the utilitarian view of mathematics, learning how to do mathematics can become more important than understanding the underlying principles. Thus mathematics is characterized as

- a tool for solving problems
- the underpinning of scientific and technological study
- providing ways to model real situations.

By no means all the pressure for school mathematics to move away from its purist influences come from the political field. Many in the mathematical world share the view that mathematics should be presented as something that is useful, and this view was highly influential in the introductions of General Certificate of Secondary Education (GCSE) and the National Curriculum. Hence mathematics began to be taught more through applications and contextual situations with the aim of increasing pupil motivation through demonstrating relevance (for example, Burkhardt, 1981; Mason, et al., 1982). According to this view, mathematics is less about knowing and more about doing. There is an acceptance that pupils should study the pure mathematical skills, but it is the applications that bring the subject to life. This philosophy of teaching mathematics is backed up by pointing to the wide range of applications, 'the social sciences, biology and medicine, management, and, it seems, every field of human endeavour' where mathematics makes a contribution (Burghes and Wood, 1984).

The 2007 revision of the mathematics National Curriculum still promotes the idea that mathematics is, above all, useful. There is an acknowledgement that mathematics has developed as 'a means of solving problems and also for its own sake' (QCA, 2007: 139), but the importance of mathematics is affirmed mainly through its usefulness: in business and finance, science and engineering, and in public decision-making. Critics decry the current preference for usefulness, where if a mathematical topic is not used in everyday life, then it is omitted from the curriculum. Typical of this criticism is the view that modern curricula have 'replaced the joy of arithmetic with the utilitarianism of numeracy' (Lingard, 2000: 40). The Smith Report (Smith, 2004) opens with several paragraphs about the place of mathematics within the curriculum. But the spirit of the times is perhaps reflected in the fact that only the first paragraph is devoted to a discussion of mathematics for its own sake. There then follow seven further paragraphs devoted to the usefulness of mathematics in a variety of fields – for the knowledge economy, for science, technology and engineering, and for the workplace. Contrast this with the summary of definitions of mathematics given by Orton (1994: 11): 'an organised body of knowledge, an abstract system of ideas, a useful tool, a key to understanding the world, a way of thinking, a deductive system, an intellectual challenge, a language, the purest possible logic, an aesthetic experience, a creation of the human mind', where the utility of the subject is only a minor aspect.

Although the utilitarian view of mathematics has been the main influence on the curriculum in recent years, it is still widely acknowledged that mathematics should be presented as a subject in its own right, a subject that can inspire and challenge at all levels. Two of the quotes chosen to introduce the 1999 version of the mathematics National Curriculum make a clear effort to indicate that mathematics is both interesting in itself and useful in solving problems.

> Mathematics is the study of patterns abstracted from the world around us – so anything we learn in maths has literally thousands of applications, in arts, sciences, finance, health and leisure! (Ruth Lawrence, quoted in DfEE, 1999a: 15)

> Nobody has to worry that pure mathematics won't be used. Mathematics – even some of the most abstruse mathematics that we thought would never be used – is now used every time you use your credit card, every time you use your computer. (Andrew Wiles, quoted in DfEE, 1999a: 15)

In addition, it can be argued (for example, Wigner, 1967) that the very fact that mathematics is so useful in describing the physical world is itself bordering on the mysterious. If the whole universe is a mathematical structure, then we are likely to wonder why this is the case. Hence the usefulness of mathematics brings us back to a study of the nature of mathematics itself.

So mathematics is a study of patterns, relationships and rich interconnected ideas (the purist view). It is also a tool for solving problems in a wide range of contexts (the utilitarian view). There is a third common answer to the question of what mathematics is, which says that mathematics is a means of communication. Mathematical language is a wonderful way of communicating ideas, which works across international boundaries, and is not subject to individual interpretations of meaning. Adrian Smith describes mathematics as providing 'a powerful universal language and intellectual toolkit for abstraction, generalisation and synthesis' (Smith, 2004: 11). Using mathematics, we 'convey ideas to each other that words can't handle' (Alison Wolf, quoted in DfEE, 1999a: 15).

The 2007 National Curriculum makes explicit reference to teaching the ability to communicate findings effectively, as part of ensuring that pupils are able to use mathematics to describe (and hence analyse and change) the world (QCA, 2007).

Mathematics as a language has many facets. Within the English language, as in others, mathematics uses its own specialist vocabulary which helps to communicate specific ideas in a precise and unambiguous way. Developing this mathematical vocabulary is necessary if pupils are to have access to learning higher levels of mathematics, where specialists will routinely use this vocabulary. Another facet of mathematics as a language is algebra. This is a truly international language and is something that helps to bind the international mathematical community together. The use of Arabic letters for unknowns is universal, even where spoken languages use different scripts. Similarly, symbolic conventions like powers, roots, integrals, and so on, are recognized by the international community, so teaching mathematics helps pupils to have access to this rich body of internationally communicated ideas.

Another dimension to the debate about the nature of mathematics is the extent to which mathematics is a body of knowledge as opposed to a way of working. For example, in a book about mathematical investigations, Gardiner (1987) presents a series of problems that are not in themselves important, but 'what is important is the way the problems are studied'. Many in the mathematics education community agree with Gardiner that much teaching overemphasizes the content elements of the subject to the detriment of developing mathematical processes. They argue that it is more important to learn, for example, the skill of working systematically than the meaning of rotational symmetry. One is a mathematical fact; the other is a process that is useful in doing a range of mathematics.

WHY SHOULD MATHEMATICS BE TAUGHT?

All teachers are under pressure to produce good examination results, which can cause some to feel that a good set of results is the main purpose of their teaching. Although clearly this aspect of the job is high profile, it is important for you to consider the broader picture and examine why mathematics holds its position as part of the core curriculum.

If mathematics is mainly a tool for solving problems, then its reason for being in the curriculum is clear; it is so that pupils can acquire the skills they need to solve problems. If, on the other hand, mathematics is a fascinating body of knowledge or a means for appreciating patterns, then the reason for teaching it must be that it forms part of culture, and that an understanding of mathematics is required before anyone can be considered fully educated. This is clearly a more difficult idea to articulate, but is nevertheless a perfectly reasonable justification for teaching the subject.

The Mathematical Association identify a series of mathematical goals that define what mathematics teachers are trying to achieve.

The student should develop the ability to:

- Read and understand a piece of mathematics
- Communicate clearly and precisely using appropriate media
- Work clearly and logically using appropriate language and notation
- Use appropriate methods for manipulating numbers and symbols
- Operate with shapes both in reality and in the imagination
- Apply the sequence 'do, examine, predict, test, generalise, prove'
- Construct and test mathematical models of real life situations
- Analyse problems and select appropriate techniques for their solution
- Use mathematical skills in everyday life
- Use mechanical, technological and intellectual tools efficiently.
  (Mathematical Association, 1995: 8)

This list seems to include all the expected references to utilitarian aims, and makes clear reference to mathematical communication, but could be seen to under-represent the purist perspective. 'Work clearly and logically' is a mathematical skill concerned equally with thinking and with solving problems, and the concepts of generalizing and proving are key ideas from pure mathematics, but there is only one mention of the word 'understanding', and no explicit reference to appreciation of, or interest in, the subject.

The two bullet points on communication and the mathematical skills in everyday life are clearly important. On a basic level, mathematical language is part of everyday communication, and includes the huge number of graphic presentations used in the media to convey information. Hence it is important to teach mathematics so that pupils become informed citizens, who are able to understand information presented to them in a variety of graphical forms.

The importance of mathematics is stressed in the 2007 revision of the National Curriculum, which refers to mathematics as useful in the workplace and fundamental to national prosperity (QCA, 2007). But after a paragraph that is largely dominated by a utilitarian view of the subject, there is a short statement that mathematics is a creative discipline that 'can stimulate moments of pleasure and wonder for all pupils when they solve a problem for the first time, discover a more elegant solution, or notice hidden connections' (QCA, 2007: 139).

Teaching mathematics is sometimes justified by the argument that it trains the mind (for example, QMUL, 2007; Smith, 2004), and is thus an aid to learning in other disciplines. As a justification in itself, this seems to overstate the case, and we need evidence of exactly what this training of the mind really means. It is more commonly accepted that acquiring general thinking skills is a cross-curricular aim of education rather than a justification for teaching any one particular subject.

Finally, in this section, we should mention the more general humanistic justifications for teaching mathematics. A study of mathematics contributes to societal values, how people feel about themselves and their environment (Bishop, 1991). Mathematics can provide people with a feeling of control over their environment, and therefore it increases a sense of power through knowledge. We are able to control events because we feel that they are predictable. Second, the study of mathematics suggests that problems can be solved, if not in full then in part. Mathematics thus reinforces the view that advances in society are possible and that aspirations to a better way of life are realistic. Third, mathematics reinforces a belief in rationalism. Things can be explained through logical argument; we can convince others of the correctness of our thinking through reason. Put together, these three justifications mean that mathematics helps us to feel more comfortable about the world where we live.

Point for reflection

Examine your own background to learning mathematics. In a utilitarian age, it is easy to justify mathematics in terms of its usefulness, but as specialist mathematicians, we should consider that the subject stands strongly in its own right. How would you convince someone that school mathematics should be studied because it is a worthwhile area of study that is part of human culture?

NUMERACY AND MATHEMATICS

'Numeracy' is one of those words whose meaning seems to have changed in recent years. Formerly, it was used to represent that subset of mathematics involving numbers, particularly understanding what numbers mean, and being able to perform calculations.

It then started to be used as a shorthand for basic numeracy, understood as the sort of 'everyday' mathematics that all school leavers would need to cope with. This is the sense in which the word is used in the Cockcroft Report. In Cockcroft (1982), numeracy is being comfortable working with numbers, but also it is the set of mathematical skills used in daily life. This definition is itself open to interpretation, but most would concede that essential mathematics includes aspects of interpreting data, or using graphs, maps and scales that are not predominantly number work. It is in this sense that politicians and the media often use the word.

When, in 1996, the government set up a review into the teaching of mathematics in primary schools, the title chosen was the National Numeracy Project. Numeracy's connection with number work is retained in the working definition given by Askew et al. (1997), that numeracy is the ability to 'process, communicate, and interpret numerical information in a variety of contexts', but as the National Numeracy Project came to an end, its name was partly retained in the title of the *National Numeracy Strategy: Framework for Teaching Mathematics* (DfEE, 1999b). Hence in primary schools, the word 'numeracy' has become almost synonymous with the word 'mathematics'. Being numerate is understood as the ability to do mathematics (rather than any subset of mathematics).

There is some debate about whether there is still any useful distinction to be made in the use of the two words 'numeracy' and 'mathematics'. The discussion given by Tanner and Jones (2000) sees numeracy as a foundation for the whole of mathematics, rather than the whole thing. Numeracy involves 'an interaction between mathematical facts, mathematical processes, metacognitive self-knowledge, and affective aspects including self-confidence and the enjoyment *of number work*' (Tanner and Jones, 2000: 146 my italics). My own view is that numeracy is virtually synonymous with mathematics, but with two differences. The first distinction is that numeracy is a slightly more active word than mathematics. Numeracy is less likely to be understood as a body of knowledge, and is more associated with doing mathematics. The second distinction is that numeracy has an (undefined) upper limit. Higher levels of study will always be called mathematics; lower levels of study may be called mathematics or numeracy.

The lack of a short verb to describe being numerate has caused difficulties for those wanting a headline or soundbite. In 1997, the Department for Education and Employment described the main functions of education as ensuring that every child can read, write and add up (DfEE, 1997). Mathematical basics have here been reduced to the very basic! In another example, when an employers' leader criticized the levels of school leavers' English and mathematics, one newspaper headline read, 'Bosses say school leavers can't read write or count' (Stewart, 2005). The rest of the article makes no reference to the ability to count, but refers instead to mathematics and problem-solving skills. The work that goes on in mathematics classrooms is thoroughly trivialized by this soundbite usage, where an ability with basic mathematics is equated to the ability to add up or to count.

MATHEMATICS IN THE CURRICULUM

The main reason why mathematics retains its place in the curriculum is that it is seen as useful, even though an analysis of the curriculum shows that very little of the content is used by most people in a normal week. Unfortunately, the emphasis on usefulness has not transferred to outcomes; although pupils may be able to perform mathematical operations in schools, they are often unable to transfer these skills to other social contexts (Lave, 1988). This inability to apply mathematics lies at the heart of the argument for greater emphasis on functional mathematics for all.

Functional skills are seen as the core elements of English, mathematics and ICT that enable individuals to access further education, be effective in the workplace and confident in their everyday life. Ongoing reform of the 14–19 curriculum involves separating out 'functional mathematics', and building onto that the other aspects of the subject. Current plans are that functional mathematics will be taught in all qualification routes from September 2010.

Functional mathematics is more demanding than what in the past has been called basic skills or basic numeracy. To be successful in basic numeracy, candidates had to show that they could perform certain mathematical tasks that were seen as essential for everyday life, such as calculating percentages or interpreting graphs. Functional mathematics is concerned with those same skills, but also the ability to apply skills, to explain why and to justify conclusions. In other words, functional mathematics increases the importance of effectively communicating mathematical ideas. For example, tests of functional mathematics will examine candidates' ability to:

- use mathematics in different contexts
- draw conclusions and justify them
- interpret results and discuss their validity.

Under the reformed 14–19 curriculum, the study of functional mathematics to level 2 standard (the equivalent of a grade C or above at GCSE) becomes an entitlement (but not a requirement) for all post-16 students.

EVIDENCE FROM THE RESEARCH

The philosophy of mathematics is a rich area for discussion. We have discussed the nature of the subject in terms of the purist/utilitarian viewpoints already, but there is also considerable debate about the extent to which mathematics is a social activity.

Traditional philosophers of mathematics treat it as a subject that stands on its own. It needs no input from other disciplines; it remains constant over time, and it is not affected by social constructs in any way. 'A theorem is true regardless of whether it is proven by a human, a computer or an alien' (Tegmark, 2003: 13). Others (for example, Hersh, 1998) argue the contrary: that mathematics must be understood as a human activity that has evolved historically, and which takes place in a social and cultural context. Such writers contend that there is a human dimension to the way in which mathematicians work.

This is one of the key discussions of mathematical philosophy. One group believes that that mathematical truth is certain, that it is incontestable and entirely objective. For example, Kassem (2001: 72) reports 'a deep seated notion that the subject is value-free, independent of society and an exemplification of absolute truth'. This is known as the truth view of mathematics. Holders of this view are accused of an idealized view of the subject, ignoring how mathematics is, in favour of how it ought to be (Körner, 1960). The more commonly accepted view today is that mathematics is constructed; its truths are subject to argument, and may at any time in the future be challenged and revised. This is known as the constructivist view of mathematics.

All agree that all mathematical truths are proved from axioms, using the rules of inference. The constructivists argue that there is a fundamental fallacy in regarding mathematics as absolute truth. All mathematics uses deductive proof to demonstrate truths based on axiomatic starting points. But whatever axioms are chosen, they are simply chosen and not absolute. Examples of axioms may be that $1 + 1 = 2$, or that the number of natural numbers is infinite. These may be thought to be above question, but their existence weakens the absolute truth view of mathematics. Ernest (1991: 13) argues that 'deductive logic only transmits truth, it does not inject it, and the conclusion of a logical proof is at best as certain as its weakest premise'.

Lakatos (1978) demonstrates the weakness of seeking certainty in mathematics. Any mathematical system depends on a set of assumptions. In order to prove an assumption we need to make earlier assumptions, and so on. We can never be free of the assumptions. The role of the mathematician is to reduce the number of assumptions to the smallest number possible.

> Mathematical truth ultimately depends on an irreducible set of assumptions, which are adopted without demonstration. But to qualify as true knowledge, the assumptions require a warrant for their assertion. But there is no valid warrant for mathematical knowledge other than demonstration and proof. Therefore the assumptions are beliefs, not knowledge and remain open to challenge, and thus to doubt. (Ernest, 1991: 14)

There is one further weakness in the truth view of mathematics: just as axioms are stated without proof, so the rules of deductive logic are themselves unprovable. Thus the foundations of mathematics as an unquestionable truth are weakened further.

So if we reject the philosophy of mathematics as truth, it becomes necessary to articulate a philosophy that mathematical truths are open to argument and can be refined over time. According to Hersh (1979), mathematical philosophy should not be about seeking universal truth. It should seek to give an account of mathematical knowledge as it really is: fallible, evolving and as subject to argument as every other branch of knowledge.

As discussed earlier in the chapter, mathematics is more than a body of knowledge; it is also an activity of gaining knowledge and understanding. As soon as we embrace this change in viewpoint, then mathematics becomes a human activity. Older philosophers saw mathematics as separate from other fields of human learning, but once it is accepted that mathematics is not infallible, the subject becomes part of the broader human knowledge that includes the sciences. According to this perspective, mathematics is part of society and hence a product of the culture that produced it. The development of mathematics is then subject to societal influences; it has values and cultural influences.

Putting a greater emphasis on the social side of mathematics has been propounded as a way of making the subject more interesting to more pupils. Lingard (2000) makes a strong case that learning about the history of mathematics may help motivation and hence achievement. The history of mathematics shows that the subject has developed over time (and is still developing) and reminds pupils that mathematicians are human.

If mathematics consists of a set of universal and incontrovertible truths, then it should not include apparent inconsistencies. At a simple level, it is possible to argue that the recurring decimal 0.99999… is equal to one, and also that it is slightly less than one (see, for example, the argument on the nrich website – a link for which is provided on the website for this book at www.sagepub.co.uk/secondary. One famous challenge to the position of mathematics as a body of logical truths comes in the form of Russell's paradox. This suggests that we can separate out all sets in two piles, pile one for sets that are members of themselves and pile two for sets that are not members of themselves. If we then consider the set of all sets that are not members of themselves, then we have a paradox. We do not know which pile this set belongs in, because it appears to be a member of itself if and only if it is not a member of itself. The paradox illustrates the counter-intuitive fact: it is possible to find illogicalities in mathematics!

Point for reflection

Consider the extent to which mathematics is influenced by society. If mathematics is constructed rather than an absolute body of truth, then the social context of the time should influence how mathematics develops, and the sort of mathematical dialogue that goes on. Would mathematics develop in a totalitarian society in the same way as in a liberal democracy? Consider examples of how the mathematics would be independent of context, and examples where the contrary is the case.

Further reading

Orton, A. (1994) 'The aims of teaching mathematics', in A. Orton and G. Wain (eds), *Issues in Teaching Mathematics*. London: Cassell.

Orton's fairly short chapter is an interesting summary of the reasons for teaching mathematics, including discussion of the extent to which practice in schools is dominated by utilitarian aims. The author examines different ideas about the nature of mathematics, with particular emphasis on the distinction between learning a body of knowledge and learning mathematical processes. The chapter puts mathematics into the context of the aims of education as a whole, and also includes a section on mathematics as a language.

Ernest, P. (1991) *The Philosophy of Mathematics Education*. Basingstoke: Falmer Press

The author is an acknowledged expert in the field of philosophy in mathematics education, and in this book he covers the big questions about the nature of mathematics and why we teach it. He compares different external influences on the mathematics curriculum, from both a purist and a utilitarian standpoint. He also considers the extent to which mathematics is a set of truths, and argues that mathematics should be regarded as a constructed entity, within a general philosophy of 'social constructivism'.

Useful websites

Live links to these sites can be found on the companion website.

The Professional Standards for QTS can be found on the website of the Training and Development Agency for Schools (TDA), at http://www.tda.gov.uk/teachers/professionalstandards.aspx

A copy of the Smith Report on mathematics can be found online at http://www.mathsinquiry.org.uk/

The nrich website, run from Cambridge University, has discussion, articles, and enrichment problems that are linked in with the school curriculum. The home page is https://nrich.maths.org/. The page with the arguments on whether 0.9 recurring is equal to 1 or less than 1 is at https://nrich.maths.org/discus/messages/67613/68880.html? 1143990391

References

Askew, M., Brown, M., Rhodes, V., Wiliam, D. and Johnson, D. (1997) *Effective Teachers of Numeracy: Report of a Study carried out for the Teacher Training Agency*. London: King's College.

Bell, E.T. (1953) *Men of Mathematics*. London: Penguin.

Bishop, A. (1991) 'Mathematics education in its cultural context', in M. Harris (ed.), *School Mathematics and Work*. Basingstoke: Falmer.

Burghes, D.N and Wood, A.D. (1984) *Mathematical Models in the Social, Management and Life Sciences*. Chichester: Ellis Horwood.

Burkhardt, H. (1981) *The Real World and Mathematics*. Glasgow: Blackie.

Chambers, P. (2007) 'Mathematics trainee teachers', *Edge Hill Occasional Papers*, Autumn. Ormskirk: Edge Hill University.

Cockcroft, W.H. (1982) *Mathematics Counts*. (Cockcroft Report) London: HMSO.

Department for Education and Employment (DfEE) (1997) *Excellence in Schools*. London: HMSO.

Department for Education and Employment (DfEE) (1999a) *The National Curriculum for England: Mathematics*. London: HMSO.

Department for Education and Employment (DfEE) (1999b) *The National Numeracy Strategy: Framework for Teaching Mathematics from Reception to Year 6*. London: Department for Education and Employment.

Ernest, P. (1991) *The Philosophy of Mathematics Education*. Basingstoke: Falmer Press.

Gardiner, A. (1987) *Discovering Mathematics: The Art of Investigation*. Oxford: Oxford University Press.

Hersh, R. (1998) *What is Mathematics, Really*? London: Vintage.

Körner, S. (1960) *The Philosophy of Mathematics*. London: Hutchinson.

Kassem, D. (2001) 'Ethnicity and mathematics education', in P. Gates (ed.), *Issues in Teaching Mathematics*. London: RoutledgeFalmer.

Lakatos, I. (1978) *Mathematics, Science and Epistemology*. Cambridge: Cambridge University Press.

Lave, J. (1988) *Cognition in Practice*. Cambridge: Cambridge University Press.

Lingard, D. (2000) 'The history of mathematics; an essential component of the mathematics curriculum at all levels', *Australian Mathematics Teacher*, 56(1) 40–4.

Mason, J., Burton, L. and Stacey, K. (1982) *Thinking Mathematically*. London: Addison Wesley.

Mathematical Association (1995) *Why, What, How? Some Basic Questions for Mathematics Teaching*. Leicester: Mathematical Association.

Orton, A. (1994) 'The aims of teaching mathematics', in A. Orton and G. Wain (eds), *Issues in Teaching Mathematics*. London: Cassell.

Pedoe, D. (1958) *The Gentle Art of Mathematics*. London: Penguin.

Qualifications and Curriculum Authority (QCA) (2007) *Mathematics Programme of Study: Key Stage 3*. Available for download at www.qca.org.uk/qca_12216.aspx (accessed 23 August 2007).

Queen Mary University of London (QMUL) (2007) *Prospectus: Mathematical Sciences*. London: Queen Mary University of London.

Scopes, P.G. (1973) *Mathematics in Secondary Schools*. Cambridge: Cambridge University Press.

Smith, A. (2004) *Making Mathematics Count: The Report of Professor Adrian Smith's Inquiry into Post-14 Mathematics Education*. (Smith Report) London: HMSO.

Stewart, H. (2005) Bosses say school leavers can't read, write or count. Online at http://education.guardian.co.uk/gcses/story/0,,1554020,00.html (24 Nov 2007).

Tanner, H. and Jones, S. (2000) *Becoming a Successful Teacher of Mathematics*. London: RoutledgeFalmer.

Training and Development Agency for schools (TDA) (2007) *Professional Standards for Teachers: Why Sit Still in your Career?* London: Training and Development Agency for Schools.

Tegmark, M. (2003) 'Parallel universes', in J.D. Barrow, P.C.W. Davies and C.L. Harper (eds), *Science and Ultimate Reality: From Quantum to Cosmos*. New York: Cambridge University Press.

Wigner, E.P. (1967) *Symmetries and Reflections*. Cambridge, MA: MIT Press.

2

WHAT TO TEACH IN A MATHEMATICS LESSON, AND THE STUDY OF PROOF

This chapter:

- discusses how mathematics teaching fits in to the Every Child Matters framework
- summarizes your responsibility for safeguarding children
- gives a summary of the background to the National Curriculum
- describes the structure of the National Curriculum
- discusses the issue of progression in mathematics
- challenges you to develop further your understanding of mathematical proof
- discusses the role of proof in mathematical education.

EVERY CHILD MATTERS

A very fundamental change to the organization of education and children's services has taken place as a result of a national initiative, led by government, called Every Child Matters (DfES, 2003). The Every Child Matters (ECM) initiative aims to bring together the full range of children's services, including education, childcare and social services, and unite them in a common purpose. The intention is to bring together provision that was previously separate, and hence avoid the situation where agencies do not communicate with each other. When agencies do not communicate effectively, it has been found that individual children, particularly the most vulnerable, may be failed by the system.

The ECM agenda means better information sharing across different agencies. It has led to Ofsted, previously the Office for Standards in Education, being given a broader brief than it had before. The new Ofsted – the Office for Standards in Education, Children's Services and Skills – came into being in April 2007, and brings together four formerly separate inspectorates. In its broader remit, Ofsted inspects and regulates care for children and young people, and inspects education and training for learners of all ages.

In addition, the government has published a common core of skills and knowledge for the children's workforce (DfES, 2005), describing the skills that are required by all people who work with children, whether in schools, social services or children's support groups. The ECM agenda affirms the link between emotional well-being and learning, and requires a response from every school. The initiative should influence the lives of all young people, with schools adopting a positive approach to sharing information about pupils with other professionals and agencies.

SAFEGUARDING

Within the ECM framework, schools have a statutory responsibility to make arrangements to safeguard and promote the welfare of pupils. Within the school, there will be one person designated with responsibility for child protection, and you must get to know who this is. As a teacher, you must work within the school's child protection policies, and respond to things that you see or hear during your time in school which give you cause for concern.

For the purposes of the Child Protection Register, child abuse is divided into emotional abuse, neglect, physical injury and sexual abuse. Your responsibility as a teacher includes acting when you see signs of any abuse, or even when you begin to suspect (possibly through something that you have heard) that a pupil is suffering abuse. As an example, bruising to the mouth, ears or neck should arouse suspicion and indicate the need for you to report the matter to the child protection officer. More difficult to spot are signs of other abuse. Sudden changes in behaviour, self-harm or sexually aggressive behaviour towards other pupils may be symptoms of sexual abuse, or they may not, but if you have a genuine concern that a child may be the victim of abuse, then you must not ignore it.

It is possible that a pupil will confide in you. Your reaction to any allegation of abuse is vitally important; the pupil's statements should always be taken seriously, never dismissed or downplayed. Bear in mind the guidance that you should treat children as no less reliable than adults.

You might witness what appears to be inappropriate touching of a child by a teacher. You must report this. You should do this either directly to the child protection officer in the school, or immediately inform your supervising tutor, who will pass on your concerns to the child protection officer. Although this process may be distressing, it is the welfare of the child that must be paramount.

A MATHEMATICAL PERSPECTIVE ON THE EVERY CHILD MATTERS OUTCOMES

Each school as a whole should be focused on what are called the five ECM outcomes: staying safe, being healthy, enjoying and achieving, making a positive contribution and achieving economic well-being. Similarly, every department and every teacher should be aware that these five outcomes are fundamental to all provision for young people. All mathematics departments need to consider how the mathematics curriculum contributes to achieving these outcomes.

Staying safe

Staying safe means ensuring that pupils are free from abuse, bullying and discrimination. To a large extent, the context for this is set by the ethos of the school, but it is vitally important that every teacher plays a part in challenging antisocial behaviour and promoting a safe and secure environment. Both around the school and within the classroom, you must intervene to prevent bullying, to challenge stereotyped views and to prevent any pupil from suffering discrimination.

Clearly, ensuring that the mathematics classroom is a safe environment is vitally important. As a trainee in a new school, you need from the first day to become familiar with emergency procedures – for example the evacuation procedure if there is a fire. Even though you are not in charge of a class from day one, you are a responsible adult and have a role in supervising children and young people in an emergency.

Within your mathematics classroom, the safety challenges are not so great as those faced in, for example, science lessons, but they still need to be considered carefully. In essence the safety issues for you are the fundamental issues that apply to every teacher: proper supervision of pupils in the classroom, intervening to protect pupils from harm and managing the teaching space so that potential hazards are avoided.

If the mathematics learning is to take place in a non-classroom environment (especially outside the school), then there are many other safety issues that need to be considered, including risk assessment. In these circumstances, as a trainee or newly qualified teacher, you are strongly advised to take advice from an experienced colleague in the school.

Being healthy

Schools are judged on the extent to which they enable pupils to develop healthy lifestyles. A healthy lifestyle includes being physically, mentally and sexually healthy, and choosing not to take illegal drugs. Good schools promote healthy eating and provide plenty of opportunities for pupils to be physically active; drug education and sex education are well delivered and effective.

Mathematics lessons are less likely to have a major impact on the promotion of healthy living than some other lessons, but good health can be promoted in mathematics by making the most of the opportunities that arise. Where a mathematical topic involves an element of discussion, the lesson can be planned to include examples that involve reflecting on health issues.

It is quite possible to promote good health in several statistical topics. On a departmental level, long-term plans can provide guidance on appropriate topics, including a departmental policy to use real data wherever possible. You can, for example, promote healthy eating by selecting and analysing relevant data, such as the ingredients of breakfast cereals or crisps. Given such data, pupils can make comparisons based, for example, around the percentage fat content of different foodstuffs, together with discussion of the data and conclusions.

Enjoying and achieving

In general terms, pupils at school should attend regularly, enjoy their learning, and develop personally and socially. In addition, they should also make the most of their opportunities to learn; they should achieve well in their school subjects.

Enjoying and achieving are two fundamental aspects of all lessons in school, and certainly that applies to mathematics lessons. It could be said that you are not training to teach mathematics, you are training to help pupils to enjoy mathematics and to achieve success in mathematics.

There is very little that is subject-specific about enjoying and achieving. All good teachers attempt to make their lessons enjoyable, through selecting work that is challenging and activities that are interesting. Achievement is at the heart of education. In mathematics, as in other subjects, the best teachers structure their teaching to maximize the achievement of all individuals within the class. They set targets, monitor progress and support individuals in difficulty for the very purpose of helping pupils to achieve both good examination results and a wider appreciation of the subject.

Making a positive contribution

We want pupils to become responsible citizens, active and involved in their communities. For this purpose, and because it is desirable in itself, we want pupils to play a full and active role in their school community, with positive attitudes to taking part and making the most of the available opportunities. Good schools encourage their pupils to take an active part in decision-making via bodies such as school councils. They promote involvement in the community through fund-raising for local charities. They introduce schemes that help pupils to develop a pride in their environment, and also support initiatives that come from the pupils themselves. Pupils who play an active role are more likely to behave well, form positive relationships and develop self-confidence.

In many schools, teachers provide additional opportunities for pupils to make a positive contribution. One example from the mathematics subject area is setting a weekly mathematics challenge that is open to all pupils, with a prize for the best entries. Another example is the mathematics club, where recreational mathematics problems can be tackled in an informal atmosphere.

Many schools provide opportunities for their pupils to enter national mathematics competitions, and such competitions have very big numbers of entries. One example run from the mathematics department at Edge Hill University is the Edge Hill Challenge. In order to enter the competition, pupils need to work in small groups, and present their results by means of a poster. In the final stages groups have to explain their work orally to a panel of judges. The Edge Hill Challenge started in 2000 and in 2007 had several hundred entries involving over 1,500 pupils. Other schools promote mathematics by arranging external trips and visits. These visits include promotion days or taster days in universities or colleges, and master classes for the most able pupils.

Some trainees underestimate the importance of fostering a positive attitude in their pupils. They sometimes appear apologetic when setting homework ('this will only take you about 10 minutes') or they present some mathematical topic in a negative light ('you probably don't like fractions'). You must strive to avoid this. Pupils will enjoy their learning more if you present a positive image of the subject; they will respond well to your enthusiasm. You should encourage pupils to take an active role in your lessons wherever possible. For example, you can organize lessons that involve participation in classroom activities and independent tasks, but more than anything, you should encourage pupils to put forward ideas and to volunteer for tasks.

Achieving economic well-being

Recent reforms of the 14–19 curriculum have tried to re-establish the link between education and employment in the minds of young people, and the introduction of work-related learning as a compulsory part of the Key Stage 4 curriculum for all pupils has given vocational education an added status. But achieving economic well-being is more than just work-related learning. It also involves being able to access further education or training, having the key skills required by employers and having a positive attitude to enterprise. Inspection evidence suggests that schools provide 'insufficient sustained effort' to improving communication skills or the application of number across the curriculum (Ofsted, 2006), and need to improve this aspect of preparing pupils for achieving economic well-being.

Research suggests that people with an A level qualification in mathematics (even at modest grades) go on to earn significantly more than their peers (Vignoles, 1999), so it could be argued that the study of mathematics can itself contribute to economic well-being. But within the subject, it is easy to find examples of where mathematics teachers can promote economic well-being. For instance, the ability to calculate and understand number is at the heart of money management. In your lessons, you should plan to ensure that their number work includes examples in financial contexts.

Long-term planning should take account of developing enterprise, which involves money management and risk assessment. Enterprise education forms part of a compulsory work-related learning element within the overall 14–19 curriculum, and mathematics teaching can make a significant contribution. Evidence (Ofsted, 2006) suggests that schools need to do more to promote enterprise education to avoid it remaining on the margins of the curriculum. In 2006, inspectors found that many teachers were unclear about what this involved.

All mathematics departments need to consider how they can develop skills in these areas. This may involve making more explicit links with other subjects at particular points in the year, for example when interpreting statistical data or using measuring equipment, or providing particular activities with risk assessment as a focus.

Point for reflection

Make sure that you know and understand the five Every Child Matters outcomes. In the sections above, we have given examples of how mathematics lessons can contribute towards achieving the outcomes. Think about additional examples in each of the categories, giving consideration to specific lesson content, illustrative materials or personal approaches to teaching. In your first school visit, find out how the mathematics department has responded to the Every Child Matters agenda.

Point for reflection

THE DEVELOPMENT OF THE NATIONAL CURRICULUM IN MATHEMATICS

Since 1989, mathematics teaching in secondary schools has been prescribed by the National Curriculum. The introduction of the National Curriculum was an attempt to ensure that all pupils had access to the same curriculum, and was backed by a legal requirement for all maintained schools to follow it. In mathematics this meant that examination boards had far less opportunity to offer varied types of mathematics content and, as a result, teachers had less opportunity to select the type of mathematics they felt suited their pupils.

For example, in 1988 the Southern Examining Group, one of the leading GCSE examination boards, offered three different GCSE options in mathematics. Other examination boards, of which there were several, offered a similar range of alternatives. The school could choose any one of these alternative syllabuses and prepare for the examination by teaching the particular topics listed on the syllabus. Teachers chose an option according to which one they thought would enable their pupils to do well or, possibly, to suit their underlying philosophy of what mathematics is. Work in the early years of secondary schooling was often determined by working backwards from the GCSE syllabus, with each school determining the order in which topics were introduced and the year in which they were first encountered.

It is easy to see that the introduction of the National Curriculum gave much more structure to the curriculum and that the pupils' experience of mathematics was far less dependent upon choices made by their teachers. Although there were some regrets about a loss of freedom, most mathematics teachers welcomed the change. They valued the structured progression provided by the National Curriculum, while accepting that the content was, in broad terms, acceptable. It is fair to say that, among mathematics teachers, the content of the National Curriculum caused some discussion but little controversy.

A lot of the new structuring involved assigning levels to particular topics and strengthening the progression from one idea to another within a particular strand of thinking. The allocation of levels owed a lot to recent research carried out by the Assessment of Performance Unit, which conducted large-scale national tests at ages 11 and 14 (APU, 1980a; 1980b). These tests provided evidence of a 'facility' for a large number of mathematical questions. The facility for a question is simply the percentage of the sample group who were able to provide the correct answer to that question. In broad terms, if a question had a low facility, then it was generally assigned to a higher level within the hierarchy of the mathematics curriculum.

Since 1989, the mathematics National Curriculum has undergone several revisions (in 1993, 1997, 1999 and 2007), but the overall principles have remained the same. What is more, it is notable how little the content has changed in the various revisions; when changes have been introduced, they have been more to do with the way the curriculum is structured (for example, bringing all subjects into a common structure) than anything else.

The 2007 secondary curriculum review (which provides the programme of study taught from September 2008) draws together all National Curriculum subjects through a common set of curriculum aims, based on the five Every Child Matters outcomes. These three curriculum aims are given at the start of each programme of study, whatever age and whatever subject, with the expectation that teaching and learning in all subjects should help learners achieve these aims. So mathematics teaching, along with all other subjects, aims to develop:

- successful learners who enjoy learning, make progress and achieve
- confident individuals who are able to live safe, healthy and fulfilling lives
- responsible citizens who make a positive contribution to society (QCA, 2007a; 2007b).

All teachers should see their subject as contributing to a child's general education, and the National Curriculum encourages inter-subject links wherever possible.

The content of the curriculum, called the programme of study, is divided into sections in both Key Stage 3 and Key Stage 4. Statements in each of the key stages reaffirm the importance of mathematics, giving reasons for studying the subject, and present a set of key concepts that underpin the subject. These concepts identify what pupils need to understand in order to 'deepen and broaden their knowledge, skills and understanding' in mathematics. The key concepts are:

- competence – being able to work appropriately and accurately
- creativity – combining approaches and working in unfamiliar ways
- applications and implications of mathematics – appreciating how and why we engage in mathematics, and the historical roots of the subject
- critical understanding – understanding mathematical modelling.

Unfortunately, there is no indication of the relative importance of the four key concepts. As a result, it may be that the first in the list retains its hold on curriculum time.

KEY PROCESSES

As well as key concepts, the curriculum identifies a set of key processes, described as the skills that should be developed through learning mathematics. These skills are listed as:

curriculum *identified (2007?)*
key processes

- representing situations mathematically, including selecting appropriate approaches
- analysing – using mathematical reasoning and appropriate procedures
- interpreting and evaluating – evaluating evidence and justifying findings
- communicating and reflecting.

Representational skills involve being able to think how mathematics can help to solve a problem. They also include the ability to explore alternative approaches, to amend ways of working in the light of experience and to break down a complex problem into more manageable stages. Pupils should be taught that they can often gain understanding of a complex problem by working on a simple case and building up to the general case. In statistics, they should understand how to pose appropriate questions and how to collect data efficiently avoiding bias.

Analysis includes the ability to make and test conjectures, including generalizations, using inductive reasoning. Pupils should be able to construct a mathematical argument, showing how they have deduced one statement from another. They should draw together their knowledge from different parts of mathematics. Analysis skills also include supporting mathematical arguments with correct, accurate calculations and/or graphical representations, using technology where appropriate. Pupils should be taught to use routinely their skills of estimation and approximation, and to check their answers to see if they are reasonable.

Interpreting and evaluating is about being able to assess the strength of an argument, to appreciate its limitations. It is about understanding the difference between evidence and proof. We want all pupils to be able to respond to weak arguments and generalizations. For example, when faced with the statement that 'boys are taller than girls', pupils should be able to say what evidence or further information they would need in order to assess the strength of the claim. They should also be able to critically examine the strategies adopted, by looking at the efficiency and possibly the validity of the methodology.

Communicating and reflecting involves comparing alternative methods of solution and representation. It involves reflecting on previous mathematical experiences, and identifying similarities to and differences from the current work. Above all, it involves pupils being able to express their ideas clearly and concisely, in a way that is suitable for the intended audience.

THE STRUCTURE OF THE NATIONAL CURRICULUM

There are slight differences in the range and content of mathematics that pupils encounter at the different key stages. At Key Stages 3 and 4, the curriculum content is organized into three mathematical categories:

- Number and Algebra
- Geometry and Measures (formerly, to 2008, Shape, Space and Measures)
- Statistics (formerly Handling Data).

At Key Stage 1, there is no content in the Statistics section, and at Key Stages 1 and 2, the heading Number and Algebra is replaced by Number.

Supporting guidance is provided for each programme of study on how to develop coherent approaches to teaching and learning. This includes examples of how the mathematics programme of study links to the whole-school curriculum, contributing to curriculum aims, personal, learning and thinking skills, personal development and functional skills.

The programme of study also provides support and guidance on ensuring that the curriculum is coherent and motivating for pupils. It is intended that all schools should provide opportunities for pupils to work on problems that show mathematics being applied to solve problems in other subjects. This may involve 'traditional' subjects such as science, or general problems from an enterprise project, for example. It is also specified that pupils should be solving problems that arise from contexts beyond the school, such as holiday planning or product design.

One criticism of the National Curriculum has been that it encourages an atomized approach to mathematics, where pupils learn a series of mini-skills that they find hard to bring together. This is not entirely without foundation, and the guidance for the 2008 National Curriculum makes it clear that you should avoid the atomized approach; you should draw links wherever possible, and should also provide pupils with the opportunity to work on extended problems. You should give all pupils experience of problems that draw together learning from different parts of the mathematics programme of study. One example is for pupils to engage in the 'handling data cycle', which involves:

- specifying the problem and planning
- collecting data
- processing and presenting the data
- interpreting and discussing the results.

This cycle represents the stages in a statistical investigation, and draws together several key mathematical processes. As part of the process, pupils may also need to apply specific techniques such as calculating averages and presenting information in graphical form.

There are plenty of opportunities for drawing links between mathematical topics. Several links, such as between decimals and percentages, will be obvious to you, but may need making explicit to the pupils. Other links are less obvious.

Table 2.1   National Curriculum Target Levels

Age	End of Key Stage	Expected level
7	1	2
11	2	4
14	3	5–6

Examples are: linking factors with area calculations (the number of rectangles with integer sides that have an area of, say, 40 cm^2), linking the idea of a square in geometry with squaring in number and algebra and linking inverse operations in calculation with inverse transformations. You should aim to make such links wherever possible.

In the Key Stage 3 programme of study, attainment is described in levels – level 4 to level 8 – with work beyond level 8 described as 'exceptional performance'. Level 1 work corresponds to the earliest foundations of mathematics that pupils will encounter in their early years of schooling. Level 4 is the level that corresponds to the expected level of attainment at the end of Key Stage 2, so in secondary schools, the curriculum will normally build on level 4 work. Table 2.1 summarizes the target levels.

As Table 2.1 makes clear, the expectation is that pupils enter Key Stage 3 having demonstrated level 4 outcomes and will progress by the end of the key stage to show attainment at either level 5 or level 6. Of course, this is only a guide, and it is expected to find teaching at Key Stage 3 focusing on work described by levels ranging from 3 to 7, depending on the age and ability of the pupils (DfEE, 1999).

Assessment of the Key Stage 3 programme of study is organized into four attainment targets, the three headings: number and algebra, geometry and measures, and statistics, plus an additional one called mathematical processes and applications. This last attainment target tests pupils' abilities in the skills of working mathematically, such as explaining, justifying, generalizing and reflecting. Each attainment target contains a level descriptor for each level of attainment, so that you can assess individual pupils against National Curriculum levels.

Unfortunately, the grading system has a discontinuity between the way that pupil attainment is reported at ages 14 and 16. At age 14, all pupils are assigned a National Curriculum level to describe their overall performance, but the use of levels is discontinued in Key Stage 4, where pupils' targets and progress are instead focused on GCSE grades A* to G.

PROGRESSION IN MATHEMATICS

Mathematics is one of the subjects, like modern languages, where learning is hierarchical. It is impossible to perform calculus without a thorough understanding of algebra; it is impossible to understand algebra without a basic competence in arithmetic. Even within a topic such as algebra, the skills needed to solve quadratic equations depend on an understanding of how algebraic terms combine, and the use of brackets. The introduction of the National Curriculum strengthened the idea of progression, particularly between key stages. The Key Stage 3 National Strategy framework for mathematics (now subsumed within the Secondary National Strategy) has made the progression within key stages more explicit (DfEE, 2001).

In your early days in the classroom, you will find it difficult to come to terms with the prior learning that the pupils need for your particular lesson. You may be able to identify what the pupils need to know, but it will be difficult to plan the lesson, because you do not know the class well enough. Being told by the class teacher that the class has 'done percentages' is only part of the story. You will need to estimate the thoroughness of the pupils' understanding and how many of the class will need further support before they can move on.

A very useful activity that you can do while training is to identify a progression of ideas in a particular area of mathematics. In fact, you would be well advised to try to do this for as many topics as you can; it helps you to become more familiar with the curriculum and helps to reinforce in your own mind the connections between related topics. In the following pages we examine the topic of probability as an example and chart the progression that pupils are taken through as they move through the levels in the National Curriculum.

In probability it is not difficult to identify two overall aspects that need to be understood: pupils calculate the probability of an event, and then calculate the probability of combined events. But it is much more difficult to put in the detail about how ideas of probability are developed over several years in the school curriculum. The bulleted list here describes the prescribed order of introducing new ideas, and how this strand of mathematics fits together. In general, each bulleted statement gives a development on the one before.

- Pupils develop an understanding of the words 'fair', 'more likely', 'less likely', 'certain' and 'impossible' to describe the outcome of events. For example, pupils may discuss which is more likely: that it will snow tomorrow or rain tomorrow; that a coin will come down heads or tails; or that on the way home from school they will see an elephant or a dog.
- Pupils understand the word probability, and know that probabilities are described as fractions between zero and one. This usually involves the use of a probability scale drawn as

a line on the display board, with one end labelled zero and the other end labelled one. Pupils may then be asked to estimate the probability of a range of events, and represent each probability as a point on the probability scale. It is important at this stage to try to establish the links between the word 'impossible' and zero probability, and between 'certain' and a probability of one.

- Pupils calculate the probability of equally likely outcomes. For example, given that there are 10 beads in a bag, seven red and three yellow, they understand that the probability of drawing a red bead is seven-tenths.

Notice the progression of ideas in these three bullet points. The first bullet requires pupils to compare probabilities, the second to estimate probabilities and the third to calculate probabilities. Pupils should realize that sometimes probabilities can be calculated and that sometimes they cannot; if the latter, they have to then be estimated using experimental evidence. It is also important to get across the point that if we repeat an experiment, then we may obtain different results. The progression of ideas continues:

- Pupils can set up a diagram to display all the outcomes of a pair of experiments. They can then use it to calculate the probability of a particular outcome. For example, pupils can set out in grid form the outcomes from rolling a pair of dice, and use it to calculate the probability of rolling a score of ten.
- Pupils know that probabilities add up to one. They can use the probability of an event happening to calculate the probability of it not happening.
- Pupils know the relationship between relative frequency and probability. Trainees are often unable to articulate this relationship themselves when they embark upon their training. You need to know two things in relation to this aspect of probability theory. First, relative frequency describes the outcome of an experiment, which may change when the experiment is repeated, whereas probability is a theoretical construct that holds a single value. If a fair coin is tossed 100 times then the relative frequency of a head is the number of heads obtained divided by 100; the probability of a head is always one-half. The second thing that you need to know is that the relative frequency will get closer to the probability as the number of trials increases. Stated mathematically:

$$\text{Relative frequency} \rightarrow \text{Probability, as } n \rightarrow \infty$$

In general terms, this is what the pupils need to know, although it might be presented to them in a rather less formal style. The sort of question that they need to be able to answer is:

Three friends wish to estimate the probability of a basketball player scoring with a free shot. A notes that the player scores seven times out of the ten shots seen, so concludes that the probability is $\frac{7}{10}$ or 0.7.

B notes that the player scores 20 times out of the 25 shots seen, so concludes that the probability is $\frac{20}{25}$ or 0.8.

C notes that the player scores 68 times out of the 100 shots seen, so concludes that the probability is $\frac{68}{100}$ or 0.68.

Who do you think has the best estimate of the probability and why?

At this level, pupils are expected to realize that an estimate based on more trials will give a better estimate.

- Pupils can calculate the probability of a combined event by combining probabilities. For example, they can use a tree diagram to answer questions on the probability of two independent events.
- Pupils understand that they can add probabilities to find the probability of event A or event B happening as long as events A and B are mutually exclusive.
- Pupils use tree diagrams to calculate combined probabilities, when conditional probability is involved (for example, selection without replacement).

Working through the curriculum progression for individual topics is very useful, but it is also useful to think about what other mathematical ideas are being used to underpin the learning in this topic. For the topic of probability, pupils need to have some understanding of fractions, and the equivalence of fractions, decimals and percentages. For higher-level work, they need to be able to add and multiply fractions and decimals.

Point for reflection

Consider how pupils build up their understanding of graphical representations. It is easy to identify using co-ordinates as a key starting point, but think about the progression from points to lines to regions, and the different representations that pupils need to be familiar with.

Printed below is a short exercise for you to try. You should look at the questions described on the left of the sheet, which all are associated with graphical representations. Your task is to try to identify a progression of difficulty in the questions. In this case, the progression is described by reference to National Curriculum levels.

You may be interested to see if others agree with your allocation of levels. When you have finished, look up the correct levels on the website, (www.sagepub.co.uk/secondary) and reflect on how successful you have been and where you found the task difficult.

Graphical representations activity

Assign a level to each of the following school work.

One is at level 4
One is at level 5
Four are at level 6
Two are at level 7
Five are at level 8 (roughly equivalent to a GCSE grade B) or above.

Illustrative question	Level
Sketch the graph of $y = x^2 + 3$	
Use a mapping diagram to illustrate the mapping $x \rightarrow 4x + 3$	
Sketch the graph of $y = \sin x$. On the same axes, show the graph of $y = \sin 2x$	
Sketch the graph of $y = \frac{1}{x}$	
Show the following information on a distance–time graph. Emily visits her friend Alice who lives 10 miles away. She leaves home at 1 p.m. and travels at 12 mph for 4 miles. She stops for 5 minutes, and then carries on at a constant speed to reach Alice's house at 1.47 p.m.	
Plot the graph of $y = 4x + 3$, by calculating co-ordinate pairs	
Show on a graph the solution set for the inequalities $$y \leq 3x + 1$$ $$x + y \geq 11$$	
Use a graphical method to solve the simultaneous equations $$y = 3x + 1$$ $$x + y = 11$$	
Plot the point $(-6, 4)$ on a co-ordinate diagram	
Which is steeper, the graph of $y = 4x + 3$ or the graph of $y = 2x - 2$? Explain.	
Sketch the graph of $y = 4x + 3$	
Plot the point $(6, 4)$ on a co-ordinate diagram	
Show on a number line the solution to the inequality $x - 1 < -2$	

PROOF IN THE SCHOOL CURRICULUM

Having looked at structure and progression in the National Curriculum, we shall now concentrate of one key aspect of mathematics: the idea of mathematical proof. It has been chosen as the focus in this section because trainees often have weak experiences of proof, as evidenced by the following quotes from recent trainees:

> I don't remember doing any proofs at school at all. My first experience of a proof was during my first year at university.
>
> The two areas of the National Curriculum that I immediately picked out as worries were circle theorems and proof.
>
> I was happy with almost all of the GCSE paper that we did in the first week, but I wasn't sure what was expected on the proof question, and decided to make that a focus for my subject development work during my PGCE.

One of the criticisms of the early National Curriculum versions was that they gave too little emphasis to the notion of proof (see, for example, Gardiner, 1993). Proof, it is argued, is a fundamental idea in mathematics, and in a thorough study of the subject 'it is not possible to avoid proof' (Open University, 1971: 23). In the 1990s, university tutors complained that even able mathematicians starting out on a degree course in mathematics had little concept of constructing a proof, or even what was meant by a proof. As a result of this and other pressures from the mathematics community, the school curriculum was changed to include more work on proof. In the 1999 revision of the National Curriculum and in the 2007 curriculum review, reference to proof is made explicit (DfEE, 1999; QCA, 2007a; 2007b).

The importance of proof is affirmed by Waring (2000), who argues that one of the main reasons for teaching mathematics is that it can provide learners with experience of logical reasoning, and she welcomes the introduction of proof to the National Curriculum. Through discussion of proof, she argues, pupils acquire a deeper understanding of mathematical concepts and therefore require less time in performing routine tasks that demonstrate skills. She goes further in claiming that 'proof-orientated mathematics is an alternative approach to teaching mathematics' (p. 239). Other helpful examples and discussion of proof at secondary school level are given by the Mathematical Association (MA, 2005) and the Association of Teachers of Mathematics (Giles, 2002).

From 2003, examinations at Key Stage 3 and GCSE have included explicit references to proof. An example from the 2003 specimen paper for the Higher Tier is:

If $p = \sqrt{a}$, where a is an integer, prove that it is always possible to find a number q, $p \neq q$, so that pq is also an integer.

If you are a little alarmed by this question, then it is an indication that proof is an area of mathematics that you need to work on. If your experience of proof is weak, you may not have seen rigorous proofs of standard school mathematics. For example, consider whether you have ever seen a proof that the angles of a triangle add up to 180°. The result is usually justified in the classroom in one of two ways:

- By pupils drawing several triangles, measuring the angles, and adding up the three angles. In each case, they discover that the angle sum is always close to 180°.
- The teacher or the pupils cut out a triangle from card. They tear off the three corners and fit the angles together along a straight line. They discover that, taken together, the angles form a straight line.

Point for reflection

Consider the two ways of introducing the angle sum of a triangle in the classroom described in the above bullet points. Decide whether either of them has any extra merit in comparison with the other. Finally, consider whether either of these approaches forms a proof. Think how you would justify your answer to another person.

PROOF AND JUSTIFICATION

Of the two activities described in the bullets above, the first is fine as a justification, but does not work as a proof. The reason is that however many triangles we draw, there may be a special triangle that is the exception to the rule, and we may have missed it. It is also clear that we want an exact result, and the measurement method can only suggest that the angle sum is approximately 180°.

The second activity similarly falls short of the requirements of a proof. Again, there may be a particular triangle where the corners do not fit together on a straight line, and we have not happened to find it. Also, the fact that the angles appear to fit on a straight line is not sufficient for mathematical proof. Our

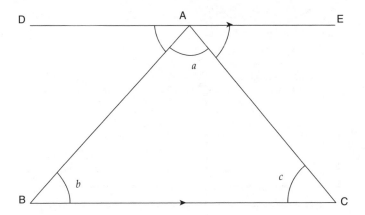

Figure 2.1 Angles in a triangle

method is not exact; it may be that the angle sum is 180.0001°, and that the diagram is, in fact, misleading.

A proof is provided by Figure 2.1 and argument below. Here, the argument that convinces us that the angle sum is 180° does not depend on the particular triangle that we have chosen, and there is no approximation in the result.

The proof could go as follows:

> In Figure 2.1, triangle ABC has angles a, b and c, and DE is parallel to BC. Our deductions tell us that:
>
>   Angle EAC = c (EAC and ACB are alternate angles, with DE parallel to BC)
>   Angle DAB = b (DAB and ABC are alternate angles, with DE parallel to BC)
>   Angle BAC + Angle DAB + Angle EAC = 180° (angles on a straight line)
>
> So, a + b + c = 180
> Therefore the angles in the triangle add up to 180°.

This level of argument is within the capability of many Year 7 pupils. The proof, of course, depends on the pupils being familiar with the angle properties of parallel lines with transversals. In the past, this may have been taught after pupils have learnt about the angles in a triangle property but, with a slight adjustment to the order of working, this elegant proof can be used in the classroom.

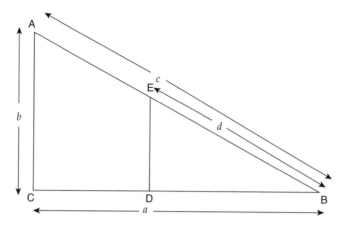

Figure 2.2 Similar triangles

An additional emphasis on proof does, however, have its dangers. One is that the proof is presented to the pupils with little more than an explanation of how one step follows from the previous line. This line-by-line approach may mean that pupils can follow the argument, but it makes it very unlikely that they will see how the proof is constructed. Concentrating on the mechanics of the argument can detract from the beauty of the argument as a whole. Every proof should be accompanied by some insight into the problem (Coles, 2005). In fact, the insight into the problem that is provided by discussion around the proof can be at least as important as the proof itself.

One of the interesting aspects of mathematics is how new techniques can be applied to familiar situations. There are many examples of this in the area of proof. One example is the use of similar triangles to prove Pythagoras' theorem. We need the result that the ratio of the areas of similar shapes is the square of the ratio of corresponding sides.

For example, in Figure 2.2, the triangles ABC and EBD are similar, with side c being the side in ABC that corresponds to the side marked d in EBD. So the ratio of lengths in triangle EBD to lengths in triangle ABC is $\frac{d}{c}$. For areas we use the square of this ratio, so the ratio of the triangle areas is given by: $\frac{Area\ EBD}{Area\ ABC} = \left(\frac{d}{c}\right)^2$.

We now use this result in a different diagram (Figure 2.3), where the three triangles ABC, ACP and CBP are similar. For brevity, we omit the proof that these three triangles are in fact similar, which involves showing that each triangle has one angle equal to angle A, one angle equal to angle B and one right angle.

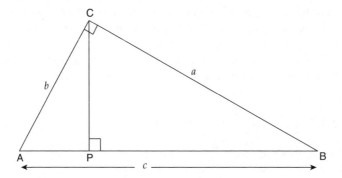

Figure 2.3 Pythagoras' theorem using similar triangles

The ratio of corresponding sides for triangles CBP and ABC is $\frac{a}{c}$, so the ratio of the areas for these two triangles is $\left(\frac{a}{c}\right)^2$

Let the area of the large triangle ABC = X. Clearly, Area of CBP + Area of ACP = Area of ABC.

Using similar triangles,

$$\left(\frac{a}{c}\right)^2 \times X + \left(\frac{b}{c}\right)^2 \times X = X$$

Dividing each term by X,

$$\left(\frac{a}{c}\right)^2 + \left(\frac{b}{c}\right)^2 = 1$$

Multiplying out, we obtain $a^2 + b^2 = c^2$

There are many proofs of Pythagoras' theorem (certainly over 50). It is difficult to give an exact number, since several proofs have a lot in common with each other, so it is not always obvious what constitutes a distinct proof. The topic does, however, provide you with the opportunity to choose between proof and justification (Chambers, 1999), and to choose from several alternatives for both proof and justification.

PROOF AND FALLACY

Proof does mean different things to different people. In particular, outside of mathematics, 'proved' is used to mean 'accepted as true beyond reasonable doubt'. In contrast, a mathematician will not accept something as proved if there is any doubt at all. Consider the argument presented below, which is adapted from an illustration by Professor John Cassels of Cambridge University. The presentation highlights how a mathematician can satirize the kind of proof accepted elsewhere.

Statement: Every odd integer > 1 is prime

Proof: The economists' proof runs as follows: 3 is prime, 5 is prime, 7 is prime. Three cases in a row is surely enough for any economist.

If, however, we imagine an idealized economist, who would not be satisfied by the preceding, then the rest of the proof runs as follows. Look at the next odd integer, 9. Well it is admittedly not a prime; there must be some unusual factor of some kind operating. Let us go on looking at the figures: 11 is prime, 13 is prime. Two more instances, so 9 must have been a freak result, and the conjecture must be true.

Sometimes, presenting arguments in a mathematical way makes them look more convincing. Consider the following mathematical argument that purports to prove that every natural number is interesting. When you have read it through, reflect on where the mathematical argument breaks down.

Statement: Every natural number is interesting

Proof: There are certainly interesting natural numbers. 1 is interesting because it is the only natural number whose reciprocal is the same as the number itself, 2 is the only prime which is even, 3 is a triangular number, and so on.

Suppose the statement is false. Then there must be some natural numbers which are not interesting.

Let x_0 be the smallest of these numbers. Then x_0 has the property that it is the smallest uninteresting number – a fact that makes it very interesting indeed. Hence, the supposition that the statement is false has led to a contradiction. Therefore, the statement cannot be false, and has been proved to be true.

In this case, it is the use of language that provides the weak link in the argument. The word 'interesting' is ill-defined, and it is therefore possible to have something defined as interesting *because* of the fact that it is uninteresting!

Consider the following mathematical argument, which seems to prove that $1 = 2$. The deductions at each stage appear to follow the normal rules of algebra. See if you can spot the flaw in the deductive reasoning.

Statement: 1 = 2

Proof: Let $a = b$
$$\Rightarrow ab = b^2$$
$$\Rightarrow ab - a^2 = b^2 - a^2$$
$$\Rightarrow a(b - a) = (b + a)(b - a)$$
$$\Rightarrow a = b + a$$
$$\Rightarrow a = 2a$$
$$\Rightarrow 1 = 2$$

Consider whether you could use this 'proof' in school. If so, what level of work would the pupils need to know in order to find the flaw in the argument?

EVIDENCE FROM THE RESEARCH

There has been plenty of recent research and discussion around the area of proof. Much concentrates on pupils' perceptions of what constitutes a proof. Lulu Healy and Celia Hoyles (2000) report that even high-attaining 14–15-year-old pupils are poor at constructing proofs. Pupils tend to blur the distinction between empiricism and proof, with many seeing an empirical argument as sufficient evidence to prove a statement. Consider the following simple example:

Prove that the sum of two odd numbers is always even.

One common approach to this problem is to provide several examples of pairs of odd numbers, demonstrate that the statement is true for all of the examples given, and state that therefore it is always true. Perhaps not surprisingly, the more the pupils believe in the original statement, then the more likely they are to think that it does not need any rigorous approach to prove it (Healy and Hoyles, 2000). If the result is obvious, as in the example of two odd numbers adding up to an even number, the pupils see it as simple mathematics, and hence not requiring any higher-level mathematics to justify it.

Claire Baldwin (2005) lists four misconceptions about proof that she encountered when working with able pupils in Years 8 and 11. These are that:

- proof is a sequence of steps that leads to the answer
- proof needs algebra to be correct
- providing several examples is sufficient to prove a result
- proof is the same as providing convincing evidence.

She provides interesting evidence of different attitudes to proof between pupils who had been taught according to the principles and structure of the National Strategy and those who had not. She reports that the Year 8 pupils were more likely to engage in debate about proof, whereas the Year 11 pupils had never met the idea of a proof before they had started their GCSE work, and found the ideas very unfamiliar. Year 8 pupils were at least as competent in constructing proofs as Year 11 pupils in the sample tested. One clear conclusion suggested by the study is that pupils are more likely to understand and recall a proof if they have had an active role in constructing the proof in the first place, rather than being simply shown a proof as a demonstration.

One criticism of the current treatment of proof in school mathematics is that it is introduced too late. When proof is introduced, it can seem alien and unfamiliar (Ball et al., 2002), and unrelated to any mathematics that pupils have met in the past. Stylianides (2007) focuses on how notions of proof can be introduced to the curriculum for pupils in the 7 to 11 age range. Although formal proofs may not be appropriate at this stage, he argues that proof can be conceptualized according to two key principles. The first principle is that proof should be intellectually honest – that is, mathematically correct and not trying to underrate the learners' capabilities. The second principle is that notions of proof should form a continuum of development through different ages.

Stylianides discusses what could constitute a proof, and identifies a class of arguments that could be called proofs for younger pupils, paying crucial attention to the social aspect that 'an argument that could count as proof should be convincing to the students on the basis of socially accepted rules of discourse' (2007: 12). The idea of developing skills of reasoning is very much part of the National Curriculum. Waring's description (2000) of the progression as being from learning about proof to learning to prove also emphasizes the need to introduce skills of reasoning in a structured way. In particular, she identifies an informal stage in the learning of proof that concentrates on a discussion of the key ideas.

There is little doubt that pupils find proof difficult, and that many prefer empirical arguments (Dreyfus, 1999; Porteous, 1990). Even when presented with the ideas of deductive proof, or when they have constructed a general proof, many pupils fail to appreciate the general nature of the argument, and feel that additional examples are necessary to complete the argument (Balacheff, 1990; Healy and Hoyles, 2000)

The fact that proof in society means something different from proof in mathematics may offer an explanation for why proof is difficult. In societal terms, several examples of an occurrence may be sufficient to prove that something is true. For example, there is convincing evidence that global warming has occurred over the past 50 years and that human activity is responsible. Many people would consider that the evidence proves this as a fact. This is a much looser understanding of proof than would be acceptable in mathematics. This sort of distinction has led to the consideration of proof in a social context, with the understanding that different levels of evidence are needed in different situations (Hanna, 1991; Nardi and Iannone, 2006).

Further reading

Cheminais, R. (2006) *Every Child Matters: A Practical Guide for Teachers*. London: David Fulton.

In this book, Rita Cheminais examines the impact of the Every Child Matters agenda for teachers. The book provides an overview of the main changes that have taken place or are in process, and how these impact on practice in schools and other educational settings. There is a review of the notion of personalized learning opportunities for pupils, and a summary of how teachers need to interact with other professionals within schools and from external services. The author provides advice and practical resources that are designed to support teachers wanting to know more about their responsibilities in the Every Child Matters framework.

Waring, S. (2000) *Can You Prove It? Developing Concepts of Proof in Primary and Secondary Schools*. Leicester: Mathematical Association.

This interesting book justifies why proof should be taught as part of the mathematics curriculum. It then suggests a three-stage process for developing skills in proof: learning about proof; learning to prove; and improving proof skills. A large number of proofs are provided, all relevant to the existing mathematics curriculum, some familiar and some less so. The author acknowledges that many younger teachers have never experienced proof themselves at school level, and seeks to raise awareness about the importance of proof among this group and others. She suggests a model for teaching proof that demonstrates the progression of ideas, and which provides the skills needed by a fully functioning mathematical thinker.

🌐 *Useful websites*

Live links to these sites can be found on the companion website.

The Every Child Matters website is at http://www.everychildmatters.gov.uk/

A specific link to the Every Child Matters Green Paper is at http://www.everychildmatters. gov.uk/_files/EBE7EEAC90382663E0D5BBF24C99A7AC.pdf

The common core of skills and knowledge for the children's workforce is at http://www.everychildmatters.gov.uk/deliveringservices/commoncore/

The booklet *What To Do If You're Worried a Child is being Abused – Summary*, is a guide for all who work with children, published in 2006 by the then Department for Education and Skills. You can download a copy from http://publications.teachernet.gov.uk/ default.aspx?PageFunction=productdetails&PageMode=publications&Product Id=DFES-04319-2006&

Documents relating to the National Curriculum can be found via the QCA website at http://www.qca.org.uk/

Specific reference to proof in the context of Pythagoras' theorem is at http://www. m-a .org.uk/docs/library/2074.pdf

References

Assessment of Performance Unit (APU) (1980a) *Mathematical Development – Primary Survey Report No. 1*. London: HMSO.

Assessment of Performance Unit (APU) (1980b) *Mathematical Development – Secondary Survey Report No. 1*. London: HMSO.

Balacheff, N. (1990) 'Beyond a psychological approach: the psychology of mathematics education', *For the Learning of Mathematics*, 10: 2–8.

Baldwin, C. (2005) 'Are we making progress? Proof', *Mathematics in School*, 34(1): 9–13.

Ball, D., Hoyles, C., Jahnke, H. and Movshovitz-Hadar, N. (2002) 'The teaching of proof', in *Proceedings of the International Congress of Mathematicians*. Vol. 3. Beijing: Higher Education Press.

Chambers, P. (1999) 'Teaching Pythagoras' theorem', *Mathematics in School*, 28(4): 22–4.

Cheminais, R. (2006) *Every Child Matters: A Practical Guide for Teachers*. London: David Fulton.

Coles, A. (2005) 'Proof and insight', *Mathematics Teaching*, 190, March: 11.

Department for Education and Employment (DfEE) (1999) *The National Curriculum for England: Mathematics*. London: HMSO.

Department for Education and Employment (DfEE) (2001) *Key Stage 3 National Strategy: Framework for Teaching Mathematics Years 7, 8 and 9*. London: Department for Education and Employment.

Department for Education and Skills (DfES) (2003) *Every Child Matters*. Green Paper. London: HMSO.

Department for Education and Skills (DfES) (2005) *Every Child Matters: Common Core of Skills and Knowledge for the Children's Workforce*. London: Department for Education and Skills.

Dreyfus, T. (1999) 'Why Johnny can't prove', *Educational Studies in Mathematics*, 38: 85–109.

Gardiner, A. (1993) 'Recurring themes in school mathematics – reasons and reasoning', *Mathematics in School*, 22(1): 20–1.

Giles, G. (2002) *Proof in Elementary Geometry*. Derby: Association of Teachers of Mathematics.

Hanna, G. (1991) 'Mathematical proof', in D. Tall (ed.), *Advanced Mathematical Thinking*. London: Kluwer Academic.

Healy, L. and Hoyles, C. (2000) 'A study of proof conceptions in algebra', *Journal for Research in Mathematics Education*, 31(4): 396–428.

Hersh, R. (1979) Some Proposals for Reviving the Philosophy of Mathematics, *Advances in Mathematics* 31: 31-50.

Mathematical Association (MA) (2005) *Are You Sure? Learning About Proof*. Leicester: Mathematical Association.

Nardi, E. and Iannone, P. (2006) *How to Prove It: A Brief Guide for Teaching Proof to Year 1 Mathematics Undergraduates*. Norwich: University of East Anglia.

Office for Standards in Education (Ofsted) (2006) *The Annual Report of Her Majesty's Chief Inspector of Schools 2005/06*. London: Office for Standards in Education.

Open University (1971) *Mathematics Foundation Course Unit 17: Logic II – Proof*. Bletchley: Open University Press.

Porteous, K. (1990) 'What do children really believe?', *Educational Studies in Mathematics*, 21(6): 589–98.

Qualifications and Curriculum Authority (QCA) (2007a) 'Mathematics Programme of study: Key Stage 3'. Available for download at http://www.qca.org.uk/qca_12216.aspx (accessed 23 August 2007)

Qualifications and Curriculum Authority (QCA) (2007b) 'Mathematics Programme of study: Key Stage 4'. Available for download at http://www.qca.org.uk/qca_12217.aspx (accessed August 2007).

Stylianides, A. (2007) 'The notion of proof in the context of elementary school mathematics', *Educational Studies in Mathematics*, 65(1): 1–20.

Vignoles, A. (1999) 'A levels: does less mean more?', *CentrePiece Magazine*, Spring: 8–11.

Waring, S. (2000) *Can You Prove It? Developing Concepts of Proof in Primary and Secondary Schools*. Leicester: Mathematical Association.

3 PLANNING TO TEACH A MATHEMATICS LESSON

This chapter:

- discusses definitions of long-term, medium-term and short-term planning
- provides examples of good practice in medium-term and short-term planning
- discusses the processes of planning
- summarizes with a flow chart that is designed to help you through your early experiences of planning lessons
- examines how a number of more general issues, such as curricular links and differentiation, have an impact on lesson planning.

Anyone who has ever addressed a group of people will appreciate the need to be well prepared, and teachers in particular are aware that well-planned lessons are the most likely to be successful. During your training you will need to spend more time on your planning than experienced teachers, for the simple reason that you do not have experience to help you. As Keith Jones (2005) says, for you, planning needs to be explicit and detailed, particularly in the early stages of taking over classes, because you do not have a bank of memories and notes from earlier, similar lessons, which you can adapt to the needs of the current class. Skills of planning come easily to some trainee teachers; they are shown some guidelines, and they can then produce plans that take account of the important issues and form the basis of a good lesson. Other trainees can be given exactly the same guidance, and yet find it extremely difficult to produce plans that look coherent and pay sufficient attention to detail.

Different terminologies for planning have been around for a long time, so it is perhaps helpful that the Key Stage 3 National Strategy: Framework for Teaching Mathematics (hereafter referred to as the Framework) identifies three connected levels of planning: long-term, medium-term and short-term, which it defines in a useful way (DfEE, 2001). In the past, it has been difficult to say exactly what is meant by the phrase 'long-term planning'. How long is long term? Using the Framework definitions, teachers now know that they are not likely to be misunderstood, at least, not by other teachers.

The Professional Standards for QTS (TDA, 2007) include three statements under the 'Planning' heading. You need to show that you can:

- plan for progression across the age and ability range for which you are trained, designing effective learning sequences within lessons and across a series of lessons and demonstrating secure subject/curriculum knowledge
- design opportunities for learners to develop their literacy, numeracy and ICT skills
- plan homework or other out-of-class work to sustain learners' progress and to extend and consolidate their learning.

This chapter concentrates mainly on the first of these three statements.

LONG-TERM PLANNING

The Framework describes long-term planning as an outline of what needs to be taught each year. For many schools, this is largely a matter of using the key objectives and content for Years 7 to 9 as listed in the Framework, and then for Years 10 and 11 using the relevant GCSE syllabus to list the topics that need to be covered. But this is not the full picture. Many schools choose to differentiate the planned activities at this stage, to take account of the different objectives for different ability groups. For example, as stated in the Strategy document, 'pupils in Year 7 who have yet to achieve level 4 may need to follow a programme of work based largely on objectives in the Year 5 and Year 6 yearly teaching programmes, leaving the higher level work – particularly algebra – until later in Key Stage 3' (DfEE, 2001: 47). Many mathematics departments feel that the structure suggested in the Strategy does not suit the pupils in their school or, more likely, it does not suit all the pupils in their school, and consequently they adapt the given plans in some way.

Having decided on the mathematical objectives for the year, the department staff must decide what will be taught in order to help pupils attain the objectives. Most teachers are good at this; they take guidance from others, identify mathematical progression across the key stages and list the relevant mathematical topics in a coherent way. Where many mathematics departments are weaker is in putting these long-term plans into the context of the children's overall learning, such as the Every Child Matters outcomes and education for citizenship.

Long-term planning should address the key concepts listed at the beginning of the 2008 National Curriculum (QCA, 2007): competence, creativity, applications and implications of mathematics and critical understanding. Most of these key concepts are fairly easy to incorporate into a mathematics scheme of work, but they need to be considered on a year-by-year basis to ensure a coherent approach. For example, a good scheme of work will include reference to where creativity can be promoted in each year, and should provide guidance on how pupils can develop their understanding of the historical and cultural roots of mathematics. Long-term plans in mathematics should also provide guidance on how mathematics lessons can develop pupils' skills in literacy and ICT.

The National Curriculum requires all schools to teach about mathematical process skills. This happens most effectively if such teaching is incorporated into long-term plans. Within many topics, it is possible to plan opportunities for pupils to explore, reason and explain their mathematical thinking, either orally or in writing. Problem-solving and thinking skills are developed through presenting extended problems, where pupils try things out and experiment, and where they go through several stages of work in exploring the problem and presenting their solution. The Framework suggests that such work should take up 15–20 per cent of teaching time, and be spread across work on number, algebra, geometry and statistics, so clearly a good deal of planning is required to ensure that this happens.

Mathematics departments can also play a part in developing citizenship education. Most departments have a paragraph on citizenship written into their handbooks; some go further and make reference to citizenship in their schemes of work. One example of developing citizenship through mathematics lessons is work on money management and interest rates, which can be related to becoming an active citizen. Similarly, work on interpreting data contributes to pupils' ability to make informed choices, and helps pupils to avoid being taken in by misleading advertisements or presentations. Other examples include comparing methods of statistical enquiry, ensuring that sampling methods are not biased and investigating pollution through the analysis of statistical data.

Good long-term planning helps not only with balance and progression, but also provides guidance on good practice and a range of teaching ideas. An overview from school inspections concludes that:

The best schemes ensure consistency of teaching and lead to smooth progression in learning because they:

- make clear the prerequisite knowledge on which each unit or programme is based and how learning should progress
- contain a broad range of rich and stimulating classroom tasks with clear learning outcomes
- require the use of a range of teaching and learning approaches
- integrate reasoning, investigative and problem-solving skills, recognising that these are essential to mathematical thinking
- include appropriate ICT experiences at various stages to enhance the learning of mathematics
- make reference to the development of cross-curricular skills such as literacy and ICT.
(Ofsted, 2005: 9)

MEDIUM-TERM PLANNING

When long-term planning is complete, the department has decided what mathematics is going to be taught in each year, and how and when whole-school issues are to be addressed. Medium-term planning then puts more detail on this. The year's work is split into what is to be taught each term or half term, ensuring progression during the year and ensuring that there is a reasonable balance of topics in each half term. For example, it is clearly desirable to split up the work on algebra in a given year into separate units of work, each lasting perhaps three weeks, and to place the different algebra units at different times within the year, rather than do them all in one go.

The Framework document (DfEE, 2001) provides guidelines on how to carry out medium term planning by providing planning charts. On the Standards website is a set of sample medium-term plans, which schools can use in their entirety if they wish. In practice, many schools take the given examples as a starting point for their medium-term plans. They use the guidance, but adapt the plans to the needs of their school and their pupils.

For most trainee teachers and newly qualified teachers, the planning up to this stage has generally been done for them by the department in their school. When you arrive in school, you are likely to be given a copy of the departmental handbook and a scheme of work that lists, often in much detail, what is to be taught to each class and when. Your task, given that you are in the school for a limited number of weeks, is to ascertain which part of the scheme of work you will be responsible for teaching, and to map out lesson by lesson how your teaching is going to cover the material in the weeks available to you. It is good practice at this stage to give thought to what the main objective of each lesson will be and what resources will be used. It is also useful to think about where homework needs to be set and to plan what homework might be given.

Here is one experienced teacher's approach to medium-term planning:

When I plan a series of lessons, I look at the scheme of work and look at the description of the topic, and then I break that down into smaller units. I tend to have my starters linked in some way into the main part of my lesson, whether it is reviewing prior knowledge or linking in with a related area of the curriculum. For example, today I did a lesson on trigonometry, and so my starter focused on Pythagoras' theorem. This was so that, at the end of the lesson, we could easily see when to use trigonometry and when to use Pythagoras. The plenary then focused on whether the pupils had understood which we would use when. Wherever possible, I make links with other areas of the subject.

Once I have broken the topic down, I tend to think it through and note down a framework of things that I know that I want to cover, and the key areas. If there is a key idea that I want to make sure that the pupils understand, then I write that into my notes for the lesson.

This illustrates an analysis of the subject matter that structures the new material, and considers the pace at which new ideas are introduced. It also illustrates clearly a determination to avoid teaching a topic in isolation, by making explicit links with prior learning.

Two examples of trainees' planning at this level are given below. Notice that in each example, there is evidence of forward planning, ensuring that individual lesson plans will fit together to make a coherent progression of ideas. Different individuals will inevitably produce medium-term plans that are different in appearance, but you should ensure that your plans identify how many lessons are due to be spent on each topic and which lessons these are (with dates). Your plans should show how that topic is developed in a series of stepped objectives, and how the topic is going to be assessed. A further example of a medium-term plan is given on the website, (www.sagepub. co.uk/secondary) together with electronic versions of these two plans, so that you can adapt them for your own use.

Medium-Term Teaching Plan

Measures Unit 2 (12 Lessons) Year 9

Lesson	Topics to be Covered	Homework	Resource	NC Reference
Lesson 1 (Mon)	Circumference of a circle. Formula for circumference		Measure diameters and circumferences of objects to calculate pi. PPT presentation	Ma3/4h Find circumferences of circles
Lesson 2 (Tue)	Using the formula for circumference of circle. History of pi	Prepared w/s. 5 questions for Monday	PPT starter. Ex 6b in textbook PPT worded problem	As above
Lesson 3 (Wed)	Worded questions on circumference		Worksheet (10 ticks) – worded questions	As above
Lesson 4 (Thurs)	Worded questions on circumference. Extended question: group activity on designing a mini-trundle wheel	Questions from practice book	10 ticks worded questions (to finish) Problem sheet	Ma3/1b,c (Using and applying maths)

(Continued)

Lesson	Topics to be Covered	Homework	Resource	NC Reference
Lesson 5 (Mon)	Area of a circle. Formula for area. Practice calculating areas		Notebook presentation on area of circle Ex 6c q 2, 4, 5, 6 PPT Presentation	Ma3/4h Find areas enclosed by circles
Lesson 6 (Tue)	Metric units for area and volume. Area Volume Capacity	Revise for test	PPT Starter for missing units. PPT for unit conversions Ex 6d text books	Ma3/4i Convert between area measures
Lesson 7 (Wed)	Conversion between related metric units		PPT conversions Ex 6d textbooks	Ma3/4i Convert between area measures
Lesson 8 (Thurs)	TEST ON CIRCUMFERENCE AND AREA OF CIRCLES		Test questions using TestBase	
Lesson 9 (Mon)	Review test. Consolidation of conversions, including imperial units		10 mental questions on conversions. Prepared worksheet	Ma3/4i Convert between area measures
Lesson 10 (Tue)	Volume and surface area of prisms Definition of a prism	Worksheet Questions 1–5	PPT for definition of prism Selection of prisms to demonstrate Worksheet (to prepare)	Ma3/4g Calculate Volumes of right prisms
Lesson 11 (Wed)	Recap of VOLUME of prisms		Visual aids – various prism packages Worksheet	Ma3/4g Calculate volumes of right prisms
Lesson 12 (Thurs)	Recap on SURFACE AREA of prisms	Worded questions 6 and 7	PPT for surface area of prisms Worksheet	

(Continued)

YEAR 7 SET 2 - MEDIUM-TERM PLAN

Lesson No	Date	Lesson Topic	Learning Objectives	Resources	National Curriculum Reference
1	08/01	Algebra	Use the rules of algebra to write algebraic formulae correctly	Board pens, text books, exercise books	KS3, Ma, 5a 'distinguish the different roles played by letter symbols in algebra'
2	09/01	Algebra	i. Use tables to spot patterns ii. Link patterns in geometry and number iii. Express problems in algebraic form	'Quick questions', worksheets, textbooks, exercise books, board pens, rulers	KS, Ma2, 1b: 'breakdown a complex calculation into simpler steps before attempting to solve it' 5f 'derive a formula'
3	15/01	Algebra	i. relate a pattern to a table ii. find a rule from a table in words iii. write the rule as an algebraic formula	OHP, acetates and pens, board pens, text and exercise books	As above
4	16/01	Algebra	i. Substitute numbers for letters in an algebraic formula.	Board pens, text books, exercise books	KS3, Ma2, 5f 'substitute numbers into a formula
5	17/01	Algebra	i. Substitute numbers into expressions ii. Substitute numbers to solve formulas iii. Getting information from worded questions	Text books 7.2, exercise books, magic squares starter sheet, board pens	As above

Lesson No	Date	Lesson Topic	Learning Objectives	Resources	National Curriculum Reference
6	19/01	Algebra	i. to review worded algebra substitution questions ii. To revise and practise all algebraic knowledge learnt	Projector, PowerPoint presentation, text books, exercise books, homework booklets, board pens	As above
7	22/01	Negative numbers	i. Identify negative numbers ii. Order negative numbers	Text books, exercise books, board pens, plenary number cards	KS3, Ma2, 2a 'understand and use negative integers both as positions and translations on a number line; order integers'
8	23/01	Negative numbers	i. use a number line to find the difference between two numbers, including both positive and negative numbers ii. use a calculator to find the difference between two numbers including –ve numbers	Text books, exercise books, board pens, calculators, worksheets	As above
9	29/01	Negative Numbers	i. add and subtract	Text books 7.7, exercise books,	As above

(Continued)

(Continued)

Lesson No	Date	Lesson Topic	Learning Objectives	Resources	National Curriculum Reference
			negative numbers ii. To use negative numbers in other contexts	board pens, projector, PowerPoint presentation, starter sheets	
10	30/01	Negative numbers	i. Plot points in all four quadrants ii. Reflect shapes in the axes	Rulers, pencils, projector, set up on the whiteboard not the screen	As above
11	31/01	Negative numbers	i. Plot co-ordinates correctly and join up and extend straight lines. ii. Given the equation of a line, find the *y* co-ordinate value given the *x* co-ordinate value	Text books, exercise books, rulers, pencils/pens, projector, board pens.	KS3, Ma2, As above e) 'understand that one co-ordinate identifies a point on the number line, two co-ordinates identify a point in a plane and three co-ordinates identify a point in space; use axes and co-ordinates to specify points in all four quadrants; locate points with given co-ordinates; find the co-ordinates of points identified by geometrical information

Lesson No	Date	Lesson Topic	Learning Objectives	Resources	National Curriculum Reference
12	02/02	Negative numbers	i. Write down the rules of lines, given co-ordinates. ii. Find the point of intersection of two lines	Projector (if possible), text books, exercise books, board pens, rulers, pencils	As above
14	05/01	Revision	i. Put data into a tally chart, pictograms, bar charts, pie charts, scatter diagrams, correlation. ii. Algebra: writing rules in algebra, rules of algebra, collecting terms, substitution iii. Negative numbers; >,<, ordering numbers, using a calculator, plotting points in four quadrants, rules of lines, point of intersection.	Text books, exercise books, projector, PowerPoint presentation on revision	N/A
15	06/02	Unit Test	i. To develop skills for future examinations	Test papers, pens/pencils	N/A
16	19/02	Units of length: scale drawing	i. to know how many feet are in a yard, how	Metre rule, ruler, board pens	KS3, Ma3, 4a) 'convert measurements from one unit to

(Continued)

(Continued)

Lesson No	Date	Lesson Topic	Learning Objectives	Resources	National Curriculum Reference
			many inches in a foot, etc. ii. convert between feet, inches and yards		another; know rough metric equivalents of pounds, feet, miles, pint and gallons, make sensible estimates of a range of measurements in everyday settings'
17	20/02	Units of length: scale drawing	i. know how many mm are in a centimetre etc ii. convert between mm, cm, m and km	Text books, exercise books, board pens	As above
18	21/02	Unit test review	Review test, Pupils will review their own work, and correct their mistakes	Test papers, board pens	As above
19	23/02	Units of length: scale drawing	i. Estimate conversions using rough approximations. ii. Convert from the imperial system to the metric system	Text books, exercise books, board pens, calculators – borrow from room 12.	As above

Good medium-term plans also provide some indication of the resources that will be used lesson by lesson. Regrettably, it remains the case that some schools base their medium-term planning around the use of a single textbook. It is easy to see how this can make life easier for the teachers planning the scheme of work, but it often proves to be a severe limiting factor on teaching styles and content. In 1992, inspectors reported that textbooks were the dominant influence in forming the curriculum in many schools (HMI, 1992). Inspectors criticized teachers for claiming that the textbooks had done the planning for them, and that, as a result, they did not need to undertake any further detailed planning. In the late 1990s, a national initiative to improve departmental planning involved training for heads of department, with guidance on developing schemes of work.

It is likely that fewer schools today would fall into the category described by Millet and Johnson (1996: 59) as 'scheme driven' planners, where the published textbook forms the starting point for departmental planning. It does, however, remain an issue, with more recent inspection evidence still identifying a common weakness in departmental planning as 'over-reliance on published materials that are adopted uncritically and not audited to ensure they match pupils' needs and prior experiences' (Ofsted, 2005: 9).

The examples given show how the trainees plan to use a textbook as one source of material, but they have made decisions about how and where the textbook should be supplemented by additional or alternative material. Even within a single topic, taking a single textbook as the only teaching resource is sometimes seen as a weakness. If you choose to rely on a single source, you are saying that the textbook writer has done everything right and their approach cannot be improved upon in any way. Your job is always to be selective about how to present a particular lesson, to use professional judgement that takes account of the needs of the class that you are teaching. So medium-term plans need to show that you have selected materials from a range of sources and have supplemented these with some original material where necessary or useful.

In the examples, the trainees make reference to the National Curriculum (DfEE, 1999) or to the Framework. By doing this, they ensure that the level of work is correct, and that it fits in with prior learning. They also ensure that they know how the work is developed further in future years. By specifying what homework is to be set and when, the trainees make sure that homework planning is not left to the last minute, but is given a high priority. This aspect of forward planning also helps with managing the marking load, by ensuring that it is spread over the course of a week.

Some medium-term plans include information beyond that which is given in these two examples. Some provide extra detail about differentiation, possibly identifying separate core objectives and extension objectives for the series of lessons. Others provide more about specific starter or plenary activities, or cross-curricular links (see, for example, Laing and MacInnes, 2000). It is also helpful to consider styles of working, making decisions about whether there will be an opportunity for practical work, pupil discussion or other forms of group work. Whatever headings you choose, you should take the school's planning and add in sufficient detail for it to form a useful, workable plan for a series of lessons.

SHORT-TERM PLANNING

A key challenge to all inexperienced teachers is how to plan individual lessons. In the early stages of your teaching career, you need to write out these plans in far more detail than will be necessary for experienced teachers. There are several reasons for this. First, writing things down (particularly following set prompts) promotes detailed thinking about all the aspects of a lesson. Planning that has not been written down will often miss some detail about how the lesson will progress. Second, writing things down clarifies thinking in the same way that putting ideas into words aids learning. The process of writing out the plan helps to focus your mind on the key features of the lesson.

Knowing that the lesson is well planned enables you to approach it with far more confidence than if it is only partly prepared, and confidence itself is a major factor in how well you come across to the pupils. Finally, a written plan is an extremely useful aide-mémoire to use during the lesson. It can be referred to at different parts of the lesson, for example to remind you which examples you plan to go through with the whole class or which page to use in the textbook. What seem small points can make a significant difference to how the lesson flows and the image that you present to the pupils.

Just because you see little evidence of written planning, you may be misled into thinking that experienced teachers do not plan their lessons. They do! Where their experience helps is in being able to hold a lot of this planning in their minds, supported by whatever notes may be necessary. As your experience increases, you will find the amount of detail that you need to write in your lesson plans reduces.

While the detailed format of a lesson plan will be subject to individual interpretation, there is considerable consensus on what a good lesson plan should contain. Asking a group of teachers what they would expect from a trainee's lesson plan, invariably generates a list that includes the following headings:

- class details
- objectives
- starter/main/plenary activities
- reference to the National Curriculum or examination syllabus
- equipment or resources needed
- differentiation
- assessment.

 A very similar list (although strangely omitting any reference to planned assessment) appears in National Strategy guidance (DfES, 2002). Other headings are suggested as well, and written plans can usefully include a section on one or more of the following:

- key words, mathematical vocabulary, literacy development
- learning outcomes
- learning styles
- teacher activity and pupil activity
- cross-curricular links
- key questions to ask
- possible misconceptions, likely errors
- prior learning
- deployment of additional staff
- homework.

A key element to a lesson plan is the list of objectives. You have to be clear about the main purpose of the lesson, and what the pupils will be able to do by the end of the lesson. Many trainees are not sufficiently precise in their use of lesson objectives or they trivialize the objectives. Others write down objectives that cannot possibly be measured, thus making it impossible to evaluate the lesson. Some examples of weak objectives (with an indication in brackets of why they are weak) are:

Objectives:
Pupils will be able to

- Make up equations and solve them. (How difficult are these equations?)
- Recognize and visualize line symmetry of two-dimensional shapes. (We can probably test whether they can recognize symmetry, but it would be very difficult to know whether pupils were able to visualize symmetry.)
- Complete Chapter 10 Exercise 3.2. (This is very precise and measurable, but does not have any mathematical learning attached to it.)
- Understand Pythagoras' theorem. (Do we want them to be able to state it, use it, or apply it in a range of contexts? More detail is needed.)
- Bisect a line, an angle and construct a triangle given three sides. (This is fine, but is better written as three separate objectives, which can be measured separately.)

One, two or at the most three objectives are usually sufficient for a single lesson. More than that and it is likely that the lesson will be lacking sufficient focus. It is often useful to create differentiated objectives, along the lines of:

By the end of this lesson:

All pupils will be able to calculate the hypotenuse of a right-angled triangle, given the other two sides.
Some pupils will be able to calculate the third side of a right-angled triangle, given the other two sides.
A few pupils will be able to apply Pythagoras' theorem in a range of contexts.

It can be useful to distinguish between lesson objectives and learning outcomes. Lesson objectives are what the pupils should understand or be able to do by the end of the lesson; learning outcomes are the evidence to show that the pupils have achieved the objectives. The distinction is sometimes summarized by the acronyms:

WALT – we are learning today (for the lesson objectives)
WILF – what I am looking for (for the learning outcomes).

This can help with communication to the class about the lesson objectives. The WALT statements are the learning objectives; the WILF statements are the success criteria. Sharing the WILF criteria with the pupils lets them see how they can achieve the objectives. Make up your own mind whether you think that the distinction between objectives and learning outcomes is helpful.

Point for reflection

Many people recommend that a good starting point for planning is to list objectives. It has been argued (Jones and Smith, 1997) that this can have the drawback of leading to mechanistic teaching, where opportunities for being creative in the classroom may be missed. Reflect upon the extent to which you agree with this. Suggest ways that you can ensure that your itemized objectives do not lead to itemized learning.

PLANNING MATHEMATICALLY

Having decided on the objectives of the lesson, you need to think in detail about the mathematics that will be included. The objectives identify what you want the pupils to learn, but not how that learning will take place. As a next step, it helps to list on paper all the possible ways that the mathematics can be taught, so that each can be considered in turn and assessed according to its merits and drawbacks.

Here is how experienced teachers describe their thinking at this stage of the planning process:

If I have done something that worked well, I tend to stick to that way of putting the mathematics across. But I do tend to have more than one way of doing different things, and it would depend on the ability of the group, and individuals within the group as to how I decided to teach each individual topic.

I think a lot about the mathematics and the assessment, as they tend to be the key things. I plan carefully for the maths content of the lesson. With experience you see the pitfalls and problems that are likely to occur because you have been there and done it before.

In my planning, I think hard about where the problems are going to come up. I identify what the key ideas are, and where there are going to be stumbling blocks. I often think back to the different methods I have used in the past, and compare how effective they were. I usually think that I can improve on the way that I taught it last time.

Many trainee teachers have very limited ideas about the different mathematical approaches to teaching a particular topic. Unless you have undertaken extensive lesson observations, you are likely to start your thinking by referring back to the way that you were taught the topic when you were at school. During training you need to develop your knowledge of alternative approaches by sharing ideas with others, or perhaps by asking your mentor to provide a list of alternative approaches for you to evaluate.

Consider, for example, a lesson where the objective is that pupils will be able to multiply a pair of linear algebraic expressions. Discussion with groups of trainees usually brings the following suggestions for ways to teach the mathematics:

1.	$(x + 5)(x - 2) = x(x - 2) + 5(x - 2)$ $\qquad\qquad\quad = x^2 - 2x + 5x - 10$ $\qquad\qquad\quad = x^2 + 3x - 10$ The 'splitting' method
2.	FOIL – a mnemonic for 'first, outer, inner, last', the four pairs of terms that need to be multiplied
3.	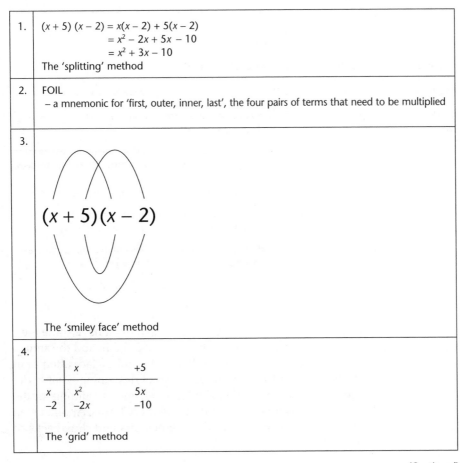 The 'smiley face' method
4.	 $$\begin{array}{c c c} & x & +5 \\ \hline x & x^2 & 5x \\ -2 & -2x & -10 \end{array}$$ The 'grid' method

(Continued)

5.

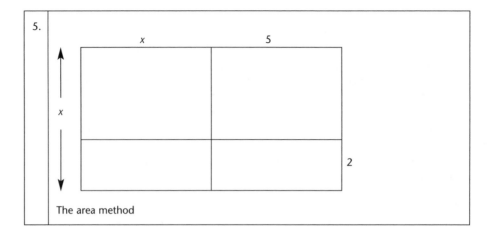

The area method

Table 3.1 Benefits and drawbacks of each method

Method	Benefits	Drawbacks
1. The 'splitting' method	Logical, mathematical approach. Develops algebraic skills.	Could be dull
2. FOIL	Easy to remember	Just a mnemonic. No links with other mathematical ideas
3. The 'smiley face' method	Easy to remember. Amusing	An unfamiliar presentation
4. The 'grid' method	Links well with grid method for multiplying numbers	Has an informal appearance
5. The area method	Nice pictorial approach. Links well with knowledge of areas	Illustration is more complex for negative terms

All five of these approaches are in current use, so each must have some merits. There is clearly a difference between methods 2 and 3 (FOIL and the smiley face) and the other three methods. Neither FOIL nor the smiley face attempt to explain why the method works; they are simply ways of describing what to do. The other three methods make links with prior learning, and are aiming for the learners to understand what is meant by multiplying these terms. Another step in the planning process may then be to assess the benefits and drawbacks of each method (Table 3.1).

Having decided upon the mathematical approach to be employed, the next step in the planning process is to think about the structure of the lesson. This will depend heavily on the amount of time available, but let us consider, for example, planning a 60-minute lesson on multiplying out linear terms. Say you have decided to employ method 1, the splitting method, with the intention of using the smiley face illustration at the end of the lesson. You need to plan how the time in the lesson will be spent. You want the lesson to involve as much pupil activity as possible, but also to employ some direct interactive teaching methods. You also want the method used to make sense to the pupils, rather than just showing them a method for getting the correct answer.

A suitable starter would be a short revision activity on the topic of algebraic terms. For example, you could plan to spend 5 minutes on the activity below.

Find the equivalent pairs:

A	$4(x - 5)$	1	$4x - 4$
B	$4(x - 1)$	2	$-2x^2 - 10x$
C	$x(x + 2)$	3	$6x - 10$
D	$2(3x - 5)$	4	$12x - 8$
E	$x(3 + x)$	5	$4x - 20$
F	$-4(2 - 3x)$	6	$4 - x$
G	$-2x(x + 5)$	7	$x^2 + 3x$
H	$-(x - 4)$	8	$x^2 + 2x$

This activity is one that you expect the class to do with relatively few errors, but you may still wish to spend a few minutes discussing the answers and getting pupils to explain and justify their answers.

For the main activity, one possible approach is to write up on the display board the two mathematical expressions

$$A = (x + 6)(x - 1)$$
$$B = x^2 + 5x - 6,$$

and ask pupils to select a value for x. For the given value of x, you ask the pupils to evaluate each of the expressions, and then you challenge them to find what happens for other values of x. Having established that there is an intuitive case for the two expressions being equal, you can engage in the mathematical justification chosen from the above list of alternatives.

At the planning stage, it is vital that not only is the mathematical approach well thought through, but also that the particular examples are carefully chosen. In the case of multiplying out brackets, one approach to the choice of examples is to consider first only linear factors containing positive coefficients and positive integers such as $(x + 3) (x + 6)$. Only when pupils are secure with the mathematical ideas of multiplying out the brackets will you develop the ideas to cover more general cases. This illustrates a general principle that trainee teachers sometimes take some time to grasp: pupils need new ideas to be introduced slowly; too many new ideas at once and they can be overwhelmed. In this case, when the pupils have shown success in multiplying out linear factors with all terms positive, the lesson can move on to consider cases such as $(x + 4) (x - 5)$, $(x - 2) (x - 1)$. Depending on the class, this may be as far as you decide to go in one lesson. Questions of the type $(2x + 1) (2x - 5)$, $(4 - 3x)$ $(2 - x)$, $(x - 1) (3 + 7x)$, where the extra difficulty comes from coefficients of x other than one, and different orderings of the terms within each factor, may be included as extension work.

The choice of mathematical approach may be influenced by factors other than personal choice; you need also to consider prior learning. One particular approach may fit in with the way the topics have been introduced in the past, whereas other approaches may sit rather uncomfortably with previous related learning. To some extent you can do this by looking at the school's scheme of work or the Framework to see how the progression of ideas in this topic is developed. But almost certainly, you will need to talk to the class teacher about the class, the previous work that they have done, and the approaches that have been used.

Above almost all other things, you should use your planning time to ensure that the mathematics contained in your lesson is correct in every detail. Your language must be precise and accurate, and your explanations must be flawless in their logic. Take time to check this, even when you are confident with the fundamentals of the mathematics involved; it is in the detail that you are more likely to make an error.

The two lesson plans given below are examples of how complete plans can look. Each comes from a different trainee, and has its own style, but both include the same important features that were listed earlier, such as lesson objectives, equipment needed and how learning will be assessed. Notice that the plans here both give anticipated timings for the different parts of the lesson. These can give enormous support during the lesson, either to help you to stick to the plan or to be aware of how you are adapting the plan according to the circumstances. Electronic versions of these, and additional lesson plans, are available on the website that accompanies this book.

Lesson plan

Year Group: 7	Ability Set: 2 of 4	Number of Pupils: 24	Room: 6
Date: Friday 12th January 2007		Duration: 50 minutes	Period 2

National Curriculum:

MA4 – Handling data 1
(a, e, f), 3(a)
Level 4

Learning Objectives: Pupils will be able to …
- Put raw data into a grouped frequency table
- Represent the frequency table in a bar chart

Homework:
* To write a brief report on the investigation that was carried out in the previous lesson
* Due date: Monday 15th January

Working Resources:

Collins textbook
A4 Squared paper

Individual Pupils:

Follow up Molly to check overdue homework.

Equipment:

Promethean Board
Whiteboard
Board Ruler

Key Vocabulary:

Grouped Frequency Table, raw data, classes, sample, frequency

---

STARTER

09:50 am

1. Explain the rules of the loop game and how one person answers to the question of another
2. Give out the spare cards to selected pupils
3. Introduce a timer to see how quickly it is completed

Allocated Time: 10 minutes

MAIN ACTIVITY

Phase 1
10:00 am

1. Arrange the pupils in the same groups as previous lesson to complete the bar chart representing the results from the survey (*about 5 to 10 minutes*). (*Extension: write a brief report explaining the investigation that was carried out and the results that they obtained. A list of points to include will be displayed on the board.*)

(Continued)

2. Call class's attention and instruct them to get their planners out, and write in details about homework. Hand out the homework sheets and ask the children to complete it in the back of their exercise books. (*3 to 5 minutes*).

Phase 2

1. Get the pupils to write down the title 'Grouped Frequencies', together with the date.
2. **LO to be able to produce grouped frequency tables, and represent on a bar chart.**
3. Go through the example on power point presentation 'grouped frequency tables', pausing to ask questions.
4. Key questions:

   • How could we display this data in a sensible manner?
   • What about the different values – would it be easy/suitable to draw a bar chart with such a large range/variety of values?
   • What would make it easier to display these results on a bar chart?
   • What kind of groups could we split them into?
   • How could we record this in a table?
   • What labels should we use for the axes?

   (The pupils should be ready to attempt the exercise by 10:25 am)
5. Set the class Questions 1 and 2 from exercise 8C, page 88. (Extension: Question 3)

   Allocated Time: 35 minutes

PLENARY

10:35 am

1. Ask what is a class? What size classes should you choose?
2. Why do we need to draw a grouped frequency table?
3. How would we know which values have been included in the different bars or classes?

   Allocated Time: 5 minutes

ASSESSMENT

   ✓ As the class is working through the set task I will be walking around the class monitoring progress and answering any questions

   ✓ Providing feedback to individuals by checking their grouped frequency tables as I am going around the class

   ✓ The class will be showing each other their work at the beginning of the lesson and discussion their findings.

   ✓ The homework has been designed to consolidate the work covered mainly in the previous lesson, but finished off in this lesson. This will be discussed at the beginning of Monday's lesson when I will also be taking in the pupils books to mark them.

Lesson plan – area of triangles

Year: 7	Ability: Set 2	Number of pupils : 26
Date : 17.01	Period : 1	Duration : 50 minutes

Aims

Pupils will:

  – Know where the formula for the area of triangles is derived from
  – Use this formula to find the area of different triangles

Objectives

Pupils will be able to:

  – Find the area of right angled triangles
  – Find the area of other triangles

Keywords: Area, square centimetre, perpendicular, base, height.

National Curriculum reference: MA3 Level 5

Resources: OHP for starter activity, prepared resource, homework sheets, pencils, rulers, post it notes and thought wall.

Starter Activity: 9:05 am (5–10 minutes)

Matching angle facts OHP. Girls versus boys, pupils take turns to pick grid references and try to match the angle facts. Run through exactly what to do first. May need to discuss statements (e.g. vertically opposite angles).

Main Activity: 9:15 am (30–35 minutes)

Pupils copy title, date and objectives. Recap how to find the area of a rectangle. Then draw a right angled triangle on the board. 2 minute brainstorm for each pupil to think how to find the area and discuss with a neighbour. Share ideas. Formalize into a formula. Example to show that it works, with base 4 cm and height 3 cm. **Ex 10F pg 208**. For question 1, I may need to discuss what perpendicular means. After 15–20 minutes stop the class and cover an example of a non-right-angled triangle, use prepared resource to demonstrate that the formula used is the same. Follow up work from **Ex 10G, pg 210**. Any pupils who finish the exercise may begin prepared extension sheet.

Differentiation: prepared extension sheet, prepared notes for BB.

Plenary: (9:50 am (5 minutes)

Give each child a post it note and ask them to write how they feel they have done in today's lesson. They can stick these onto the thought wall.

Homework: N/A

Assessment

Assessment of prior knowledge in the starter activity. Questioning in the main activity and the starter activity, asking children to come to the front of the class and marking work when on task.

ISSUES IN PLANNING

An often neglected aspect of planning is to consider what might be called the bigger picture. It is good practice to ask yourself the question, 'Why are we doing this piece of mathematics?', because this is a question that pupils frequently ask. In many cases (for example algebraic topics), one answer is that it builds up mathematical understanding and helps us to solve problems. Other topics have more obvious answers, such as transformations in design work or prime numbers in cryptography.

Another useful area of reflection is how the lesson can be linked in with other areas of mathematics, other school subjects or life outside school. The Framework emphasizes the need to present the subject as more than a set of isolated topics. Pupils need to be shown explicitly links with other areas of mathematics, with good planning ensuring that 'mathematical ideas are presented in an interrelated way, not in isolation from each other' (DfEE, 2001: 46).

A collection of visual aids is helpful in showing how mathematics is linked to situations outside school. During the training year(s) and in the early years of teaching, it is well worth collecting supporting examples of mathematics from the media or the Internet. Goulding (2004) provides some useful suggestions for a file of resources:

- a local bus timetable
- a train timetable
- a list of foreign exchange rates
- temperatures around the world
- sports results
- pages from catalogues
- a page from an A–Z of the area near to the school
- a photocopy of a map of the locality.

The Internet provides an excellent source of back-up material for mathematics lessons. This is especially true for graphs, charts and lists of data, but also applies to other areas of mathematics such as tessellations, symmetry, or maps and scales.

Having used the objectives to plan the main mathematical content of the lesson, you need to consider whether the planned work is suitable for all pupils in the class. In many cases, you will have conceived the plan as focusing on the needs of the middle range of ability in the class, and you now need to look again at the plan to see how it relates to the needs of different groups.

Even when mathematics teaching is organized in classes that are set by ability, there is always a range of ability within a class, and a range of individual needs above that, and, as Haggarty (2002) says, you need to make a conscious effort to avoid having your lessons suit only the middle ability range within the class.

The plan is likely to need adapting to take account of the needs of all learners. In mathematics, this differentiated planning often means providing support materials for the least able, and providing extension work for the most able, but it can also make provision for pupils with different preferred learning styles. Kinchin (2007) reports a 'general agreement' that individuals differ in their preferences for gathering and processing information. These different learning styles are often categorized onto three headings: visual, auditory and kinaesthetic. The pupils described as visual learners learn most effectively when information is presented to them in the form of pictures or diagrams. Auditory learners learn through listening, both to the teacher and to other pupils. Kinaesthetic learners learn best when they have some physical materials to manipulate or move around.

Visual learners are often well catered for in mathematics lessons, where teachers usually support the spoken word with a diagram or a piece of mathematics to look at. Auditory learners respond well when the teacher sets up opportunities for group discussion or encourages pupils to explain their methods to the rest of the class. Kinaesthetic learners respond well to physical activity. There are many examples in mathematics, such as matching cards, using multi-link cubes, measuring, or constructing shapes and solids. In your planning, consider whether your teaching style tends towards one particular learning style, and ensure that, over time, you give all pupils opportunities to learn in their own preferred style. In addition, try to encourage pupils to become more flexible in their learning styles, since research suggests that 'the most successful pupils are those who can access and process information in a variety of ways' (DfES, 2004: 8).

A commonly seen approach to catering for different abilities is to allow (or expect) a different pace of working within a normal class setting. This does not mean that pupils are accelerating continually, as often used to happen in the early years of secondary school, where pupils worked individually through a mathematics scheme at their own pace. It means that the pupils, within individual lessons, are working at different rates and that some will finish the core work more quickly than others. Good planning takes this into account by providing extension activities that may involve more searching questions or additional activities. Importantly when setting more tasks on the same topic, the plan needs to ensure that such work really does lead to further learning, so the extension work must be more challenging or in an unfamiliar context, or lead to a more general understanding of the topic. Sadly, in some lessons many able or fast-working pupils are given 'more of the same' to keep them busy while other pupils complete the core work.

General support for individual pupils involves understanding what the pupils can already do, and what particular strengths, weaknesses and needs have been identified in the past. The particular needs of some pupils are documented in Individual Education Plans; the needs of others may be less formally recognized in school or departmental records. At the planning stage, you should consider how the lesson might need adapting for special needs. For example, to help illustrate a particular mathematical idea, it may be helpful to bring to the lesson specific resources. In a lesson on rotational symmetry, you might plan to support the least able by providing multi-link cubes so that the pupil can build the shape and rotate it. All pupils benefit from learning opportunities which are well matched to their needs and abilities, but this is particularly important for pupils who have special educational needs (SCAA, 1996).

Lesson planning performs another important function in catering for the needs of all. It is at the planning stage that you need to consider the support that can be provided by any additional adults in the classroom. Making the most of this support is not an easy task, but in the best planned lessons the work of teaching assistants is managed, rather than left to their (perhaps considerable) professional expertise.

It is vitally important to think carefully about the class that the lesson is planned for, and reflect whether the planned activities exclude any individuals from taking a full part in the lesson. This may include considering whether gender or cultural backgrounds will have any effect on participation in the lesson. It may also include considering whether all learning styles are accommodated, and whether there are particular language demands that will cause difficulties for those with poorly developed language skills or those for whom English is an additional language.

One aspect of planning that is often fairly weak among trainees is planning for assessment. Most planning templates include an 'Assessment' heading, which helps you to focus attention on how you are going to assess the pupils' progress. Be careful that you avoid the temptation to copy and paste the same phrase under this heading in every plan. A phrase such as, 'give out answers; ask questions in the plenary', has nothing wrong with it, as long as it is not thought to apply to every lesson. At the planning stage, you need to consider a range of different ways in which the learning can be assessed during the lesson. Examples may include

- use of questioning to gauge understanding
- looking at exercise books to monitor successful completion of written work
- listening to discussion between pupils
- interacting with pupils on a one-to-one basis
- taking note of the pupils' assessment of their own learning
- a show of hands to indicate a number of correct answers
- a plenary activity that focuses on assessing learning.

In the early stages of working in a school, you should include in your plans a list of the equipment that you will need in the lesson. This may seem like a trivial level of planning, but writing down the equipment and resources that are needed makes it far less likely that you will have to rush off at the last minute to locate some vital piece of equipment. Equipment is a particular problem for you as a trainee teacher, because you are always working in someone else's classroom, and may not know where the teacher keeps the stock of protractors, pencils, calculators, multi-link cubes or whatever. Teaching in a number of different rooms, as will usually be the case, means that you have to know where each teacher keeps each piece of equipment – a challenge for anyone.

HOMEWORK

Your plans should give due consideration to the setting of homework. It is not good practice to think about what to set for homework during the lesson! Think of the two purposes of homework as being to consolidate and extend learning; it may be appropriate to set work on what has been learnt most of the time, but you should also, from time to time, set work that is more challenging. It is good to set an occasional homework that involves pupils in finding out or in trying to apply their knowledge in new ways.

You should not routinely set homework that asks pupils to finish off the exercise that they are doing. Although this may be appropriate on occasion, it is not appropriate as a regular practice. 'Finishing off' homeworks are likely to give the most able pupils little to do; it is better to plan your homework with the whole class in mind, and as a piece of work that is separate from classwork.

SUMMARY OF THE PLANNING PROCESS

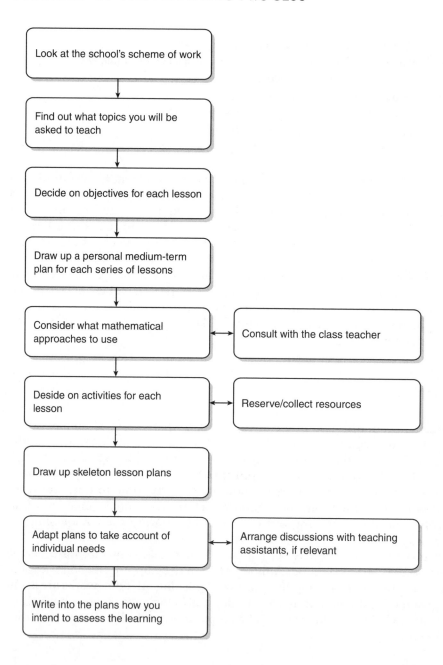

EVIDENCE FROM THE RESEARCH

The Framework has provided considerable guidance with planning on a whole-school basis and on a departmental basis. This level of planning has an impact on individual teachers' planning but, more importantly, it helps to ensure consistency of teaching. Inspection evidence suggests that most schools have adequate schemes of work, but many could be further developed. Inspectors report that in many departments, schemes of work are not sufficiently well developed to give non-specialist or inexperienced teachers the support that they need (Ofsted, 2005). In the best schools, departments use their to follow scheme of work as a basis for a wide range of staff development activities, where teachers discuss different mathematical approaches, share successful lesson ideas and develop good practice as a team.

Much research into the efficacy of lesson planning is general to all teachers. For example, a practical guide to planning is provided by John (1993), who discusses the expected contents of a lesson plan and provides several possible alternative layouts that can be copied or adapted.

We referred earlier to students starting their teacher training with ideas on how to teach a topic heavily influenced by their own experience at school. John (1991) takes this a stage further and reports how trainees not only remember mathematical approaches, but also ideas about the structure of a lesson and how pupils learn. Trainees bring with them to their training courses a set of preconceived ideas about what a mathematics lesson is like. They find it difficult to reject their own view out of hand, despite advice and guidance from others. This means that an emphasis on lesson objectives and non-traditional approaches in the training course may be insufficient to challenge the traditional view of a mathematics lesson as a pattern of exposition, examples and practice (Jones and Smith, 1997). Even though their training course may provide guidance on alternative approaches, trainees are reluctant to move away from what is seen as a safe approach.

Research on learning styles is relevant to teaching in all subjects, but it is helpful to have evidence to support the use of resources and visual aids. Cano-Garcia and Hughes (2000) demonstrate how different learning styles affect academic achievement, and Marzano et al. (2001) summarize the research that learning is helped by visual representations, giving examples of graphs, diagrams and equipment. Aubusson et al. (1997) give evidence of the value of kinaesthetic activities. Paivio (1990) describes two ways that the brain receives information: through language and through visual imagery. In mathematics, most teaching situations demand that pupils engage in both forms of processing, and it is in processing information in two ways that learning is most effective.

Point for reflection

Point for reflection

Consider the lessons that you have observed up to now, and consider what planning went into making the lessons. In particular, contrast two lessons that you have seen – one that went well and one that went less well. Are you able to identify differences in the quality of the planning that went into the lessons?

Further reading

Jones, K. (2005) 'Planning for mathematics learning', in S. Johnston-Wilder, P. Johnston-Wilder, D. Pimm and J. Westwell (eds), *Learning to Teach Mathematics in the Secondary School*. Oxford: Routledge.

This chapter provides a good review of how to plan a series of lessons, and how to plan an individual lesson. It includes an attempt to model good planning by describing how experienced teachers plan. Interspersed among the text are 15 tasks for the reader to undertake, ranging from the fairly brief, 'Write down five (or more) reasons for planning lessons' to much more lengthy tasks such as reviewing a series of lessons, examining each lesson to check that every pupil can feel included in the activities, and analysing how the teacher has differentiated within the lesson.

Goulding, M. (2004) *Learning to Teach Mathematics in the Secondary School*. London: David Fulton.

This book contains a wealth of advice for the trainee teacher, including plenty of helpful advice on planning lessons. In the chapter that focuses specifically on planning, the author characterizes planning as reconciling the two notions: what understanding pupils bring to the lesson, and what learning the teacher wants to take place. The guidance presented is particularly focused on short-term planning. The book offers several examples of lesson plans, with useful commentaries on the strengths and weaknesses of each.

Useful websites

Live links to these sites can be found on the companion website.

The Teachernet website is a forum for a wide range of educational issues. In the mathematics section, you will find plenty of guidance and interesting resources for teaching mathematics at http://www.teachernet.gov.uk/teachingandlearning/subjects/maths/

The Standards website is an essential for all trainees. Here you will find National Strategy publications, including the Framework for Teaching Mathematics. http://www.standards. dfes.gov.uk/secondary/ will give you the choice of Key Stage 3 or Key Stage 4, before you then select the mathematics option. Advice on planning lessons can be found within the Framework on pages 44–56.

The sample medium-term plans can be downloaded at http://www.standards.dfes.gov.uk/secondary/keystage3/all/respub/ma_samplepln

Further guidance on general issues relating to planning can be found in the training module (Module 3) that can be downloaded from http://www.standards.dfes.gov.uk/secondary/keystage3/all/respub/fs_trmat

Information on learning styles (Unit 19) can be downloaded from http://www.standards. dfes.gov.uk/secondary/keystage3/all/respub/sec_pptl0

References

Aubusson, P., Foswill, S., Bart, R. and Perkovic, L. (1997) 'What happens when students do simulation role-play in science?', *Research in Science Education*, 27: 565–79.

Cano-Garcia, F. and Hughes, E.H. (2000) 'Learning and thinking styles: an analysis of their inter-relationship and influences on academic achievement', *Educational Psychology*, 20(4): 413–30.

Department for Education and Employment (DfEE) (1999) *The National Curriculum for England: Mathematics*. London: HMSO.

Department for Education and Employment (DfEE) (2001) *Key Stage 3 National Strategy: Framework for Teaching Mathematics Years 7, 8 and 9*. London: Department for Education and Employment.

Department for Education and Skills (DfES) (2002) *Training Materials for the Foundation Subjects. Module 3: Planning Lessons*. London: Department for Education and Skills.

Department for Education and Skills (DfES) (2004) *Pedagogy and Practice: Teaching and Learning in Secondary Schools. Unit 19: Learning Styles*. London: Department for Education and Skills.

Goulding, M. (2004) *Learning to Teach Mathematics in the Secondary School*. London: David Fulton.

Haggarty, L. (2002) 'Differentaiation', in L. Haggarty (ed.) *Aspects of Teaching Secondary Mathematics: Persectives on Practice*. London: Routledge.

Her Majesty's Inspectorate (HMI) (1992) *Mathematics Key Stages 1, 2 and 3. A Report by HM Inspectorate on the Second Year 1990–1*. London: HMSO.

John, P.D. (1991) 'A qualitative study of British student teachers' lesson planning perspectives', *Journal of Education for Teaching*, 17(3): 301–20.

John, P.D. (1993) *Lesson Planning for Teachers*. London: Cassell.

Jones, K. (2005) 'Planning for mathematics learning', in S. Johnston-Wilder, P. Johnston-Wilder, D. Pimm and J. Westwell (eds), *Learning to Teach Mathematics in the Secondary School*. Oxford: Routledge.

Jones, K. and Smith, K. (1997) 'Student teachers learning to plan mathematics lessons', paper presented at the annual conference of the Association of Mathematics Education Teachers (AMET), Leicester.

Kinchin, G.D. (2007) 'Understanding learning', in V. Ellis (ed.), *Achieving QTS: Learning and Teaching in Secondary Schools*. Exeter: Learning Matters.

Laing, G.B. and MacInnes, I. (2000) 'Another illustration of refraction', *School Science Review*, 82(299): 100–1.

Marzano, R.J., Pickering, D.J. and Pollock, J.E. (2001) *Classroom Instruction that Works*. Alexandria, VA: Association for Supervision and Curriculum Development.

Millett, A. and Johnson, D. (1996) 'Solving teachers' problems? The role of the commercial mathematics scheme', in D. Johnson and A. Millett (eds), *Implementing the National Curriculum, Policy, Politics and Practice*. London: Paul Chapman Publishing.

Office for Standards in Education (Ofsted) (2005) *Mathematics in Secondary Schools, Schools subject reports, The Annual Report of Her Majesty's Chief Inspector of Schools 2004/05*: Online at www.ofsted.gov.uk.

Paivio, A. (1990) *Mental Representations: A Dual Coding Approach*. New York: Oxford University Press.

Qualifications and Curriculum Authority (QCA) (2007) 'Mathematics Programme of Study: Key Stage 3'. Available for download at http://www.qca.org.uk/qca_12216.aspx (accessed 23 August 2007).

School Curriculum and Assessment Authority (SCAA) (1996) *Consistency in Teacher Assessment: Supporting Pupils with Special Educational Needs*. London: School Curriculum and Assessment Authority.

Training and Development Agency for Schools (TDA) (2007) *Professional Standards for Teachers: Why Sit Still in your Career?* London: Training and Development Agency for Schools.

4 THE ELEMENTS OF A MATHEMATICS LESSON

This chapter:

- examines how teachers organize the teaching time in mathematics lessons
- discusses reasons for employing starter and plenary activities
- gives examples of effective starters and plenaries
- discusses why plenaries are difficult and suggests ways of avoiding possible pitfalls
- illustrates practice by referring to a sample lesson.

All lessons take place within specified time limits, and these provide constraints for all teachers. In mathematics, timetable structures usually lead to lessons of about one hour's duration, and this chapter considers ways in which you can structure that time to best effect. Traditionally, a mathematics lesson consists of the teacher explaining some new piece of mathematics, and the pupils working through a series of written questions. At the end of the lesson, the teacher may provide some answers, and check who has got the work correct. This style of lesson has been challenged in recent years for being too predictable and unimaginative. It is also criticized for making insufficient use of the full range of effective learning strategies (which is discussed more fully in Chapter 5).

In practice, any well-planned lesson contains several different elements, which should combine together to form a coherent learning experience for the pupils. The Framework (DfEE, 2001) provides clear guidance on structuring a mathematics lesson. In a section entitled, 'A typical lesson', it recommends dividing a lesson into three parts: a beginning, a middle and an end. These three parts are described as:

- an oral and mental starter (about 5 to 10 minutes)
- the main teaching activity (about 25 to 40 minutes)
- a final plenary to round off the lesson (from 5 to 15 minutes).

This suggested structure is presented as 'typical', and should not be followed mechanistically. Unfortunately, this style of structuring a lesson has become too dominant a theme in the minds of some teachers, who characterize the recommendations of the Framework as being 'the three-part lesson'. This does a great disservice to the Framework, which is presenting recommendations about styles of teaching, learning and assessment that go far beyond a suggested lesson structure. It is certainly not expected that all mathematics lessons will follow the three-part lesson structure, and you should plan a structure that is appropriate to your lesson. This may, for example, have four parts to it, or contain a plenary activity that takes place in the middle of the lesson.

Various adaptations of the three-part lesson have been suggested in recent years, sometimes in the headings used to describe the different stages, and sometimes changing the structure to a four-(or more)-part lesson. These structures include (in no particular order):

1. Starter	1. Starter	1. Starter
2. Teacher introduction	2. Main activity	2. Attack
3. Pupil practice	3. Plenary	3. Consolidation
4. Plenary	4. Reflection on learning	4. Plenary

1. Entry activity	1. Starter	1. Start
2. Main	2. Discussion	2. Exploration
3. Review	3. Consolidation	3. Reflection
	4. Activity	4. Plenary
	5. Review and challenge	

There is little value in discussing the relative merits of these alternative ways to organize a lesson; all can provide helpful guidelines for planning lessons. The important thing is to realize that many well-structured lessons do not have three parts!

In this chapter, we illustrate, through reference to a sample mathematics lesson, how a lesson can be structured to provide a range of activities. The illustrative lesson is available for viewing on the website, split into eight short sections. It takes place in a mixed 11–16 comprehensive school in an urban setting in the north-west of England; the class are a Year 8 group, set 5 out of 6. Most of the planned work for the term is at National Curriculum level 5, with some level 6 work included to stretch their thinking. Pupils in the class are expected to attain level 5 or level 6 in the Year 9 Standard Tests. Two pupils in the class have special educational needs that identify dyslexia and writing difficulties as requiring support, but there is no additional teacher to support these pupils in this lesson. The lesson has a recognizable starter and plenary, and the main part of the lesson has three distinct phases, involving discussion, consolidation and independent work.

THE STARTER ACTIVITY

The starter activity in mathematics is often referred to as an oral and mental starter. This suggests an activity that involves interaction between the teacher and the pupils, where pupils are encouraged to work mentally and explain their thinking verbally. In practice, starter activities take a whole range of different forms, including:

- an oral revision of basic arithmetic facts, such as multiplication tables or the meanings of arithmetic operations
- a revision of previously learnt work on the lesson topic
- a revision of previously learnt work that the teacher chooses to revisit, such as estimating answers to calculations or practising using correct mathematical vocabulary
- a mathematical puzzle
- a statement, or the presentation of some data, as a focus for discussion
- a challenge that leads into the main learning objective of the lesson, possibly through illustrating that previously learnt work is insufficient for a more complex problem.

The starter activity may relate to and lead into the main part of the lesson, or it may be unconnected with the rest of the lesson. There is scope to vary its length, but it is unwise to allow an activity that is unrelated to the main part of the lesson to run on for more than 10 minutes. For obvious reasons, if the starter activity is not contributing to the main lesson objectives, then it should not form a substantial part of the lesson. It is, however, perfectly acceptable to plan a lesson where the starter and the main lesson are unconnected, as long as the objectives for each part are clear.

A different style of implementing a starter activity is in evidence in some schools, particularly schools in challenging circumstances. In these schools, mathematics lessons begin with an entry activity, which is already written up on a board or computer screen. As pupils arrive and sit at their desks, they are asked to settle down straight away and to put their attention to the given task. This approach has the advantage that it caters well for pupils arriving in small numbers over a period of 5 minutes or more, and means that everyone is given purposeful work from the minute they sit down in the class. The task often invites a written response that revisits recent work, or revision work that will be useful in the main part of the lesson. Research evidence suggests that this way of working, using an initial activity partly as a management technique, contributes to creating a calm learning atmosphere (Muijs and Reynolds, 2005). The drawback is that the activity is less likely to involve whole-class discussion or interaction, and therefore the oral and mental aspect of the starter activity is weakened.

If the purpose of the starter activity is to get the lesson off to a brisk start, then it needs to be planned with this in mind. It is useful, for example, to have a prepared visual display that can be shown quickly. It is helpful to choose an activity that needs a minimum amount of explanation about what to do; it should be an easily accessible task that engages the pupils quickly. It is also useful to prepare any questions that you intend to use, possibly with the intention of involving as many pupils as possible in giving responses.

In the sample lesson, the class are working on the topic of probability. In the previous lesson, pupils were writing down the probability of equally likely outcomes, and then cancelling down the fractions to their simplest forms. The task at the beginning of this lesson is a quick five-minute starter to remind the pupils about fractions, to remind them that they can write fractions in a simpler form sometimes, with the additional aim of getting the group focused quickly on their mathematics. The teacher uses a computer projection onto the display board, and projects the two sets of fractions shown below. The task is for the pupils to match together pairs of equivalent fractions.

All the class are involved in this same activity. Pupils are told to spend 3 minutes thinking about the pairings. The instructions given to the class are

---

I want you to match up the fractions on the left with their equivalent fractions on the right. We did this last lesson so remember you are looking for equivalent fractions. You are going to cancel down, and you are going to draw a line to join up one of the fractions on the left to one of the fractions on the right. You have 3 minutes starting now.

$$\frac{15}{20} \qquad \frac{1}{2}$$

$$\frac{4}{20} \qquad \frac{2}{3}$$

$$\frac{30}{60} \qquad \frac{3}{4}$$

$$\frac{8}{12} \qquad \frac{1}{7}$$

$$\frac{4}{28} \qquad \frac{1}{5}$$

During the 3 minutes of the activity the teacher first picks out a boy who has been absent recently, goes over to his desk, and spends a minute with him making sure that he can engage with the activity.

> David, you have not been in have you, so I will give you a hand. Have a look at the fractions on the left, and see if you can find what the equivalent fraction is on the right. You have missed a bit of this haven't you, David? Have a look at this, now can you see any fractions on this side that might be the same as a half?
> (David points to 30/60)
> Is it that? Yes, good, OK so match that one up, and you can actually draw on the sheet, drawing a line to match them. I do not mind if you want to talk to the person next to you as well.

The teacher uses the rest of the time to provide encouragement to the group, by giving plenty of positive feedback about the work that she can see. In addition, she is very keen to maintain some pace in the working. In order to achieve this, she makes extensive use of the short-term timed target that she set at the beginning of the activity, giving regular reminders about how long the pupils have to complete the activity. She also monitors progress by looking at the pupils' work, asking questions to individuals, and responding to questions.

> We all seem to have matched up a half. That is good. That's right so far yes, good. 2½ minutes to go.
>
> Miss, is this right?
>
> Yes, that is right so far, Jake. Let's have a look. Which was the factor of these two numbers? Which times tables were you looking at?
>
> Twos
>
> Is there a bigger number that goes into these other than two? Yes. Which?
>
> Four.
>
> How many fours go into eight? Two. How many fours go into 12? Three. That is it. You're OK. Two minutes to try to match it up. Brilliant. Some of us are nearly there.
> Hannah how are you doing? Yes that's good, that one is right. That one is not a half, because what number goes into that? (Hannah points.) It's that one, yes, so change that one. Are you OK with these, David? Yes, good.
> Just over one minute left, everybody, looks good, yes. OK, just wait for everyone to finish. Are you OK, Ellie? Good, just check the last two, just have a think about the last two.
> OK, just 30 seconds now. Double check them even if you think they are right, just double check. Have a look at the person's next to you. Do you agree with what they have got, if not who's right? Can you convince the other person why you are right?

Point for reflection

Point for reflection

Watch part 1 of the sample lesson on the website. Reflect on what has made this an effective lesson starter, thinking in particular about:

- the preparation that has gone into this starter activity
- how well it engages the attention of the pupils
- the use of short-term timed targets
- the use of managed discussion between pupils.

Consider alternative ways that the teacher could have conducted a revision of cancelling fractions as a five to ten minute activity.

THE MAIN TEACHING ACTIVITY

Main teaching – discussion phase

The main activity, as the name suggests, is what takes place for most of the lesson. It is often broken down into smaller chunks of time, and may contain several different activities. Clearly this part of the lesson will focus on the main lesson objectives, and may incorporate a range of learning strategies. It is good practice to share the lesson objectives with the pupils, so that they know the main purpose of the lesson. Objectives should be presented to pupils as easy-to-understand short statements, and usually backed up with some verbal explanation. In some schools, the objectives are written on a special board at the front of the classroom; often, they are presented via a computer display screen.

In the sample lesson, the focus of the main part of the lesson is to consider cases where the probability cannot be calculated using equally likely outcomes. Pupils are asked to reflect on estimating probabilities. In order to start off their thinking, the pupils are given a discussion task, displayed on the board, which says:

> There are pizzas, salad and curry on sale in the canteen today, so the probability that I will choose pizza must be **one out of three** or **1/3**

The lesson continues:

Now I want you to talk with the people near you for 30 seconds about whether you agree or disagree with that and why? So read it again. You have 30 seconds to discuss that.
    Hands down, you are discussing for 30 seconds. Adam, talk to Beth. 15 seconds, I want some good explanations in a minute whether you agree or disagree and why.

Clearly the task has been designed to generate some disagreement. Pupils are given a focused discussion task that involves pupils discussing in groups for 30 seconds, and then contributing to a class discussion managed by the teacher for another 5 minutes.

OK, stop talking and hands up with your answers.

The first person to venture an answer agrees with the statement given, 'because there are three items being served and one of them is pizza'. The teacher has to convince this pupil that their logic is flawed, but does not want to discourage future contributions by saying that the answer is wrong. She employs a very useful technique that avoids being judgemental: she asks whether other members of the class agree or not. But to begin with, she repeats the question and the answer given, so that all the class remain part of the discussion.

There are three items on sale and one of them is pizza so I'm going to go in and there is a one in three chance I am going to choose pizza. Is there anybody who disagrees?

Daniel: You might like something better than pizza.

Yes! Actually, I like pizza more than I like salad. In fact if there were pizza, salad and curry on sale I would probably never pick salad. I would probably choose pizza and then if I felt like something different I would probably choose curry. So does anybody else now after listening to what Daniel said disagree with the statement?

David: You might not like salad or curry at all, and could be allergic to something on the pizza.

I might be allergic to it or I might not like it at all. Who in here doesn't like curry? (Several hands go up.)
    Do you not like curry, Ellie? So the chance you that you would choose curry, would it be a one in three chance? Is it a 1/3 chance that you would pick curry? What is the chance that you would pick curry?

(Continued)

(Continued)

Ellie: Impossible.

OK, so what is the difference between this situation and everything we have been looking at so far? Because we have been able to work out the probability so far, but at the moment can we say what the probability that this person would pick pizza is? Can we say what it is?

Class: No

Why can't we say what it is?

Daniel: Because there is more chance he would pick pizza.

Not necessarily more chance, do we know anything about this person? So what is the key word in here that is different to before? What is happening here that people have never had in the past? The word 'choose' is the difference. Yes, he or she is choosing; that is the difference.

After managing the discussion, the teacher is confident that the pupils understand the main features of the argument: that not all outcomes need to be equally likely. As a result, she draws the discussion to a conclusion.

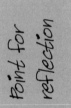

Point for reflection

Now watch the video of the sample lesson, part 3. Observe how the teacher draws out from the pupils some quite difficult answers (most of which are reproduced in the transcript above). Note the bright tone and the positive attitudes that are being fostered.

Main teaching – consolidation phase

Discussion is unpredictable, and needs managing well. Many trainees find it difficult to deal with uncertainties in the lesson, particularly unexpected answers to questions. Experienced teachers phrase the questions in a more open way, and invite comments and explanations. Often, the teacher will want to tie together the key ideas from the discussion, extracting the important features, and giving them added emphasis.

What has everything been in the past, when we have taken a card out of a pack, or when we have rolled dice, it has been ... ? There has been a key word in the past that when we have been doing this I say, I am going to take a card out of the pack, at ... ?

Class: Random.

Well done, it is random. Are these choices random? No.

It's choosing isn't it? It's choosing what they are going to have, so it is not a one in three chance so, and this is the key thing, each of the three things pizzas, salad and curry doesn't have an equally likely chance of being chosen.

When we roll dice all the numbers have an equally chance of coming up don't they? So normally when we roll dice or when we flip a coin the chance of heads or tails coming is equally likely, but when there is some choice like this it is not equally likely.

(This is where the video of the sample lesson, part 3 ends.) The next stage of the lesson takes the discussion one stage further to consider how to find probabilities for situations where a choice is involved.

So I want to find what the probability is that somebody is going to choose pizza for their lunch in the canteen. What am I going to have to do to find that out?

Daniel: Ask everyone in the class.

I could ask everyone in the class or I could go and stand in the canteen. But I would do a survey. One way would be to stand in the canteen and count everybody who comes in and picks pizza. I could do a tally. Everybody who picks curry I could do a tally. Everybody who picks salad I could do a tally.

But the key thing is we cannot work out the probability using theory like we have done in the past if the outcomes are not equally likely.

Let's say David went to the canteen today and there were pizza, curry and salad on sale. He did a survey and there were 100 people that came to the canteen and 42 of them had pizza. Could he then maybe work out what the probability is of somebody picking pizza?

However, what if Adam then went to the canteen and did the same survey but maybe in the next hour afterwards, is Adam going to get the same results that David got? If we are talking about different people going, is Adam going to get the same results? If 42 out of the 100 people that David saw picked pizza, does it mean that 42 out of the 100 people that Adam sees pick pizza?

Class: Different people will make different choices.

(Continued)

(Continued)

So are we actually finding the probability? What are we finding then? It's not quite right to call it probability because it could change couldn't it. So it's like taking a guess. What is the mathematical word that we use? Say that again Adam, but louder.

Adam: Estimate.

Yes estimate, or find the estimated probability. That is what we do, and I'd like you to write that down now. We are finding the experimental probability or the estimated probability.

Point for reflection

Now watch the video of the sample lesson, part 4. Note the clear mathematical objective, which is shared with the class. Note also the way that the teacher asks the pupils to stop and think before they give a response. Think about how you would have prepared this section of the lesson. What questions would you have prepared?

Main teaching – independent work phase

Many lessons contain some time when pupils are working independently from the teacher. Some people might think of this as individual work, since it does not contain elements of planned paired work or group work. In practice, good teachers expect that this 'individual work' will allow opportunities for pupils to discuss the work with a neighbour. The Framework (DfEE, 2001) provides guidance for this part of a lesson by listing features that make for effective learning. Among the bulleted list of guidance are the following suggestions.

It helps if you:

- Keep the whole class busy working actively on problems, exercises or activities related to the theme of the lesson
- Encourage discussion and cooperation between pupils
- Make sure that pupils working independently know where to find resources, what to do before asking for help, and what to do if they finish early (DfEE, 2001: 30).

The last point is one that is worth emphasizing. Lessons go more smoothly if the transitions from one phase to the next are managed well, and part of that transition management is to explain the task in full, rather than in brief. For example, 'Here is a worksheet. I'd like you to try the first 10 questions' may work perfectly well on occasions, but on other occasions, these instructions will need to be supplemented by more detail. Very simple additional information can make all the difference between a class settled to their work and a class of restless pupils not quite sure what they are expected to do. Useful phrases to consider at this stage of transition include:

- Let's have a look at question one together. What is it asking us to do? (Using this approach ensures that everyone knows how to get started.)
- You'll need a protractor for question four. Put your hand up now if you will need to borrow a protractor. (This anticipates and manages the need for equipment.)
- You have 10 minutes to do these 10 questions. If anybody finishes early, then I'd like you to have a look at the questions on the computer screen, which are a bit more difficult. (Letting pupils know what is coming next avoids anyone saying, 'I've finished. What shall I do now?')
- Is there anyone does not know what they are supposed to be doing? (This encourages pupils to make a start, because they have had an opportunity to express any difficulties.)

In the sample lesson, the independent working phase occupies only about 10 minutes. For these 10 minutes, the pupils are given a set of questions on a worksheet (reproduced here), and write their answers in their books. The exercise given is quite a short one, but is sufficient to make pupils think about the main point of the lesson. The key question, 'why are these answers estimates?' is designed to make the pupils think about whether the same outcomes would occur if the survey or experiment were repeated.

Estimated probability

1. In an experiment, 60 seeds were planted but only 45 of them started to grow and 15 did not grow.

    a) What is the estimated probability that a seed will grow?
    b) What is the estimated probability that a seed will not grow?
    c) Why are your answers only estimates?

2. These are the results of a survey of 90 cars passing the school.

Colour	Red	Blue	Green	Silver	Other
Frequency	23	36	12	16	3

(Continued)

(Continued)

Estimate the probability that the next car that passes the school is

   a)   Red
   b)   Blue
   c)   Silver
   d)   Not silver

3.   In an experiment, 100 drawing pins were dropped. 73 landed point up and the rest landed point down.

   a)   Estimate the probability that the drawing pin will land point up
   b)   Estimate the probability that the drawing pin will land point down
   c)   Why are your answers only estimates?

4.   Andrew did a survey of pupils' favourite pets in his year at school.

Pet	Dog	Cat	Bird	Chimp	Other
Frequency	52	65	12	4	7

What is the estimated probability that a pupil's favourite pet is …

   a)   A cat?
   b)   A chimp?

Point for reflection

Watch the sample lesson video part 5 on the website. Based on all the clips that you have seen so far, reflect on how the teacher:

- manages transitions from one part of the lesson to another
- invites the pupils to contribute their own ideas
- assesses as the lesson progresses.

Imagine that you are in that lesson during your first week in a school. Consider how you would help the pupils' learning. What would you have done?

   Now imagine that you are assisting in the lesson, but have been given the task of working with a particular pupil who usually struggles with the work. Think of different ways that you could help that individual to keep up with the rest of the class.

THE PLENARY ACTIVITY

Plenaries are difficult. In the teaching reforms that have been encouraged by the National Strategy, the use of the plenary has been found to be less effective than other parts of the lesson (Ofsted, 2002a). Trainees in particular have found it difficult to incorporate effective plenaries into their lessons. Often the reason that this part of the lesson is less effective is because of weaknesses in planning; it has not been planned as an active part of the lesson. On other occasions, time management is inadequate, with the result that the plenary is rushed or omitted altogether because of a shortage of time at the end of the lesson.

Among the guidance provided by the National Strategy, is the suggestion that plenaries work best when they:

- are planned in advance of the lesson
- reflect the objectives for the lesson
- are employed after specific episodes in a lesson
- are used to monitor or evaluate learning in order to inform future teaching and learning
- are planned to actively involve pupils
- are varied in format and approach across a series of lessons
  (DfES, 2004a).

One useful approach to understanding plenaries can be to separate out how they help you and how they help pupils. For you, the plenary is useful for checking what has been learnt (especially in relation to the lesson objectives). By organizing a whole-class activity, you can assess the extent to which pupils have achieved the desired learning outcomes. The plenary is also an obvious opportunity for you to recap on the lesson, to summarize the key ideas, and to give emphasis to the most important points. The end of the lesson also provides an opportunity to look ahead to the next lesson, and to draw possible links with previous work or with work in other subjects. The plenary can also be used in a less formal, planned way for responding to issues that have arisen in the lesson. For example, if a particular question has caused difficulties, or if you have noticed a particular (unanticipated) misconception arising in the lesson, then the time planned for the plenary can be used for discussing the issue with a view to resolving it.

For pupils, the plenary offers an opportunity to stop and think, to try to focus on the important points from the lesson. Without a plenary of some kind, there is a danger that the pupils will leave the lesson without a clear idea of what the lesson was about. They may have copied down the objectives at the beginning of the lesson, but they are not likely to think back to them unless directed to do so in some way. The plenary should help pupils to organize their thinking, to identify the important points, and to make links with other areas of learning. It is a time for pupils to reflect on not only what they have learnt, but also how they have learnt (DfES, 2002).

As a trainee, you will observe many different teachers in the classroom. You are likely to see plenty of examples of good practice in relation to plenary sessions, but you are also likely to see plenty of missed opportunities, where teachers end lessons with little or no distinct plenary session. (One rather cynical teacher used to say that all his lessons were three-part lessons: hello; teach; goodbye.) You need to think about what sort of activities make up an effective plenary. At its most simplistic, the plenary gives a chance for you to refer back to the lesson objectives, possibly to reiterate them, and to ask pupils which objectives they think that they have achieved. This level of review may be better than nothing, but is likely to be very brief (1 or 2 minutes), and is unlikely to be seen by the pupils as an important part of the lesson. More effective are plenaries where you have planned a specific activity with the same level of thought and planning as goes into the starter activity.

It is most common to think of plenary sessions as occurring at the end of lessons. But a plenary session is not exclusively something for the end of a lesson. If you are about to move on to a new idea in the middle of the lesson, it may be appropriate to have a plenary session, with you summarizing and the whole class reflecting on their learning at that stage. In an interesting reflection on plenaries, Paul Wilson (2005) propounds the value of several mini-plenaries during the lesson that are used to illustrate key points and draw attention to misconceptions and errors.

The following is a list of suggestions for how you can avoid some of the most common pitfalls of using the plenary.

- Do not allow your plenary to be squeezed out through lack of time. Plan specific times for the various sections of the lesson, and try to stick to them. If you plan the plenary properly, then you are less likely to neglect it.
- Avoid allowing pupils to think that the lesson is over when you are presenting the plenary. Tell the pupils in advance what they are going to be doing in the plenary; make it clear that this is an important part of the lesson. Do not pack away equipment until the plenary is over.
- Make sure that as many pupils as possible are involved in the plenary. One way to achieve this is to ask everyone to write down something about the lesson (for example, what they have learnt). Make use of the pupils' reviews of the lesson. Select a few pupils to explain what the lesson has been about. This could be done directly or through asking pupils to read out their written reflections.

- Do not fall into a routine of always doing the same thing in your plenary. Go for novel plenaries that re-engage attention. Think about adapting effective starter activities that you have used.
- Beware the plenary that finishes before the end of the lesson. You may have planned an excellent plenary activity, and allowed 10 minutes at the end of the lesson. In the event, the plenary activity only takes 5 minutes, so you have 5 minutes left; you must plan how you can use such times productively. Some teachers use such times to allow the pupils to start their homework; others provide a puzzle. Doug French has provided several interesting ideas in his occasional, but long-running series of articles in *Mathematics in School*, entitled 'The creative use of odd moments'.
- See the plenary as something additional to setting homework, collecting equipment, or issuing answers to written exercises. These are all worthy activities for the end of a lesson, but should not interfere with an effective plenary.

In the sample lesson, the teacher uses three questions relating to the lesson, with the aim of helping pupils to reflect and to extend their thinking.

Looking around most of you seem to have got the idea of this, so when I collect your books in I will mark them.

There are just three more questions that I want you to answer now so that we can check that you have understood what you have done today. So you have just 2 minutes now and you don't even have to write anything down, but I want you to think about those three questions.

1. What does it mean when the outcomes of an event are not equally likely?
2. Why were our answers today called the estimated probabilities?
3. How would you find out what the probability is for there being an earthquake this year?

You have just got 60 seconds to think about it or to talk to the person near you, and then I am going to ask for some answers. You can write down your answers if you want to, or you can plan your answers in your head. We are going to have three really good answers to the questions in a minute.

In this case, the first two questions in the plenary activity help pupils to focus on what they have learnt. The third question is designed to challenge and extend. This question cannot be solved by theoretical probability, nor by conducting a survey to get data. The pupils are being asked to consider how probabilities can be estimated in such circumstances. The teacher needs to prompt the class further on this question.

> Would you stand around with pen and paper ready to do a survey, and wait for the earthquake to happen? Would you? Apart from the fact that you might die in the earthquake, you could be waiting for a long time. We know that sometimes we might not be able to use the theory of probability if the outcomes are not exactly predictable.
>
> *David*:   We could look at what earthquakes have happened before.
>
> Good! David came up with a really good idea then, we could look at when earthquakes have happened before. We might be able to do an experiment ourselves, but sometimes it makes more sense to look back at data that has already been collected for us. So we could use information about how often there has been an earthquake over the last 500 years to estimate the probability of an earthquake tomorrow.

The lesson is a successful one. The pupils have taken their learning on a stage, and the organization of the lesson has contributed to the whole experience, helping to provide a sense of purpose, a brisk pace and a variety of challenges. The lesson concludes with some organizational issues around collecting in books so that the homework can be marked, and an orderly dismissal of the class.

Points for reflection

Watch the sample lesson, part 8. Note how the plenary is a well-planned part of the lesson. Think about alternative ways that you could have organized a plenary activity for this lesson.

It is well worth spending time thinking about your approach to plenary sessions, and the activity below is designed to help you focus on some of the key issues.

In order to manage the lesson time effectively, you will need to decide how long you would allow for your plenary. Consider the following possible plenary sessions for a lesson on multiplying decimal numbers by powers of ten. For each one, decide how long you would allow in your lesson planning for the plenary.

1. I've seen two different answers to question 6.
   Some people have $1.2 \div 100 = 0.12$. Others have $1.2 \div 100 = 0.012$. (writes both on the board).
   Who can explain which is correct?
   I have on the board 5 questions and 5 answers. I need you to match up the pairs.

2. Our objectives for the lesson were:
   Be able to multiply decimal numbers by 10, 100, 1000. Have we done that? Who thinks that they have achieved that?
   Be able to divide decimals by 10, 100, 1000. Who thinks that they can do that?

3. Our work today on decimals is particularly useful in work on measurement. You will need to measure lots of things, and sometimes to change between units, and to do that, you will need the skills you have learnt today.
   Can you think of any other subjects at school, where you will need these skills?
   (Expect answers of design and technology, science.)

4. Let's look back at the key ideas from today's lesson. Tell me what you think this lesson has been about. Explain what you have learnt.
   I've put four questions on the board (3.4×10, $22.76 \div 10$, 0.361×100, $9.6 \div 1000$). I want you all to write down quickly what you think the answer is to these four questions. Let's look at what you have put.

5. I've put 10 questions on the OHP slide. They are numbered 1 to 10. I'm going to ask a question out of this set – it could be any question – and I want you to have an answer. Wally, what is the answer to Q4, $22.76 \div 10$? What is the answer to Q7, 0.361×100 – Dolly? (can use repeats of questions)

6. We've looked today at questions like these: 3.4×10, $22.76 \div 10$, 0.361×100, $9.6 \div 1000$. What we need to do next lesson is to use this to do some harder looking questions like:

   $$99.2 \times 0.1$$

   and we shall look at applying what you've learnt today to changing units of measurement, so it's very important that you remember what today's lesson was about.

7. I want you to think about what you have learnt in today's lesson. Please write down in your books a sentence saying what you have learnt. (Allow 2–3 minutes.) Now please show me how sure you are about how to do questions like these: 3.4×10, $22.76 \div 10$, 0.361×100 (on the board). Give a thumbs up for 'I'm confident that I understand this work', a thumbs down for 'I don't understand this work', and a sideways thumb for 'I think I understand, but I'm not sure'. I now want you to write down your answers to these three questions. The correct answers are ... Now reassess yourselves, and show me again using your thumbs.

Having done that, read through the different descriptions again, and decide which you think make the most effective plenary sessions, and which make the least effective. Put the seven suggestions in order, from the one that you judge the best to the one that you judge the worst. If possible, find a fellow trainee to do the same task and discuss the extent to which you agree with each other. Justify how you decided on what were the most effective activities.

EVIDENCE FROM THE RESEARCH

The Framework (DfEE, 2001) has had considerable influence on teaching mathematics, but it is not clear from reading it whether the advice it contains has any basis in research. You will be pleased to learn that it has! In the 1990s, a research project called the National Numeracy Project showed gains in learning for primary school pupils through teachers adopting a particular style of teaching. The subsequent National Numeracy Strategy (DfEE, 1999), used in a much larger number of schools, also led to a rise in standards, so it was not unreasonable to extend the guidance into Key Stage 3. Margaret Brown and colleagues (Brown et al., 2003) provide a summary of the educational research on which the Numeracy Strategy was based.

Most of the research base focuses on what activities are effective in helping pupils to learn mathematics. Much less research has focused on the impact of lesson organization and structure on learning. There is, however, some theoretical justification for having a lesson split into different sections or stages. When the characteristics of good lessons are analysed, then a well-structured lesson is one of the identified features. For example, Mortimore et al., quoted in DfES (2004c), list five factors that lead to effective outcomes in lessons. One of the five factors is structured sessions. Rosenshine and Furst (in Sotto, 1994) list eight features of good teaching, one of which is that good teachers help to structure pupils' learning, through periodically summing up of what has been done and indicating the next steps on the way forward.

The Office for Standards in Education (2002b) also describe the characteristics of good lessons, based on school inspections over a two-year period. Among other features, they identify time management as essential 'if a final session to check that learning objectives have been met is not to be curtailed and unproductive' (Ofsted, 2002b: 8). The same paper puts forward the use of an oral and mental starter as an example of good practice (following on from what is seen as good practice in primary schools).

Jones et al. (2000) are less enthusiastic about the positive effects of lesson structure. They agree that having a clear structure is one characteristic of good lessons. They also note that nearly all the lessons that they observed had an identifiable plenary session and that, in the best cases, the plenary 'contributed significantly to the learning' (Jones et al., 2000: 80). But they point out that an emphasis on lesson structure can overshadow more fundamental issues relating to effective teaching and learning. It may be that much more important than a particular form of lesson organization is the fact that the lesson is well planned, and that the teacher manages well the transitions from one stage to another. It is not the structure that is important; it is the pedagogic approach. It is just that all good pedagogical approaches are highly structured with distinct stages (DfES, 2004b).

What lesson structuring does provide most obviously is an opportunity for a variety of activities within a lesson. An unstructured lesson may mean that the pupils work on one activity for the whole lesson. So it may not be the structuring that is itself important in pupils' learning; it is that well-structured lessons help teachers to employ a range of different pedagogical approaches that they need to use for effective learning (Olson and Torrance, 1998).

Various research studies have demonstrated the importance of a dynamic start to a lesson. The start is important for two main reasons. First, it provides an initial stimulus, through perhaps the use of visual aids, which can arouse interest. Second, it helps make connections with previous learning. If pupils are to build on their existing knowledge, then it is helpful for both the teacher and the learner to know what that knowledge is. Constructing learning is strongly linked to prior experience, and a starter activity can help to make connections that will aid the learning process (Pirie and Kieran, 1989; Smith, 1998).

Making connections is particularly important in the learning of mathematics because almost all new knowledge needs to be linked to concepts that have been learnt earlier. Nobody can become mathematically able if they learn new concepts in isolation; the teacher has the key role of making these links explicit, and the best time to make links is often at the beginning and end of a lesson. It is often through skilful questioning that the teacher helps pupils to make links with previous work (Askew et al., 1997).

It is also worth noting that an effective plenary, just as much as an effective initial activity, can be a helpful aid to class management (Muijs and Reynolds, 2005). The two ends of the lesson are often the two times when disruption occurs, so making specific plans for these times has the additional benefit of helping to avoid 'switched off' behaviour, and thus making full use of the available teaching time.

There seems little research basis for a specifically three-part lesson (whole class, individual/group work, whole class). Nobody claims that this forms the only structure for a good lesson, and lessons are often broken up into far more than three parts, as in the sample lesson. Equally, there is no evidence that dividing the lesson into four or more parts is either more or less effective than the three-part lesson strategy (Muijs and Reynolds, 2005). Watson and De Geest (2005: 231) go further, concluding that the teacher's attitudes and relationships are the most important aspect of good teaching, and that the search for the most successful methods, organizations and structures for teaching mathematics 'is a misguided quest'.

The balance of research suggests that structure is itself helpful, but that no particular structure can be identified as best. Where the evidence is clear is in supporting the use of strong starts and finishes to lessons, because they play an important part in helping to join up the learning, and help pupils to see mathematics as a coherent whole, with concepts and skills that transfer to other areas of learning.

Further reading

Muijs, D. and Reynolds, D. (2005) *Effective Teaching: Evidence and Practice*. London: Sage.

This is a research-based book, but it is written in an accessible style. It covers constructivist learning theories, interactive teaching and group work, including discussion of the value of structuring lessons well. Examples are drawn from different school subjects, with particular emphasis on the role of the teacher in effective learning.

Stahl, K. (2002) *101 Red Hot Maths Starters*. London: Letts Educational.

This is a book of practical ideas, rather than an academic publication. Some of the ideas are imaginative, others are rather mundane, but this has been highly valued by many people training as mathematics teachers.

Useful websites

Live links to these sites can be found on the companion website.

The 2004 DfES Pedagogy and Practice: Teaching and Learning in Secondary Schools series of training modules cover a wide range of teaching issues. Published by the Standards Unit, they are designed to be used as self-study guides. Particularly useful here are Unit 1: Structuring learning, and Unit 5:

Starters and Plenaries. Both are very practical guides to the strategies that teachers use to structure learning. They are presented from the perspective of planning lessons, rather than providing serious theoretical justifications, but they are helpful in concentrating on planning individual episodes within a lesson. Although neither is aimed specifically at teachers of mathematics, there is an accompanying video of a Year 8 mathematics lesson. There is a link to these publications on the website accompanying this book. These units (and others in the series) can be downloaded from http://www.standards.dfes.gov.uk/secondary/keystage3/all/respub/sec_pptl0

The Suffolk Authority page http://www.suffolkmaths.co.uk/Teach_Skills.htm contains ideas for starters and plenaries, together with illustrative video clips.

References

Askew, M., Rhodes, V., Brown, M., Wiliam, D. and Johnson, D. (1997) *Effective Teachers of Numeracy: Report of a Study Carried Out for the Teacher Training Agency*. London: King's College London, School of Education.

Brown, M., Askew, M., Millett, A. and Rhodes, V. (2003) 'The key role of educational research in the development of the National Numeracy Strategy', *British Educational Research Journal*, 29(5): 362–85.

Department for Education and Employment (DfEE) (1999) *The National Numeracy Strategy: Framework for Teaching Mathematics from Reception to Year 6*. London: Department for Education and Employment.

Department for Education and Employment (DfEE) (2001) *Key Stage 3 National Strategy: Framework for Teaching Mathematics Years 7, 8 and 9*. London: Department for Education and Employment.

Department for Education and Skills (DfES) (2002) *Making Good Use of the Plenary*. London: Department for Education and Skills.

Department for Education and Skills (DfES) (2004a) *Supporting ITT Providers: The Effective Use of Plenaries*. London: Department for Education and Skills.

Department for Education and Skills (DfES) (2004b) *Pedagogy and Practice: Teaching and Learning in Secondary Schools. Unit 1: Structuring Learning*. London: Department for Education and Skills.

Department for Education and Skills (DfES) (2004c) *Pedagogy and Practice: Teaching and Learning in Secondary Schools. Unit 5: Starters and Plenaries*. London: Department for Education and Skills.

Jones, S., Tanner, H. and Treadaway, M. (2000) 'Raising standards in mathematics through effective classroom practice', paper presented to the Australian Association for Research in Education, Sydney.

Muijs, D. and Reynolds, D. (2005) *Effective Teaching: Evidence and Practice*. London: Sage.

Office for Standards in Education (Ofsted) (2002a) *The Key Stage 3 Strategy: Evaluation of the First Year of the Pilot*. London: Office for Standards in Education.

Office for Standards in Education (Ofsted) (2002b) *Good Teaching, Effective Departments: Findings from a HMI Survey of Subject Teaching in Secondary Schools 2000/01.* London: Office for Standards in Education.

Olson, D.R. and Torrance, N. (eds) (1998) *The Handbook of Education and Human Development.* London: Blackwell.

Pirie, S. and Kieren, T. (1989) 'A recursive theory of mathematical understanding', *For the Learning of Mathematics,* 9(3): 7–11.

Smith, A. (1998) *Accelerated Learning in Practice: brain-based methods for accelerating motivation and achievement.* London: Network Educational Press.

Sotto, E. (1994) *When Teaching Becomes Learning: A Theory and Practice of Teaching.* London: Cassell.

Watson, A. and De Geest, E. (2005) Principle teaching for deep progress: Improving mathematical learning beyond methods and material, *Educational studies in mathematics,* 58(2): 209–34.

Wilson, P. (2005) 'The problem with plenaries', *Mathematics in School,* 34(3): 31–2.

5   LEARNING MATHEMATICS

This chapter:

- gives a brief overview of the main learning theories
- explains the influence of social constructivism on current classroom practice
- justifies the key role of the teacher in a pupil's learning
- discusses approaches that lead to long-term learning
- gives examples of classroom activities that are consistent with and supportive of the social constructivist theory of learning
- describes one project that aims to develop pupils' thinking skills.

EARLY IDEAS

Mathematics is often described as a hierarchical subject, where later learning depends on earlier concepts being grasped. From this perspective, mathematical thinking develops in levels of understanding, and this idea finds support in the structure of the current National Curriculum. But it is a mistake to think that learning development takes place in a linear fashion. Learners need to revisit old ideas regularly, leading to a process that involves recursion as much as it involves a hierarchy of ideas (Pirie and Kieren, 1989). Learning is not like following a set route, with pupils building routinely on prior knowledge; at many stages, learners may need to drop back a level to reinforce what they have learnt before. This is particularly the case when pupils encounter mathematics in an unfamiliar context or attempt to solve complex problems. In these cases, you will find that pupils often revert to lower levels of conceptual understanding.

Behaviourist theories of learning emphasize the effect of punishments and rewards in learning. This might involve providing lots of positive reinforcement to pupils who obtain correct answers and presenting disapproval to those whose answers are incorrect. In this perspective, pupils learn through seeing examples, copying those examples and then practising until they can perform the required series of steps automatically. Behaviourism also emphasizes the strong role of triggers in learning, where a particular trigger elicits a particular response. An example related to this is solving word problems, when pupils often find it difficult to identify the operation that is implied in the context. A behaviourist approach suggests that pupils are taught to look for trigger words such as more, extra, additional – words that might suggest the correct operation to employ.

Behaviourist theories have had much influence in education generally, and certainly within mathematics education. They are at the heart of the belief that if pupils practise something often enough, then they will increase their knowledge, because they will be able to respond appropriately to similar situations. The emphasis is on developing mathematical skills, with less attention paid to encouraging the learning of concepts or strategies. As a result, the approach is useful in helping pupils to develop skills that can be done without having to think, such as the results of multiplication tables, or how to plot co-ordinate points. A key weakness is that pupils who are used to this way of working find it very difficult to deal with situations that are not quite in line with their experience; they are often unable to transfer their skills to alternative contexts. The Office for Standards in Education (2006) report dissatisfaction with 'drill and practice' lessons, which contribute to long-standing concerns about pupils' inabilities to transfer their knowledge, understanding and skills to new situations.

CONSTRUCTIVISM

Most work on learning theory makes reference to the work of Piaget. Piaget identifies four stages of cognitive development, with children moving from one stage to another when they are ready. Teaching, in this perspective, involves identifying the stage of development for each child, and using methods that are appropriate to a child at that stage of development. In secondary school mathematics, much work is focused on moving pupils from what Piaget describes as the concrete operational stage to the formal operational stage (described by Adhami et al., 1998: viii, as 'shifting up a gear'). Only when they have reached the formal operational stage are pupils able to develop fully their reasoning and deal with abstract ideas.

In Piaget's description, a child constructs knowledge based on experiences. When a child encounters a new experience, it may fit in with the child's understanding of the world or it may not. If it does fit in, then the new experience is assimilated into the existing set of knowledge. If the new experience does not fit in with previous understanding, then the child has to make some adjustments in order to accommodate the new information. The construction of this new understanding constitutes learning.

The learning theory founded on Piaget's work is called constructivism. Inevitably, constructivism has been refined and amended, and there are some fundamental differences in interpretation, but it is constructivism (in some form) that is widely accepted as best describing the process by which pupils learn mathematics. It is the constructivist viewpoint that underpins many of the changes in mathematics teaching that have taken place over the past 15 years. It is the theoretical basis behind much of the advice that you will receive about what constitutes good practice in the classroom.

In simple terms, constructivism is founded on Piaget's belief that learning is an active process, where new information is accommodated into previously understood meanings or mental images. In the classroom, you need to understand pupils' current understanding (the mental images that they have constructed to explain observed behaviour). You then need to select activities that might challenge those images (Hunter, 2006). Some activities have been found to be particularly effective in doing this, and are discussed later in the chapter.

Pupils' new experiences prompt them to construct theories to explain those experiences. Learners progress when they notice a discrepancy between what they currently believe or what is commonly believed, and what appears to be true. They then form theories about how the discrepancy can be explained (Sotto, 2007). This is not to say that the new theories are necessarily correct; it may be that the pupils' new ideas are only partially correct or, indeed, entirely erroneous. The teacher's intervention is obviously important at this stage. Pupils may need prompting to test their theories and you may be able to select particular activities that are effective in helping to avoid erroneous learning.

One part of the constructivist approach is to see learning as a function of the individual. All learners can be expected to learn at different rates, and develop mathematical concepts in line with their stages of cognitive development (Neyland, 1995). This idea has a clear influence on the way that we teach mathematics. We teach pupils in large groups, but try as much as possible to differentiate according to individual need. You need to identify pupils who are finding the work difficult, and through questioning try to probe each child's understanding. As your skills grow, you will select questions that are appropriate to take forward the understanding of individuals and groups.

SOCIAL CONSTRUCTIVISM

Many modern writers on the theories of learning mathematics prefer to adapt Piaget's ideas of cognitive development to take account of social interaction. This is known as the social constructivist viewpoint. Social constructivism takes the idea of learning in stages through constructing new understanding, and adds to it an extra dimension in the form of language and communication. Vygotsky (1987) describes the key interaction between language and learning,

initially through affirming the importance of speech in learning. His view that 'the relationship of thought and word is a vital process that involves the birth of thought in the word' (Vygotsky 1987) has been strongly influential on a whole generation of educationalists.

But Vygotsky goes further than linking thought and language. He suggests that effective learning can only take place in a social context. Mathematical knowledge forms part of a social structure within the classroom and outside, and access to that structure comes through communication. In this perspective, learning takes place on two planes: the social plane through interaction with other people, and then the internal, psychological plane. Discussion, therefore, becomes a central part of learning, much more than the teacher transmitting knowledge. As you begin your time in schools, you will see that many of the most effective mathematics lessons reflect the social constructivist view of learning.

THE ROLE OF THE TEACHER

As well as highlighting the interplay of thought and language, Vygotsky also highlights the key role played by the teacher in helping pupils to learn. The teacher is seen as providing the scaffolding, on which pupils construct their learning. This scaffolding is only effective if the work provides the right level of challenge for the pupils (and of course this might mean different activities for different groups of pupils). In the Standards Unit guidance (DfES, 2005) the teacher's role is described as being to:

- assess learners and make constructive use of prior knowledge
- choose appropriate challenges for learners
- make the purpose of activities clear
- help learners to see how they should work together in profitable ways
- encourage learners to explore and exchange ideas in an unhurried, reflective atmosphere
- encourage the discussion of alternative methods and understandings, examining their strengths and weaknesses
- remove the 'fear of failure' by welcoming mistakes as learning opportunities rather than problems to avoid
- challenge learners through effective probing questions
- manage small group and whole group discussions
- draw out the important ideas in each session
- help learners to make connections between their ideas
  (DfES, 2005: 6).

This is undoubtedly a helpful list, but like all long lists, it loses impact through its length. A shorter version that derives from the above is to describe the teacher's role as to:

- share the purpose of the lesson
- choose appropriate activities that give the right level of challenge
- manage whole-class questioning and discussion
- encourage individual ideas in a non-judgemental atmosphere
- draw together the most important learning points.

In short, you are encouraged to establish and maintain an atmosphere where pupils know the purpose of the lesson and to build non-threatening relationships. But you are also there to play a key role in the learning process: by selecting challenging activities and then intervening to help pupils develop their understanding of key ideas.

EFFECTIVE TEACHING AND LEARNING

Constructivist learning theories suggest that lessons could follow a format where the lesson moves from presentation to exploration, followed by reflection and consolidation. An initial examination of prior knowledge is followed by the presentation of a problem, together with an introduction to a set of activities to help the pupils discover rules and definitions. In the exploration phase, pupils do the activities introduced at the beginning of the lesson. After exploring, pupils go on to the reflection phase. The teacher and the pupils review what has been noticed, with the teacher posing scaffolded questions to help pupils to form conclusions. Finally, the lesson has an application and discussion phase. This involves a whole-class activity to share conclusions, where the main points are recapped. The teacher may choose to look forward to future learning and identify the possible next steps.

There is plenty of evidence (for example, Ofsted, 2006) that teachers of mathematics tend to overstress methods, routines and skills at the expense of long-term learning strategies, and that, as a result, pupils are poor at transferring their skills. Although they can be taught to answer examination questions in mathematics, pupils sometimes lack any real conceptual understanding. When faced with an unfamiliar problem, many give up. They have no opinions about how they might approach the problem, and no experience of using the opinion of others. In the following quotes, two teachers explain their observations of pupils' responses to problems:

> For example year 11 could use algorithms without having gone through the thinking processes that start with simple cause and effect, develop inference and causal reasoning and eventually move onto correlational thinking.

> They were ... likely to label themselves as stupid and give up before a rational approach could be undertaken.
> (Cassell and Kilshaw, 2004)

There is evidence that regular use of textbooks may contribute to teachers overemphasizing methods. Newton and Newton (2007) studied a range of textbooks in common use in schools with pupils aged 7–11. They report that some textbooks are helpful to the teacher in structuring their lessons, but that they are unlikely to encourage the teaching of understanding. The message from the books is that mathematics is about skill development rather than understanding.

In an interesting study of teaching styles, Watson and De Geest (2005) designed a project that introduced innovative teaching methods to low-attaining secondary school pupils. In the report on the project, they are able to identify effective common principles used by all teachers, but conclude that 'overt methods are less important than the collection of beliefs and commitments that underpin teacher choices' (Watson and De Geest, 2005: 209). They report that successful teachers focus more on long-term development rather than short-term gains, and avoid trivialising the subject.

PUPILS' ACTIVE INVOLVEMENT

One focus of the Every Child Matters agenda is to generate enjoyment of learning. One way to help pupils to enjoy their lessons is to make the lessons as active as possible, and as varied as possible. This can be illustrated through the words of a teacher with 10 years' experience, describing her lesson with a low-ability Year 7 group (mostly level 3, with some near to borderline level 4).

> There are some real characters in the group. I have two learning support assistants in there and it was a bit of a battle at first to get on top of their behaviour. They really didn't particularly like maths when I started taking them. So anything we do tends to be very interactive. I try to make each lesson as interactive as possible and keep it cut up into small units, because their concentration is not very good.

We illustrate the point by describing part of a lesson, where the teacher is keen to foster enjoyment of learning through active participation. The lesson is on co-ordinates, and the objective is for pupils to be able to read and plot co-ordinates in the first quadrant, with the possible extension to all four quadrants. The first part of the lesson is all about number lines and evenly spaced numbers on the number lines, emphasizing that:

- the numbers on the axes should not be too close together
- leaving different spaces between numbers would be wrong.

An indication of the pupils' active participation is given by the teacher's description of the lesson:

> On the board, I drew a horizontal number line, which went from 0 to 10, and pupils came up and put onto the line the numbers from 1 to 9. I then added the vertical line to make a pair of axes and we numbered the vertical axis. Pupils then came to the board in turn to show where to plot various points.

The extension to that is then to include negative numbers. The class discuss why -10 did not come next to 0 and what negative numbers mean. After drawing a horizontal number line from -10 to 10, the teacher asks where we see this kind of number line. One pupil answers 'on graphs'. After discussion, the vertical number line is added and numbered.

> Then we did the same thing as before, but with the axes for all four quadrants. Pupils came up and put points on, and demonstrated that they could do it. They just love it. They really, really enjoyed it, they are now at a stage where they actually like maths because they get out of their chairs and come and have a go on the board, which they really enjoy.
>
> Initially I expected them to be critical of each other, because some classes of that ability have pupils who mock mistakes, saying, 'you can't do it'. But this group are not at all like that. They are really tolerant of each other, so if one comes out and they cannot do it, they are perfectly happy while you explain to them how to do it, and then let them do it. They are desperate to come out and write on the whiteboard or the interactive board. They love it.

It is clear that the pupils enjoy the lesson. The teacher believes that their enjoyment is down in a large part to their interaction with the teacher and their participation in the board work.

THE RIGHT LEVEL OF CHALLENGE

As discussed above, the role of the teacher includes selecting work with an appropriate level of challenge. This might sound an obvious idea, but it is surprising how often mathematics lessons fail to provide that level of challenge. Where inspectors find mathematics lessons unsatisfactory, they find that a small number of features appear time after time. Among the characteristics of weak lessons are:

- low-level tasks which are mechanistic and can be completed by imitating a routine or procedure without any depth of thought
- insufficient time is allowed for developing understanding of mathematical concepts (Ofsted, 2002).

Many teachers see their role as trying to make mathematics appear easy, which sounds a laudable aim. Unfortunately, if mathematics is reduced too much to a step-by-step approach, then the thought processes are trivialized. Instead of constructing new understanding, pupils hardly have to think at all. Of course, some pupils prefer this sort of mathematics, but teaching of this kind gives the message, 'you can't expect to understand the mathematics, the most you can expect is to be able to get some questions right'. Pupils may in fact measure their success not by whether they have learnt anything or understood the work, but by counting how many questions they have completed in the lesson. Malcolm Swan (in DfES, 2005: 4) describes this model of teaching as transmission teaching, which 'can appear superficially effective when short-term recall is required', but is less effective for longer-term learning. At its least effective, transmission teaching encourages 'the rote memorising of disconnected rules, which are often misapplied and quickly forgotten' (ibid.: 4). Watson and De Geest (2005: 213) recommend that the complexity of mathematical concepts and methods 'should be preserved rather than simplified'. In other words, you should avoid missing out all the exceptional cases and the 'what if?' questions.

A more challenging teaching style focuses more strongly on pupils understanding the work, by posing fewer routine problems and by encouraging collaborative learning, where pupils have time to explore ideas and refine their thinking. In this style, learning becomes less linear, and is more in tune with a constructionist view of learning, where the pupil is an active participant who is exploring meanings in the mathematics. These ideas are developed further in the paragraphs below.

Point for reflection

Think about mathematics lessons that you remember from when you were a pupil. Consider the extent to which you practised routines, and the extent to which you explored ideas through discussion with others.

All pupils enjoy success in mathematics, and like the reassurance of getting questions right. Consider how it might be possible to reconcile pupils facing difficult ideas and feeling positive about their learning.

DISCUSSION AND GROUP WORK

In the social constructivist perspective, the process of using language is helpful in developing understanding, and hence the emphasis that is placed on encouraging pupils to explain their methods. Another valuable teaching tool that has its roots in constructivist thinking is the use of pupils' ideas or explanations as a basis for further discussion. Hence well-focused group work helps pupils to verbalize their ideas to others. They may then be required by other members of the group to justify their ideas in more detail.

An effective way of generating discussion is to present a problem that is likely to cause disagreement among the pupils. For example, reflecting on the sample lesson on the website (discussed in Chapter 4), the teacher explains why she presents the class with a situation that is designed to promote disagreement:

> I really wanted them to understand the difference between events that have equally likely outcomes and those that don't. So I put up a picture of a little man saying there are pizza, curry and salad on sale in the canteen, with a statement that therefore the probability I choose pizza must be one out of three.
>
> Initially I think most people agreed with the statement. The majority were going to agree, but we had one little boy in there, probably thinking actually I don't like curry or I don't want salad, and realizing that there is a choice involved. The example showed them that actually not all outcomes have an equally likely chance of coming up, so therefore we cannot use the previously learned theory. We must come up with a different way of finding the probability so the idea of doing an experiment or a survey develops.

Class discussion is easier to manage than discussion within groups, simply because the teacher is an active part of the whole-class discussion. In small groups, the teacher has to give written (or possibly verbal) prompts that initiate discussion, and give some direction as to how the group can communicate its conclusions.

MISCONCEPTIONS

Misconceptions are not the same as mistakes. Anyone can make mistakes in mathematics; mistakes can occur even when the underlying work is thoroughly understood, and are likely to be the result of carelessness or tiredness. Misconceptions are systematic errors. Misconceptions produce wrong answers but the arguments that lead to the answers can be explained, and the same error will be made time and again. In other words, misconceptions are incorrect understandings of the mathematics. Most misconceptions come about through pupils overgeneralizing a result from earlier in their mathematical education.

Let us look at an example. One of the simplest misconceptions to understand is the belief that when you multiply a number by 10, you put a nought on the end. This is, of course, true for integers, and that is the cause of the problem. Pupils at an early age learn how to multiply natural numbers by ten and, either implicitly or explicitly from the teacher, they learn that putting a nought on the end always gives the correct answer. The problem comes when pupils meet decimals, and then conclude that the result of multiplying 3.6 by 10 is 3.60.

It is easy to understand how this misconception arises, and you will find it surprisingly common. But the most interesting thing is this: just showing pupils the correct way to multiply decimals by 10 is often not sufficient to remove the misconception. This is quite hard to take in. It is natural for you, especially in the early days of your training, to want to explain correct methods, and expect that pupils will take on board what you have shown them. In other words, you would expect the pupils to accept that they are wrong because you are telling them so, and giving sound reasons.

In fact, this is what often happens in the mathematics classroom. The teacher spots that a pupil has a misconception, explains that it is wrong, and demonstrates the correct method. The pupil is able to follow the correct method and gets the correct answers for the remainder of the lesson, and possibly the next few lessons. Then a few months later, when the same topic is revisited, the pupil reverts to applying his or her own, incorrect, rule. In our example, when multiplying decimals next appears in a lesson, the pupil reverts to adding a nought on the end.

The teaching has led to short-term learning, but has not removed the misconception. When faced with a question away from the direct focus of the lesson, the pupil has reverted to a level of understanding that is familiar and believed. It is as though the misconception is part of the pupil's belief system; it is a way of working that makes sense to the pupil. It is this that makes misconceptions very difficult to remove and replace.

Berry and Graham (summarized in Tanner and Jones, 2000) report an example of teaching not removing a misconception among A level mechanics students. Even after a series of lessons on Newton's Laws, students retained the belief that the mass of an object made a difference to the time that it would take to drop a specific distance under gravity. In other words, the students hang on to their intuitive belief, which is easier to retain than to replace with something else.

COGNITIVE CONFLICT

Some writers (for example, Zaslavsky, 2005) characterize the teacher's role as being to create uncertainty in the minds of the learners. Zaslavsky describes three different kinds of uncertainty that can be generated in mathematics: competing claims; questionable conclusions; and outcomes that are difficult to verify. Introducing any of these into the classroom is difficult, because pupils often prefer the security of being sure that they are right. An additional difficulty lies in creating situations that have an appropriate level of uncertainty for the pupils concerned. You may intuitively feel that creating uncertainty should be treated with care, and that such an approach can only be taken occasionally, but you should avoid being too cautious!

The teaching approach which starts by provoking uncertainty is called cognitive conflict. The approach has been shown to be effective in helping pupils overcome misconceptions. Bell et al. (1985) used pre-testing and post-testing to compare the learning on a range of decimal concepts. One group of pupils was taught using a 'positive only' approach, which emphasized the correct methods, and focused on anticipated areas of difficulty. The other group was taught using conflict methods, where pupils were led into exposing their misconceptions, before the teacher led discussions to the resolve the conflict. The testing showed that the conflict teaching method led to significantly bigger gains in learning, measured not only on a post-test but also on a delayed post-test that aimed to test long-term retention. Thus conflict methods appear to be more effective in creating long-term learning than methods where likely errors are avoided or where they are simply mentioned in passing by the teacher.

Several researchers (summarized, for example, in Askew and Wiliam, 1995) have followed up the early work of Alan Bell and colleagues, and demonstrated that when conflicts are created, given impact and resolved through reflective discussion, then learning is more effective. As noted in the National Strategy guidance (DfES, 2002), there are two ways that teachers can respond to misconceptions in the classroom:

- by warning pupils of likely misconceptions, explaining why they are incorrect, and demonstrating the correct method
- by allowing misconceptions to occur and using them as teaching points.

Many teachers use methods that can be described by the first bullet point. Of those who use the method described in the second bullet, some go further. They do not wait for misconceptions to occur, and respond; they design activities that are likely to provoke the disclosure of misconceptions. Swan (2001) recommends posing questions that create conflict – apparent contradictions that demonstrate that something needs to be learnt.

This involves more than posing a question where different pupils will disagree. It involves creating a situation where pupils find that they get two contradictory answers, both of which seem to make sense. For example, pupils with a poor grasp of place value in decimal numbers may continue the sequence

4.1, 4.3, 4.5, 4.7, ...

with the values 4.9, 4.11, 4.13. The pupils will probably have no difficulty in describing the fact that the numbers go up in 0.2s, and if given a calculator can find that by repeated adding 0.2s, they obtain 4.9, 5.1, 5.3 as the next three terms. This is not two or more people disagreeing; in this case the two answers both make sense to the same person. In this situation, pupils are understandably puzzled, and have to accept that the contradiction must have an explanation.

A possible next step is to arrange some work for the pupils on reading scales. You may choose not to mention the link between the scales work and the unresolved conflict, or you may just confirm that the issue will be revisited later. When the pupils have worked on the scales and are confident with placing, for example, 4.11 and 4.9 in the correct places, you can then reintroduce the conflict situation and encourage pupils to come to a conclusion. You can, through skilful questioning, help pupils to see the link between the work on scales and the continued sequence, and hence help to resolve the conflict. In other words, by focusing on the cognitive conflict that occurs, you can help pupils to accommodate the new knowledge by adjusting their understanding of the decimal system. Having accommodated the new understanding, pupils are then given some new problems to solve that help them to consolidate their understanding.

Swan's (2001) suggested teaching model involves the following five steps:

1. Start by assessing pupils' initial understanding.
2. Pupils complete a task that is designed by the teacher to encourage intuitive solutions or expose common misconceptions (presenting the opportunity for cognitive conflict to occur).
3. Pupils share their methods and solutions through discussion.
4. The teacher organizes a whole-class discussion that aims to resolve the conflict.
5. Pupils consolidate their learning through applying it to new problems.

This framework corresponds closely with the ideas of social constructivism, and focuses on long-term learning based on understanding, rather than on being able to perform a set of skills.

RECOMMENDED ACTIVITIES

The National Strategy guidance on using misconceptions as a focus for learning activities (DfES, 2002) gives examples of two different kinds of classroom activity that have been found to suit this style of teaching. One is a sorting activity, which involves the pupils in grouping together different representations of the same idea. The other focuses on generalizations, and presents pupils with a series of statements that they have to categorize according to the three headings: always true, sometimes true, and never true. An example of each is given below.

1. Sorting into equivalent groups

This sort of activity is good for group work, and encourages pupils to justify their reasoning to the rest of the group. Some uncomfortable decisions have to be made, because all the cards have to be put into one of the groups, even when it might not be immediately obvious that they belong to any group. This example focuses on the common misconception that the equals sign means 'makes', leading to pupils being much less comfortable with equations of the form $12 = 2x + 3$ than they are with equations of the form $2x + 3 = 12$. The sheet here needs to be cut up into cards, shuffled, and given to pupils. The task is to sort the statements into three groups of equivalent equations.

I think of a number, add 5 and double it. The result is 24.	$10 + 2x = 24$	$2(x + 5) = 24$
I think of a number, double it and add 10. The result is 24.	$14 = 2x$	$2x + 16 = 30$
I think of a number, divide it by 2, and add 5. The result is 24	$\frac{x}{2} + 5 = 24$	$24 - \frac{x}{2} = 5$
$20 - \frac{x}{2} = 1$	$48 = x + 10$	$38 = x$
$2(x - 4) = 24$	$12 = x - 4$	$24 = 2x - 8$
$2x + 8 = 40$	$\frac{x}{2} + 1 = 9$	$10 = \frac{x}{2} + 2$

This activity is not a lesson in itself, but can be used within Swan's five-point teaching framework described above. It provides an opportunity for pupils to share their methods and ideas through discussion, before the teacher brings together the class to help resolve any areas of conflict.

2. Always, sometimes, never true

Many misconceptions arise through the incorrect generalization of mathematical ideas. For example, because of their early experience with number work, many pupils believe that multiplying a number will always make it larger, and that division will always make it smaller (for example, DfES, 2002; Dickson et al., 1984). For example, consider the question:

Fill in the blank to make this sum correct: $24 \times \underline{} = 12$.

When faced with this sort of question, many pupils say that it cannot be done; there is no solution. The activity below aims to help pupils confront this situation. The question sheet is a set of statements based around the idea of multiplying and dividing. Pupils are asked to decide, giving justifications, whether each statement is always true (true for all possible numbers), sometimes true (true for some numbers but not others), or never true (there are no numbers for which the statement is true).

Multiplying a positive number by 10 makes it larger
Multiplying a number by 10 and adding 100 makes it larger
Adding 0.1 to a number makes it larger
Halving a number makes it smaller
Multiplying a number by 10 and then dividing the result by 10 makes the number smaller
Squaring a negative number makes it larger

By looking at what rules in mathematics are general and which are not, pupils are focusing on the bigger picture. They begin to understand the idea of a counter-example, and the completeness of the number system.

3. Other activities

Clearly the two activities described above are not the only way to deliver a lesson that focuses on a constructivist approach to pupils' learning. We give brief descriptions of three other activities that you may wish to try out. Here are three types of activity that have been found to be effective.

Classifying into two-way tables

This approach focuses on a series of questions for pupils to do, but avoids presenting them as a set of routine questions. The particular presentation in this form is ideal for group discussion.

A simple example is to give pupils the grid below, together with a set of 10 numbered geometrical shapes (or pictures of everyday objects). Pupils have to put each shape into one of the boxes in the grid.

	One line of symmetry	Two lines of symmetry	More than two lines of symmetry
Rotational symmetry			
No rotational symmetry			

Pupils make up their own questions

This makes pupils think about constructing a mathematical problem, and can be helpful in understanding the problem itself. This can work as part of paired work, where pupils make up three questions for their partner to do. A variation is to ask each pupil to make up a pair of questions, one difficult and one easy. This helps pupils to focus on what aspect of the question makes it difficult.

Pupils mark a set of prepared answers to questions (Wally's answers).

Pupils are given a worksheet on which Wally has already written in his answers, together with his working or reasoning. Pupils have to decide whether each answer is correct or not. Where the answer is not correct, they have to say what the correct answer should be and explain why Wally has gone wrong. This requires much more thinking than just answering a set of questions, and focuses attention on methods as much as answers.

USING RESOURCES

As we have seen, in constructivist learning theories, pupils construct their own meaning as active learners, supported by suitable intervention from a teacher. The teacher's role is to scaffold, and the use of a teaching aid can provide the scaffolding more effectively than using just language. Edwards (1998) suggests that learning takes place through the interconnections of four modes of experience: handling objects, pictures, language and symbols. The term resources may be regarded as including two types of teaching aid: objects to handle, and visual images presented as illustration.

Resources, or teaching aids, have always played a part in mathematics classrooms, but since 1997 the evidence is that their use has noticeably increased (Ofsted, 2006). In the modern classroom, many resources are ICT based, but there is also a large range of commercially produced resources. Some resources are requirements for any mathematics department, such as rulers, protractors, compasses and calculators. Others resources are more a matter of choice as to whether the teacher makes use of them. Some teachers will make extensive use of a particular resource; others may hardly use it at all. The examples in this category are almost endless, but certainly include: dice, a counting stick, show-me boards, flash cards, spotty paper, counters and multi-link cubes.

Resources divide fairly easily into two types: those used by the teacher to demonstrate, and those used by the pupils to explore or solve problems. One benefit of using a limited set of resources is that the same resource, used in different circumstances, can help pupils to see the connections between different branches of mathematics. For example, if multi-link cubes are used to illustrate cube numbers and the volume of a cube, then it is easier for pupils to see that the two ideas are very similar. It is also helpful for pupils to see the links between different representations of mathematics: 4 cubed, 4^3, $4 \times 4 \times 4$, the volume of a cube of side 4.

Some teachers equip their classrooms with permanent visual aids in terms of displays. It is common to see a giant number line, including the negative numbers, pinned to one wall of the classroom. There are several commercially produced mathematical posters that provide illustrations that are useful in particular lessons. A few teachers make extensive use of a 'washing line', a cord that they can easily stretch across the room, and use it to peg out various numbers.

The purpose of pupils using resources is often to explore ideas for themselves, to try things out, but it also makes the lesson more enjoyable for many pupils. Pupils enjoy handling multi-link cubes, tracing paper, dice, and so on. Visual representations have a particular role to play in looking for patterns in mathematics, whether in number sequences or to help generalizations into algebra. Particular resources are also helpful in recording pupils' work. Graph paper, spotty paper and centimetre-squared paper all provide essential support for accurate recording.

It may be that resources can retain their usefulness even when they are not physically present. Clearly this is most likely to occur if the resource has been used so regularly that it has become familiar to the pupil. In this way, pupils who are used to working on a number line, may accept in later years that they do not need a number line present to do simple calculations, but may count on an imaginary number line (Delaney, 2001). Similarly, pupils who have used tracing paper to perform rotations may find that the mental imagery of an object rotating as if on tracing paper is particularly helpful in deciding the position of the image.

Of course, it is impossible to judge a resource in isolation. It is not a resource as such that makes a lesson successful. The effectiveness of the resource depends more than anything on the way that the teacher incorporates it into the lesson, helping the teacher to provide appropriate scaffolding for pupils to learn.

THINKING SKILLS

The step from concrete to formal operations is one that causes difficulties for many pupils, and particularly so in mathematics. An attempt to address this difficulty is the Cognitive Acceleration in Mathematics Education (CAME) project, initiated in 1993, with the aim of producing an intervention process that accelerates cognitive development, but also (and crucially, in the world where schools are judged by examination results) improves achievement in mathematics results (Adhami et al., 1998).

The focus of the CAME project is pupils in Years 7 and 8, and consists of 30 pre-planned lessons. The lessons use discussion-based tasks that are designed to develop children's conceptual thinking rather than being able to answer questions of a specific type. The lessons are investigational in style, but each concentrates on the development of a specific concept. In each lesson the activities generate group and whole-class discussion rather than written work, with an emphasis on methods rather than answers.

The use of the CAME project in one school forms the basis of a case study reported on the Standards website. In this school, the CAME lessons are delivered within normal mathematics lessons, but as individual stand-alone lessons once a fortnight. Following the introduction of the CAME project in this school, two teachers report:

> From comments made during parents' evenings, discussions with pupils and small scale surveys the response to these lessons has been very positive. Many pupils enjoy having their say. The emphasis on 'how did you get your answer' is less threatening than 'is your answer correct?' and hence motivation in the classroom has been improved.
> (Cassell and Kilshaw, 2004)

The Cassell and Kilshaw case study acknowledges the importance of staff development as part of the project. In their school, staff meet regularly to run through lessons coming up and to reflect upon previous lessons. They report that 'this process has been vital to the successful running of the project' (ibid.). Elsewhere, Goulding (2002) reports a more mixed response from teachers, with some clearly benefiting from the collaboration that the project generated, but others much less convinced that the project had provided useful professional collaboration.

Shayer and Adhami (2007), in a more recent evaluation, reaffirm the success of the project in improving overall results in mathematics, but argue that the reasons for the success may not be the content of the intervention lessons themselves, but more the critique of standard teaching methods that the project provides. Moreover, they contend that there is still a place for 'instructional' teaching in mathematics classrooms, and argue for an evolution of practice that integrates good instructional teaching with the teaching skills suggested in the CAME methodology.

EVIDENCE FROM THE RESEARCH

It is impossible to do justice in one chapter to all the arguments surrounding learning theories, or even all the arguments surrounding social constructivism. But you should feel comfortable that the basis for a lot of recommended classroom activities lies in the social constructivist framework. Social constructivism suggests that the following methods should be evident in the classroom: modelling, scaffolding, coaching, articulation, reflection, collaboration, exploration, problem-solving activities, and giving pupils choices (Muijs and Reynolds, 2005). In addition, rather than tackling routine questions with set answers, pupils benefit from situations where there may be many alternative approaches or multiple answers.

Vygotsky refers to learning on the social plane through discussion, with a later internalization of the learning on the psychological plane. Jaworski (2002) suggests more of an interplay between learning on the two planes. She describes individual thinking and social thinking as being two processes that alternate and interweave. In her description of social constructivism, she suggests that the thinking of a group in the classroom follows this interactive process:

> Individual thought moves in and out of the group as an individual speaks, listens, thinks ... and in the process constructs something that fits with previous conceptions or challenges them. However, as the people in the group interact, talk with and across each other, challenge, argue, disagree, ask questions, offer explanations, it can be as if knowledge grows within the group; as if knowledge is located somewhere in the group space, rather than in the heads of individuals. For any member of the group, what they know as a result of all this interaction is as much

a product of the interaction, as it is an act of individual construction.
(Jaworski, 2002: 73)

It is easy to see the emphasis that social constructivism places on planned group work and on interactions between pupils. But it does not rule out whole-class teaching as an instrument for learning. The theory can accommodate a learning situation where the class is engaged in an interactive teaching session, with the teacher directing the questioning, and using the replies given to generate new questions. In this situation, the engagement of the whole group can lead to a widespread increase of knowledge.

The more one emphasizes that pupils construct their own meaning, based on accommodating new ideas into their already understood set of knowledge, the easier it becomes to view the pupil as the active person in the classroom, and the teacher as a kind of facilitator who provides the right kind of activities and organizes what takes place, but otherwise has little effect on learning. This is, of course, not the case. In the social constructivist standpoint, the teacher has a crucial role in the learning process. Vygotsky's phrase 'zone of proximal development' is used to describe the gap between what the learner could achieve without any outside input and what the learner could achieve if given help from another person (often, although not necessarily, the teacher). The teacher's role in this perspective is to identify each child's zone of proximal development (ZPD), and to provide in each lesson the level of stimulus needed to move through the zone and hence maximize the rate of learning.

The teacher's role also involves selecting the optimal level of support that is needed to help learning. The teacher may provide a level of scaffolding to support the learning process, and part of being a good teacher is selecting the right level of support for each individual pupil.

Additionally, the teacher has a key role in organizing and structuring discussion between pupils. The discussion is most likely to be useful if it is structured with a particular learning objective in mind. In this case, the learning partner (the other pupil in the discussion) acts as a mediator in the learning process. Although still the organizer, the teacher is no longer providing direct scaffolding (Shayer, 2003). When pupils are working together on a task, they share a common zone of proximal development. It is possible for a child to learn individually by constructing new meaning up to the limits of their ZPD, but it is more likely that the learning will be mediated by the other child. In other words, the rate of one pupil's move through the ZPD is influenced by the position of the other pupil. Seeing another pupil who has understood a concept can help another pupil to internalize the concept in its entirety, when initially their understanding may have been partial.

Point for reflection

The Office for Standards in Education (2006) report that teaching and learning are good in two-thirds of mathematics lessons, but some teaching provides pupils with too much repetition and limited challenge. Improving teaching and learning is a key feature of the development plan of many departments, but teachers often find constructivist methods difficult to implement. Consider why you think that this is the case, and whether there are barriers that prevent teachers giving more emphasis to pupils' long-term learning.

Further reading

Jaworski, B. (2002) 'Social constructivism in Mathematics learning and teaching', in L. Haggarty (ed.) *Teaching Mathematics in Secondary Schools. A Reader.* London: Routledge Falmer.

In this chapter, Barbara Jaworski provides a useful overview of constructivism. She then gives more detail on why and how the theory has been adapted to take more account of the social aspects of learning. She uses illustrations from a classroom in Pakistan to show how the theoretical ideas relate to practical learning situations.

Department for Education and Skills (DfES) (2005) *Improving Learning in Mathematics: challenges and strategies* in the Standards Unit pack, *Improving Learning in Mathematics*. London: Department for Education and Skills.

This booklet is part of a whole set of teaching resources, which can also be ordered from the DfES publications department. The *Challenges and Strategies* booklet gives a very practical set of activities for use in the classroom, together with a brief overview of the theoretical background. The resources focus on active, rather than passive, learning, and aim to encourage teachers to adopt a 'challenging' approach in preference to a simple transmission of information model. There are plenty of good ideas for classroom use. See the websites below, or follow the link on this book's website.

Useful websites

Live links to these sites can be found on the companion website.

http://www.amet.ac.uk/mereview/mer07pdfs/mereview-07-Jan-1996-1.pdf

This website reproduces an article by Sylvia Johnson in the Mathematics Education Review. It discusses the extent to which trainees need to understand the theoretical basis for recommended classroom practice.

The Centre for Innovation in Mathematics Teaching at Plymouth University has a web page with detailed discussion of a number of misconceptions. These can be found at http://www.cimt.plymouth.ac.uk/resources/help/miscon.htm

http://www.teachers.tv/video/4872 An experienced teacher recommends three particular teaching resources, and explains why they are effective.

A pdf file of the book *Improving Learning in Mathematics* is at http://www.ncetm.org.uk/files/224/improving_learning_in_mathematicsi.pdf

Information on how to obtain the (free) full set of resources that go with the book is available at http://www.ncetm.org.uk/Default.aspx?page=13&module=res&mode=100&resid=1442

The 2005/6 Annual Report of Her Majesty's Chief Inspector of Schools can be downloaded from http://www.ofsted.gov.uk/portal/site/Internet/menuitem.eace3f09a603f6d9c3172a8a08c08a0c/?vgnextoid=98a6cdb5cb7ce010VgnVCM1000003507640aRCRD

A discussion of the CAME project is at http://www.standards.dfes.gov.uk/giftedandtalented/goodpractice/cs/camemaths/

References

Adhami, M., Johnson, D. and Shayer, M. (1998) *Thinking Maths*. Oxford: Heinemann.

Askew, M. and Wiliam, D. (1995) *Recent Research in Mathematics Education 5–16*. London: HMSO.

Bell, A., Swan, M., Onslow, B., Pratt, K. and Purdy, D. (1985) *Diagnostic Teaching: Teaching for Long-Term Learning*. Nottingham: Shell Centre for Mathematical Education.

Cassell, A. and Kilshaw, D. (2004) *Case Studies: The CAME Maths Project*. Online at http://www.standards.dfes.gov.uk/giftedandtalented/goodpractice/cs/camemaths/ (accessed 7 August 2007).

Delaney, K. (2001) 'Teaching Mathematics Resourcefully', in P. Gates (ed.) *Issues in Teaching Mathematics*. London: RoutledgeFalmer.

Department for Education and Skills (DfES) (2002) *Learning from Mistakes, Misunderstandings and Misconceptions in Mathematics*. London: Department for Education and Skills.

Department for Education and Skills (DfES) (2005) *Improving Learning in Mathematics: Challenges and Strategies*, in the Standards Unit pack, *Improving Learning in Mathematics*. London: Department for Education and Skills.

Dickson, L., Brown, M. and Gibson, O. (1984) *Children Learning Mathematics: A Teacher's Guide to Recent Research*. London: Cassell.

Edwards, S. (1998) *Managing Effective Teaching of Mathematics 3-8*. London: Paul Chapman.

Goulding, M. (2002) 'Developing thinking in mathematics', in L. Haggarty (ed.), *Aspects of Teaching Secondary Mathematics: Perspectives on Practice*. London: RoutledgeFalmer.

Hunter, J. (2006) 'The numeracy project: foundations and development', *ACE Papers*, issue 17, June.

Jaworski, B. (2002) 'Social constructivism in mathematics learning and teaching', in L. Haggarty (ed.), *Teaching Mathematics in Secondary Schools: A Reader*. London: RoutledgeFalmer.

Muijs, D. and Reynolds, D. (2005) *Effective Teaching: Evidence and Practice*. London: Sage.

Newton, D. and Newton, L. (2007) 'Could elementary mathematics textbooks help give attention to reasons in the classroom?', *Educational Studies in Mathematics*, 64(1): 69–84.

Neyland, J. (1995) 'Eight approaches to teaching mathematics', in J. Neyland (ed.), *Mathematics Education: A Handbook for Teachers: Vol 2*, Wellington: Wellington College of Education.

Office for Standards in Education (Ofsted) (2002) *Mathematics in Secondary Schools*. London: HMSO.

Office for Standards in Education (Ofsted) (2006) *The Annual Report of Her Majesty's Chief Inspector of Schools 2005/6*. London: Office for Standards in Education.

Pirie, S. and Kieren, T. (1989) 'A recursive theory of mathematical understanding', *For the Learning of Mathematics*, 9(3): 7–11.

Shayer, M. (2003) 'Not just Piaget; not just Vygotsky, and certainly not Vygotsky as alternative to Piaget', *Learning and Instruction*, 13: 465–85.

Shayer, M. and Adhami, M. (2007) 'Fostering cognitive development through the context of mathematics: results of the CAME Project', *Educational Studies in Mathematics*, 64(3): 265–91.

Sotto, E. (2007) *When Teaching becomes Learning: A Theory and Practice of Teaching*. London: Continuum International.

Swan, M. (2001) 'Dealing with misconceptions in mathematics', in P. Gates (ed.), *Issues in Mathematics Teaching*. London: RoutledgeFalmer.

Tanner, H. and Jones, S. (2000) *Becoming a Successful Teacher of Mathematics*. London: RoutledgeFalmer.

Vygotsky, L. (1987). *The Collected Works of L S Vygotsky Volume 1: Problems of General Psychology*. New York: Plenum Press.

Watson, A. and De Geest, E. (2005) 'Principled teaching for deep progress: improving mathematical learning beyond methods and materials', *Educational Studies in Mathematics*, 58(2): 209–34.

Zaslavsky, O. (2005) 'Seizing the opportunity to create uncertainty in the learning of mathematics', *Educational Studies in Mathematics*, 58(3): 297–391.

6 ASSESSMENT

This chapter:

- provides an overview of national testing for pupils at the end of Key Stage 3, at GCSE and at A level
- examines the background to assessment, and discusses the main reasons that assessment plays such an important part in mathematics teaching
- reviews a range of different forms of assessment
- discusses the main purposes of the Assessment for Learning initiative, including the role of self-assessment
- reviews the role of oral questioning in mathematics lessons
- makes suggestions about good practice in record-keeping and reporting to parents.

Assessment is a key feature of life in schools. It is used to make judgements of pupils' ability, judgements that may be used for selection purposes or to monitor progress. Assessment has benefits for both teachers and pupils, but also reaches beyond the schools gates more than many other aspects of school life. As a result, assessment may be used to form judgements about not only pupils, but also teachers and schools. Teachers are accountable within the school for their examination results, and because of school league tables, schools are acutely conscious of results, particularly in the GCSE examinations.

National tests are the most public face of assessment but, in fact, assessment forms parts of all mathematics lessons in some form. It is part of the teaching and learning process, with the potential to make a real difference to pupils' learning. Inspection evidence (Ofsted, 2006) suggests that teachers find assessment to be one of the most difficult aspects of their role. Inspectors find that assessment is generally weaker than teaching and learning in mathematics classrooms. Whereas teaching and learning are good in two-thirds of lessons, the corresponding figure for assessment is just over one-half. Similarly, the number of schools where assessment is unsatisfactory (10 per cent) is double the number where teaching and learning are unsatisfactory. You are likely to find that applying good practice in assessment is one of the most challenging aspects of your early years as a teacher.

NATIONAL TESTING

School league tables and external scrutiny by Ofsted seem to have made the results of national tests more important than ever for schools. Before looking at the nature of the assessments and the framework within which they work, we shall look briefly at one of the more hidden aspects of national testing: the way that national testing is used to control the curriculum and influence the practice of teachers in the classroom. One unfortunate development of the current culture of results is that teachers are less likely to broaden the curriculum in ways that they find interesting, or to pursue a piece of mathematics for the sake of interest only. Indeed, it has been found that many teachers only respond fully to initiatives when required to do so by changes in the examination (Denvir, 1988). The Secondary Curriculum and Assessment Authority (SCAA, a predecessor of the current Qualifications and Curriculum Authority) notes that, 'In many schools, it is the content of national tests, rather than of the mathematics National Curriculum, which is taken to indicate the expectations that are being set for pupils'. For example, many teachers did not respond to the drive to improve non-calculator methods of calculation until the introduction of a non-calculator paper at Key Stage 2 and Key Stage 3, and introduction of mental testing (SCAA, 1997). Similarly, it was only after the introduction of coursework into the GCSE assessment that the majority of teachers began to give their pupils experience of extended investigative work. Their motives were not pedagogical, but driven by the demands of the assessment process.

National testing in England and Wales is regulated by the Qualifications and Curriculum Authority (QCA), and in Northern Ireland by the Council for the Curriculum Examinations and Assessment (CCEA). These bodies oversee the National Qualifications Framework, which ties together all the nationally recognized qualifications into a single structure. For example, level 1 in the National Qualifications Framework corresponds with a GCSE pass at grades D to G, but importantly this level is then equated with equivalent work from other qualifications, such as National Vocational Qualifications (NVQs).

Table 6.1 National Qualifications Framework

Level	Typical qualifications	Notes
Entry level	Entry level certificate (for example in Adult Literacy)	
1	GCSE grades D–G NVQ level 1	
2	GCSE grades A*–C NVQ level 2	
3	A level pass (grades A–E) NVQ level 3	Includes various 'A level equivalent', or 'access' courses, typically studied in Further Education Colleges
4	Certificate of Higher Education	First year degree work
5	Diploma of Higher Education Foundation Degree	Includes other level 5 qualifications, such as the BTEC Higher National Diploma
6	Bachelor degrees with honours Graduate certificates and diplomas	
7	Master's degrees Postgraduate certificates and diplomas	
8	Doctorates	

Table 6.1 summarizes the National Qualifications Framework and how it is now integrated with the levels used in higher education.

The Framework is subject to regular revision. In general, the aim is to produce a Framework that is more wide-ranging than that summarized in Table 6.1, by responding to new initiatives from outside as well as inside the education system. For example, the aim is to include employer-led training schemes, which currently lie outside the National Qualifications Framework. But revisions also aim to make the Framework simpler, both to understand and to administer. From 2008, the Framework is called the Qualifications and Credit Framework, and individuals studying for qualifications are able to gain credits based on the amount of work undertaken. Individuals build up their credits as they move within the Framework, to give a more flexible system that includes different pathways and options.

The examinations boards work within the current qualifications Framework; they draw up schemes of assessment and offer them to schools and colleges. In England and Wales, the four examination boards are monitored by the QCA, whose remit includes ensuring that all boards work to a common standard and that the standard is maintained over time. There are a total of five examination boards, all better known by the short name or initials than by their full titles:

- in England and Wales:
  Edexcel
  OCR – the Oxford, Cambridge and Royal Society of Arts Board
  AQA – the Assessment and Qualifications Alliance
  WJEC – the Welsh Joint Examination Committee
- in Northern Ireland:
  CCEA (the regulatory body itself administers the examinations).

(The website for this book (www.sagepub.co.uk/secondary) contains links to each of the examination boards, where you can investigate in more detail what they have to offer.) Schools choose which of the boards to register with, and may choose different boards for different subjects if they wish. As a mathematics teacher, you are certain to be involved in preparing pupils for national examinations at some stage. This is most likely to involve pupils studying for GCSE and the Key Stage 3 assessment tests, but may also involve A level, functional mathematics or free-standing mathematics qualifications.

KEY STAGE 3 ASSESSMENT

The national tests for Key Stage 3 take place in May of Year 9. There are four tiers of entry, each aimed at a different ability group. If you have a Year 9 class, you must choose which tier of entry to select for each pupil: levels 3 to 5, 4 to 6, 5 to 7, or 6 to 8. The guidance is that you should enter a pupil who is expected to attain a level 6 result in the tier that centres on level 6 (that is, the level 5 to 7 tier). The organization of the examinations is somewhat simpler than GCSE; at each tier there are two examination papers, each lasting one hour. In each case, the first paper is a non-calculator paper and the second paper allows the use of a calculator. In addition, there is a mental test for each tier of entry. The mental test is delivered orally, with a limited time allowed for each question.

There are pupils for whom none of the available tiers of entry is appropriate, because their level of work suggests attainment at a level below level 3. For these pupils, there is a set of tasks, rather than tests, that are designed to be used to assess the ability of the pupils. Teachers supervise these tasks in a setting that is rather less formal than the tests.

The second element to the Key Stage 3 assessment is teacher assessment. When Key Stage 3 results are reported to parents, they consist of two levels: the overall level achieved in the tests, and an overall level given by the teacher. The teacher assessment level is made by combining individual grades for each of the attainment targets. In other words, you must assess, in terms of National Curriculum level, a pupil's ability in each of the attainment areas: mathematical processes and applications, number and algebra, geometry and measures and statistics. You then need to keep a record of these individual levels and be able to justify them with evidence, but only the single overall level is reported to parents. In practice, teacher levels and test levels correspond fairly closely, although teacher assessments are slightly higher (DfES, 2004b).

GCSE ASSESSMENT

The GCSE in mathematics undergoes periodic revision, and no doubt will continue to do so. From 2008, the structure of the assessment at GCSE allows for two tiers of entry. This is a change from the three tiers of entry that were available in mathematics from the introduction of GCSE in 1989 up to 2007. This change, which brings mathematics more into line with other GCSE subjects, is supported by many teachers and also by the Smith Report (Smith, 2004). The two tiers are known as the higher tier, where grades A* to D are available, and the foundation tier, where grades C to G are available. Note that a pupil who is entered for the higher tier is ungraded if the performance is below grade D.

As well as two tiers of entry, there are two forms of specification, one called linear and one called modular. Testing for the linear specification takes place in the normal way at the end of Year 11. Testing for the modular specification takes place at four different points during Years 10 and 11. The modular specification is considered more suitable for learners in post-16 education. From 2009, the assessment scheme no longer includes a coursework option. The information about the assessment for 2009 is included in Table 6.2.

Table 6.2 GCSE examination structure (linear)

	Paper 1 (50% of marks) **Non-calculator**	**Paper 2 (50% of marks)** **Calculator**
Mathematics A (linear scheme)	Foundation tier – 1 hour 30 minutes	Foundation tier – 1 hour 30 minutes
	Higher tier – 2 hours	Higher tier – 2 hours

The two tiers of entry have an overlap in the grades available. The examination boards try to ensure that, for example, a grade D on the foundation tier corresponds with a grade D on the higher tier. They do this by including some identical questions on the two tiers. When the papers have been marked, the boards look closely at candidates' performance on the common questions in order to set the grade boundaries. Despite this, there is still some concern about whether a grade obtained in one paper is equivalent to the same grade obtained on a different paper. It is reported that schools have a perception that in the old three-tier system it was easier to get a grade B on the intermediate paper than the higher paper (DfES, 2004a).

All examination boards ensure that the examination papers include a balance of questions on the different parts of the syllabus. The examination boards give weighting to the different aspects of the National Curriculum (called assessment objectives) as follows:

Number and algebra	50–55 per cent
Geometry and measures	25–30 per cent
Statistics	18–22 per cent

The testing of mathematical processes and applications is subsumed into the assessment of the other three assessment objectives, and constitutes 20 per cent of the assessment (AQA, 2007).

All modular assessments must fit in with the QCA requirement that 50 per cent of the assessment is undertaken at the end of the course. In mathematics, the modular specification consists of three modules. The first two can be taken at any one of the three sittings in November, March and June; the final module can only be taken in June. Under this scheme of assessment, the organization and the timings of the various papers is identical for the two different tiers of entry. The format of the modular scheme of assessment for the AQA examination board is summarized in Table 6.3.

Table 6.3   GCSE examination structure (modular)

Module focus	Assessment weighting	Timings
Statistics	18%	Section A (calculator) 30 minutes Section B (non-calculator) 30 minutes
Number	27%	Section A (calculator) 45 minutes Section B (non-calculator) 45 minutes
Algebra, geometry and measures	55%	Paper 1 (non-calculator) 1 hour 15 minutes Paper 2 (calculator) 1 hour 15 minutes

Point for reflection

The reason for dropping coursework assessment in mathematics is mainly because of concerns about its validity. Consider the merits and drawbacks of coursework assessment. If possible, talk to mathematics teachers about their experiences with GCSE coursework. You may be surprised to find that many mathematics teachers are pleased to see coursework removed; consider why this may be the case.

AS LEVEL AND A LEVEL ASSESSMENT

As with GCSE, assessment at AS and A level is administered by the different examination boards, under the supervision of the relevant national authority. Both AS and A level syllabuses are broken down into units of work, which are assessed separately, before the final grade is awarded through an aggregation of the unit marks. There are two core units that must form part of any AS level certification, and a further two core units that must form part of any A level certification. All four of the core units focus on pure mathematics.

AS level assessment is based on three units of work; A level assessment is based on six units. The six units studied for A level must contain the four core units of pure mathematics (two of which are at AS standard, and two of which are at A2 standard). The other two units may be selected from a wide range of options. For a qualification called A level Mathematics, the optional units must be in the applications of mathematics, and can be selected from modules in mechanics, statistics and discrete mathematics. (If the additional units are from pure mathematics, then the qualification is called A level Pure Mathematics.) The main flexibility within the system lies with the choice of these applied modules. It is possible, for example, to do two modules in mechanics (one at AS standard and one at A2 standard), or to do one module in mechanics (at AS standard) and one module in discrete mathematics (also at AS standard).

Successful study of three additional units leads to a qualification in AS Further Mathematics. Successful study of six additional units (12 units in all) leads to a qualification in A level Further Mathematics.

Assessment for almost all the units is through an examination (typically 1 hour and 30 minutes), although some units include an additional coursework element. The examination for the first core unit allows no calculating aids; for other examinations, a graphical calculator is expected. Calculators with a computer algebra facility are not allowed.

Each examination board has a committee that agrees final grade thresholds after the year's examinations have been marked. The expectation is that candidates need to score over 80 per cent to gain a grade A, 60 per cent to gain a grade C and 40 per cent to gain a grade E, but these are guidelines rather than absolutes.

Point for reflection

The use of league tables is likely to remain. Reflect on what positive and negative effects league tables might have on the way that mathematics teachers deliver their lessons.

THE PURPOSES OF ASSESSMENT

It is common to describe assessment as having three branches, each with its own purposes.

- Summative assessment is judgemental, and is often made relative to external criteria (such as National Curriculum levels). Summative assessment is used for grading and selection of individuals, and also for comparing schools, departments and individual teachers.
- Formative assessment is used to help pupils learn; it involves judgements, but those judgements are used to show the pupil how to improve. Formative assessment is often associated with target setting, where pupils monitor their own progress in relation to set criteria.
- Diagnostic assessment is a device for finding out what pupils understand and can do, with a purpose of adapting future teaching to the needs of the individual or the class.

These are useful terms that you need to understand, as they are used routinely in educational circles. The Professional Standards for Qualified Teacher Status require you to 'know a range of approaches to assessment, including the importance of formative assessment' (TDA, 2007: 9). Another way of categorising the purposes of assessment is to regard assessment as providing information to two groups of people: pupils and teachers. We shall consider each in turn.

For pupils, assessment provides feedback on how well they are doing. It helps them to measure their progress against long-term or short-term targets. It helps them to identify areas of weakness that they can then work on in order to improve their overall performance. Over time they build up a profile of their own ability and may be able to group together several areas of weakness that help them to understand why they find particular topics difficult.

There is another, often overlooked, way that assessment has an impact on pupils. This can be described as its psychological impact. When pupils see their work is marked, and that some feedback has been given, they get the message that their work is valued by the teacher. In class, a teacher who wants to look at pupils' work is one who demonstrates that they think the work is important. Assessment also has an impact on motivation. Appropriately worded feedback can provide much needed encouragement; conversely, badly written feedback can be extremely demotivating, and can lead to pupils giving up.

As a teacher, assessment enables you to evaluate the success of your teaching. If the pupils have all been successful with the assessed task, you may confidently feel that they have understood the work and are therefore ready to move on to more challenging work. Where an assessed piece of work shows uneven performance, it helps you to identify which element of the work has not been learnt successfully. In that case you are likely to adapt future teaching plans to take account of the information gained in the assessment.

Assessment helps to build up a profile of strengths and weaknesses for individual pupils. If the pupils themselves find it difficult to recall which are their own weak topic areas, then you are in a position to advise.

Although assessment is mainly for the benefit of teachers and learners, it would be foolish to ignore the other audiences. As discussed above, there are assessment requirements in the National Curriculum, but parents also are particularly interested in assessments. Parents see pupils' books and look for what comments the teacher has made; they read reports and attend parents' evenings for a report on progress. In this sense, assessment is one of your most public undertakings. Mathematics exercise books are usually taken home, and these will provide evidence of your work, as well as the pupils' work. If your books are marked regularly and show evidence of individual advice to the pupil, then it is a public demonstration of your professional performance. On the other hand, it is difficult to argue against the negative impression presented by an exercise book that shows no evidence of having been marked for several weeks.

Schools often have policies for monitoring the assessment of pupils' work. Obviously, this shows that the school values assessment for its educational purposes, but it also demonstrates an awareness of the public image that is presented by the marking of pupils' work. In one mathematics department, the monitoring system consists of samples of exercise books being given to colleagues on a regular basis.

We sampled exercise books in our department last week for Year 9. When we sample work in this way, we meet together, and bring to the meeting a random sample of books from every class that we teach. We spend time looking at how our colleagues mark work and give feedback. At the end, we share anything that we have picked up.

In our school, the monitoring is mainly done within the department. It is not just the head of department: the second in department, and anyone else, we all get involved.

We also monitor exercise books on a peer basis, usually just before Christmas, when pairs of us get together to compare our assessments. Then also when we peer observe lessons, we work sample as well. Overall, there is plenty of opportunity for us to learn from each other. It helps us to be more consistent in our approach to marking.

Similar approaches are used in many schools. It is important to present this monitoring of pupils' work as not just a check by management on teachers' work, but also as an opportunity for teachers to learn from others and improve their own practice. As a result of this sharing of good practice, the pupil experience should be improved, because of better quality of feedback and also more consistent messages from different mathematics teachers.

THE NATURE OF ASSESSMENT

In this section, we look at different types of assessment, from formal written tests to informal observations. Tests are usually taken as reliable measures of pupils' abilities, even though some claim that the pressure of the test situation can lead to underachievement (Watson, 2002). But there are other difficulties associated with setting mathematics tests. Before setting your own tests, you should be aware of the time that goes into setting public examinations. Teams of people write the questions, which are then scrutinized by independent panels. The questions are then tested on groups of pupils, to see if any unexpected problems or misunderstandings arise. If you write an end-of-term test, then you will have none of that level of validation of the questions, so you need to be aware of the possible pitfalls of written tests. These pitfalls, any one of which reduces the reliability of the results, include:

- the style or context of the question may appeal to some pupils more than others
- questions may be unintentionally ambiguous
- small details of language can affect the facility of a question
- you may underestimate the amount of time needed to complete the test.

With this in mind, it is a good idea to check any intended tests that you have written yourself with an experienced colleague, before giving them to the pupils.

Marking pupils' work is the most obvious form of assessment in use. This can be done informally, in class, with a few ticks to indicate that the work so far is correct, or more formally, by taking in a set of books, and marking a particular section of written work. The way that marking is performed varies from school to school, but within schools, there is often a marking policy, at either school or departmental level, that increases consistency between teachers. Marking policies tend to cover such things as:

- whether a mark is given, or a grade, or neither. The traditional mark out of 10, or one mark for every correct answer is becoming less common. Some departments prefer to use a grade of A to E for every piece of assessed work; others prefer to use no overall marks at all
- whether a National Curriculum level is given. Sometimes the department policy is to assign a National Curriculum level for every piece of assessed work

- always giving a mark out of the same total. Some departments scale all their marks to a percentage, so that marks for different pieces of work can be compared. The drawback of this is that it ignores the possibility that some assessments are harder than others, so a mark of 70 per cent may represent a high mark on one assessment and a low mark on another
- giving an effort grade alongside an attainment grade. This acknowledges that lessons are not just about attainment; they are also about taking an active part and trying to improve. It seeks to give credit for pupils who make a positive contribution in class or in homework
- what kind of written feedback to provide. Many departments will expect more than a simple 'good' or 'very good' at the end of a piece of assessed work. Policies usually suggest that a measure of advice should be given, indicating how the work can be improved.

Good written feedback may refer to the learning objectives selectively, or provide scaffolding for steps that have caused difficulty (DfES, 2004c). Giving full written feedback is time-consuming, and some teachers develop a routine that gives detailed marking to selected books on a systematic basis. You can also find that giving pupils a chance to respond to your comments is very effective, although the bare comment 'see me to discuss this' may not be sufficient to ensure that this dialogue happens. Below is a small sample of recent written feedback from pupils' books. In each case, the comments are constructive and supportive.

You have understood how to add fractions, and worked accurately. Well done!

There is a lot of good work here, Amy. Where I have put an equals sign, you can cancel down the answers more. You need to look for common factors other than two.

You have clearly shown that you can add fractions, but you are using a method that makes things harder than necessary. Look for the *lowest* common denominator as a first step. For example, in question 3, the lowest common denominator of 3 and 9 is 9 (not 27).

You have shown that you can enlarge a shape by a positive scale factor (level 6).

You are able to calculate lengths and angles in right-angled triangles. You need to become more secure in selecting whether to use sin, cos or tan in the mixed questions. Labelling the three sides of the triangle (O, A and H) may help.

Good, well-presented work, Jonathan. You have misunderstood the diagram in question 4; I shall see you during the lesson to discuss this.

Teacher marking – of classwork, homework or tests – remains a key aspect of assessment, but it is important not to underestimate the value of other forms of assessment. For example, the process aspects of mathematics are not easily assessed in a written test; they are more effectively assessed through an extended piece of work, where pupils have to demonstrate their problem-solving abilities.

In addition, a lot of assessment takes place on an informal level within every lesson. The key role of informal assessment is acknowledged by Ofsted, who state that:

> Good day-to-day assessment practice centres on the use in teaching of a combination of observation, questioning, discussion and marking pupils' work. Through these activities, skilful and knowledgeable subject teachers find out what pupils know, understand and can do and then decide what needs to be done to improve learning. (Ofsted, 2003: 27)

Informal assessment can be summarized by the two words: looking and listening. In more detail, informal assessment involves:

- looking in pupils' books as they are working
- listening to pupils talking to other pupils as they explain the work or engage in discussion
- monitoring responses to teacher questioning
- discussions between pupil and teacher that focus on errors made
- monitoring how well pupils apply their knowledge to unfamiliar situations.

The challenge for the teacher in many mathematics lessons is to spread this informal assessment as widely as possible. In other words, at the end of the lesson, you should aim to have made some judgement about the individual progress of each child in the class. While this is not realistic in every lesson, it is a worthy focus of your efforts, and you may need to make a conscious effort to monitor the work of pupils in each corner of the room. This monitoring may be done in many ways: for example, by marking some written work, or by a short discussion prompted by, 'How are you getting on?'

ASSESSMENT FOR LEARNING

Assessment for Learning is a relatively new phrase, coined to contrast with assessment *of* learning, and is frequently abbreviated to AfL. A definition is given by the Assessment Reform Group as: 'The process of seeking and interpreting evidence for use by learners and their teachers to decide where the learners are in their learning, where they need to go and how best to get there', (Assessment Reform Group, 2002). In particular, it uses ideas of formative assessment and makes explicit links with how the assessment helps learning. A positive link between good formative assessment and effective learning is reported in a number of studies summarized by Black and Wiliam (1998a; 1998b). Evidence suggests that the increased use of formative assessment can raise the average attainment of pupils by two grades at GCSE. More interestingly, the improvement is not uniform across the ability range; in general, it is the less able pupils who show the greatest improvements.

In a summary of research findings, the Assessment Reform Group (1999) suggests that improving learning through assessment depends on five key factors:

- giving effective feedback to pupils
- involving pupils in their own learning
- teaching that responds to the results of assessment
- recognizing that assessment has an important effect on the motivation and self-esteem of pupils
- pupils being able to assess themselves and knowing how to improve.

These five key factors are at the heart of Assessment for Learning. It is fundamental to understand that assessment for learning is a part of everyday lessons; it is not an add-on that occurs every now and then. It is part of the teacher's professional skills to use assessment for the benefit of pupils' learning, and should be recognized as such by all in the profession. Pupils become more involved in their learning when teachers share lesson objectives, share targets and share assessment criteria with pupils. One of the aims of Assessment for Learning is that the pupils are more able to assess themselves, so that they can become reflective learners, able to identify for themselves the next steps in learning that they need to take.

Evidently, progress in mathematics depends on the pupils engaging with the subject and taking an active part in lessons. We have all seen pupils who give up at the first slight difficulty, and claim to need help at every stage. Wiliam (2002) suggests that the quality of feedback can help to lessen this attitude problem by demonstrating that ability can be improved by taking particular and specific steps. Where pupils believe that their ability is fixed, they do not see the reason to try harder, so one of the purposes of feedback is to counter this attitude. We need the feedback to pupils to support a view of mathematical ability as incremental rather than fixed, by pointing to achievable targets.

Developing self-assessment skills for pupils is an important aspect of AfL. Self-assessment in this context means a lot more than simply pupils marking their own work, a technique that has been employed in mathematics classrooms for many years. Self-assessment tries to involve pupils more with assessing how well they have done, and whether they feel that they understand the work. They consider for themselves how they can improve.

One technique that is now in common use is a 'traffic lights' system to review the objectives of the lesson. At an appropriate time in the lesson (often at the end), the teacher asks the pupils to display one of three colours, red, amber or green. Often this is organized through giving pupils a set of three coloured cards (although there are many other ways). If pupils hold up a green card, it means that they have achieved a particular objective, and feel confident in their ability to move forward. An amber card means that pupils are not sure if they have achieved the objective. They may partially understand the work, and feel that they can move forward, but only with assistance. A red card means that pupils do not feel they have achieved the objective. They do not understand the work, and definitely need some extra help before they are ready to move on.

A common alternative to the traffic lights, but with exactly the same purpose is the 'smiley face' system, with a smiley face, a flat face and a sad face corresponding to the three traffic light colours. In the case of the smiley face system, pupils sometimes hand in work having provided a smiley face assessment themselves, indicating to the teacher who is marking the work, the level of their understanding.

Another key aspect of self-assessment is for pupils to know their own individual targets, both short-term and longer-term. On a lesson-by-lesson basis, targets are represented by the lesson objectives. In addition to these, you need to give each pupil specific individual targets, based on previous performance. It is wise to keep these individual targets to a small number (two or three), so that the pupil can remember what they are. You then need to monitor and revise these individual targets on a regular basis (at least every half-term). In the long term, target-setting relates to grades or levels in national tests. For example, a pupil in Year 8 should have an idea of what level they are working at in mathematics, and what level they are aiming for in the Year 9 national tests.

Overall, self-assessment encourages pupils to take more responsibility for their own learning, rather than seeing their learning as a response to what the teacher tells them to do. The use of self-assessment demonstrates that the teacher or department has a commitment to helping pupils become independent learners, identifying for themselves the skills that they need to move forward (Ofsted, 2003). In order to facilitate self-assessment, you need to build in a reflection time, that helps pupils to review their targets, to analyse the strategies that they use, and whether they are making the expected progress.

Here is an example of how a teacher describes one technique of self-assessment:

Sometimes I have used a plenary pyramid. Pupils draw a triangle and they put three new things that they have learnt at the bottom. On the next row up they put two things that they are not quite sure about still, or questions that they might have. At the top they have to identify a transferable skill. They identify something they have learnt today that they might use somewhere else. It might be in a different subject or it might be in real life somewhere, or in a job of some kind. That works quite well, because after they have done it they feed back to me what they have written. It gives me the chance to assess whether they have understood the work.

Within the self-assessment process, you need to arrange opportunities for pupils to think about how they learn. Provided that they get appropriate support, pupils are able to compare their relative success in different topics within mathematics. They can then identify possible reasons for their better performance on certain topics, and use that information to improve their performance overall. Peer assessment is another way of encouraging pupils to think about features of good work. By developing their own criteria, or by applying given criteria, they learn about how to answer questions, and are encouraged to consider how work can be improved.

Point for reflection

Consider your own work in mathematics, possibly by thinking back to your A level or your degree studies. Reflect upon what aspects of the work you were not very good at. Think not only about particular topics, like trigonometry, but about ways of working.

What advice would have helped you to improve? Consider how you could have analysed your own ways of working. Think about what targets for improvement you could have set for yourself at the time you were studying.

USE OF DATA

The use of data in schools has increased considerably in recent years, aided partly by the availability of computerized systems that help to analyse performance and compare with national norms. Schools also use data to monitor the effectiveness of initiatives and strategies, and increasingly to challenge the expectations of staff, pupils and parents (Kirkup et al., 2005). One website that you should try to look at is RAISEonline, a web-based interactive tool developed jointly by Ofsted and the government to help schools and inspectors to analyse data. Via a password, schools have access to a detailed analysis of the performance of their pupils in comparison with national norms. The RAISEonline analysis gives a good visual presentation of the data, and is particularly helpful in identifying any underperforming groups of pupils. A key feature of RAISEonline is a school's Contextual Value Added score, which compares the performance of pupils in the school with similar pupils nationally. This measure gives a good indication of how successful the school is (and is a much better indicator of a good school than the raw league table results that are published each year). RAISEonline also shows whether pupils make more progress in mathematics or English, or whether they make better progress in Key Stage 3 or Key Stage 4.

In order to aid tracking, schools make use of National Curriculum sub-levels, where each National Curriculum level is further divided into three. For example level 6 is subdivided into 6c, 6b and 6a, with 6a being the highest of the three sub-levels (leading into level 7c). Information on pupils' performance (for example in end of key stage tests) is used to project forward to an expected performance at the next key stage, and is translated into individual targets. The expected performance is based not only on prior attainment, but also on other characteristics such as gender and ethnicity. Your assessments enable you to compare the performance of your pupils (for example, in terms of National Curriculum sub-levels) with expected performance. At the end of the year, you are able to analyse the progress of your group as a whole, but also compare whether, for example, the girls in your group have underperformed, or whether the most able have achieved particularly well.

The data from the classes you teach forms a part of your performance management. In other words, the headteacher monitors whether your classes make progress that is above or below expectations. Where pupil underperformance is identified, you should expect support in analysing why it has happened, and how it can be avoided in future.

QUESTIONING

Styles of questioning and their role in the classroom are rich sources of investigation. An obvious distinction is in the use of closed questions versus open questions. It is sometimes easier for the teacher to pose closed questions, where there is one single answer that is right or wrong. But it can also cause problems, because fewer pupils tend to be involved and others may feel able to 'switch off'. Inspectors report that in lessons where assessment practice is weak, 'class discussion is often dominated by closed questions, mostly answered by the same few volunteers' (Ofsted, 2005), and the challenge to all teachers is to use questioning to encourage pupils to make a positive contribution to the lesson.

Mason (2002) explores the way that teachers use questioning as a means of control in the classroom. In itself, there is nothing wrong in this; questioning a pupil who is not engaging with the lesson may be a useful technique. But it is not the main purpose of questioning. Teachers, particularly trainees who are anxious about class control, sometimes use questions that help them to keep a tight grip on the way that the lesson is heading. In some questions, the teacher often has one particular answer in mind, and it can be extremely difficult for the pupils to guess what that answer is.

One style of questioning is an oral version of a 'cloze' activity, where pupils have a structured sentence presented and have to fill in the missing word. Many teachers use this technique very well. Instead of, 'What is another way we can say $b \times b$?', the cloze approach is to ask, 'There is another way of saying $b \times b$. We can say $b \times b$ or b ___'?. When used well this can help pupils to structure their thinking. When used badly, it can take away all the thinking from the pupil. An example is when solving a linear equation, and the teacher verbalizes all the difficult thinking, and leaves a trivial question to be answered at the end: 'So, our next step is to add three to both sides. On the left-hand side, adding three gives $2x$. On the right-hand side we have 5, so adding three gives ___?'

Open questions are considered better in general than closed questions (DfES, 2005). Open questions lead somewhere, whereas closed questions stop with the right answer. Open questions are likely to involve more of the class in the discussion, because the same question can be asked several times of several different pupils. At a simple level, open questions ask for an example, so that there are several possible answers. 'Give me an example of a factor of 40' is more open than 'What are the factors of 40?' or 'Is 10 a factor of 40?' One of the most commonly used open questions that you will hear in the mathematics classroom is, 'Can you explain how you got that?' This follow-up question helps the pupil to verbalize their thinking, helping both them and the rest of the class to understand the reasons behind the answer that they have given. In your planning, you should consider carefully the questions that you intend to use. If you do that, have a second look at the planned questions and ask yourself if they can be rephrased to make them into open questions, and how you may wish to present more probing follow-up questions.

Here are some examples of closed questions and equivalent open questions:

Closed question	*Open alternative*
What is the perimeter of this rectangle?	Can you draw me a rectangle with perimeter 20 cm?
What do the angles of a triangle add up to?	Tell me anything mathematical that you know about triangles.
What is the median of these numbers?	Find a set of 6 numbers with a median of 4.
What are the factors of 10?	Using two of the numbers on the board, complete a sentence of the form, ___ is a factor of ___.

Clearly the way that a question is phased makes a considerable difference to how it helps the teacher to assess. Different phrasings can alter the level of thought that the pupil needs to apply, the language skills needed to respond, and the level of understanding that the pupil holds.

A very useful example of alternative questioning is provided by the QCA (2003). In the example, the teacher wants to assess whether the pupils understand the properties of prime numbers, and asks, 'Is 7 a prime number?' Pupils' responses to this question are likely to be variations on yes or no. The QCA discussion continues:

> This question has not enabled the teacher to make an effective assessment of whether the pupil knows the properties of prime numbers. Changing the question to 'Why is 7 an example of a prime number?' does several things.
>
> - It helps the pupils recall their knowledge of the properties of prime numbers and the properties of 7 and compare them.
> - The answer to the question is 'Because prime numbers have exactly two factors and 7 has exactly two factors.' This response requires a higher degree of articulation than 'Err...yes, I think so.'
> - It requires pupils to explain their understanding of prime numbers and to use this to justify their reasoning.
> - It provides an opportunity to make an assessment without necessarily asking supplementary questions. The question 'Is 7 a prime number?' requires further questions before the teacher can assess the pupil's understanding.
>
> The question 'Why is 7 an example of a prime number?' is an example of the general question 'Why is x an example of y?' This is one type of question that is effective in providing assessment opportunities. Other types of questions that are also effective in providing assessment opportunities are:
>
> - how can we be sure that...?
> - what is the same and what is different about...?
> - is it ever/always true/false that...?
> - how do you...?

- how would you explain...?
- what does that tell us about...?
- what is wrong with...?
- why is...true?
  (QCA, 2003: 8-9)

In our sample lesson on probability, the teacher reviews the answers to the starter activity by means of class questioning. The pupils are trying to match together pairs of equivalent fractions.

After the 3 minutes are up, individual pupils are asked to suggest possible pairs. Notice that the teacher is not happy just to accept a correct answer; she asks the pupils to explain how they obtained their answer. The transcript below comes from the sample lesson, part 2.

OK we are going to go through them now. Are we ready? OK, look this way then 4/20. Which fraction matches that?

Ellie: One fifth.

One fifth, can you explain why, what is the factor of four and 20, what number goes into four and into 20? Not sure? But you knew it was 1/5. You can't say why, but you must have had your reasons. Who can help?

Jake: There is one four in four.

Yes go on. How many fours are there in 20?

Jake: Five.

Yes, so you used the fact that four is a factor of four and a factor of 20. So you should have 4/20 linked up with 1/5.

What about the next one? 30/60. I think for most of you, this was the first one you did.

Adam: A half.

A half, why?

Adam: Because 30 is half of 60.

That is a different way of saying it. Did anyone spot what the factors were of 30 and 60? Yes 3 is a factor of 30 and 60.

Are there any other factors? Yes 5 is a factor of 30 and 60.

Are there any other factors? Yes ten. Any others? There is a bigger factor than 10. Does anyone know it? Yes 15 well done.

Is there a bigger factor than 15? 30, good.

How many 30s go into 30?

All: One.

(Continued)

(Continued)

How many 30s go into 60?

All: Two.

OK that is another way of explaining why 30/60 should have matched up with 1/2. OK, the next one. Ian, what was the factor that you cancelled for 4/28?

Ian: 1/7

It cancels to 1/7, but what was the factor? What number goes into both four and 28?

Class: Four.

Good, and four goes into four once and four goes into 28, as Ian told us, seven times. Give yourselves ticks if you got them right. Looking around I know that most of you got them all right. Well done, that's very good. So remember, this is the work that we did last lesson. They are called equivalent fractions.

It is noticeable that the teacher avoids confirming the answer until the pupils have talked through what the answers are and why. She encourages the use of correct language like common factors, cancelling down, and equivalent fractions. Note that the pupils are reluctant to do this. They are often uncertain of the correct use of mathematical language, and are usually happier for the teacher to use the correct words than to use the correct words themselves. Here, the teacher is trying to make the pupils more familiar with the language through using it for themselves.

One of the main purposes of classroom questioning is to gauge the understanding of the pupils. It is generally assumed that if several pupils give the correct answers to the questions, then learning has taken place. The teacher may therefore assume that the pupils' conceptions match those of the teacher, whereas in fact the responses merely fit in with the limitations of the question (Wiliam, 2002). In other words, just because a pupil can answer a question correctly does not mean that their understanding goes any wider than the specific question that they have answered. Even when the questions have been skilfully planned to cover a range of ideas, there may still be an underlying misconception that has gone unnoticed.

Point for reflection

Watch part 2 of the sample lesson on the website. Observe how the teacher handles the questioning. Consider what information she is gaining from her questioning. What information are the pupils gaining from reviewing their work in this way?

RECORD-KEEPING

With an emphasis on assessment and targets, it is essential that you maintain effective records. Many schools develop a policy for record keeping that fits in with the school policy on assessment. Typically teachers keep records in mark books, but there is an increasing tendency for all records to be kept electronically on laptops. Records should normally include:

- an attendance record for mathematics lessons
- a list of homework marks
- a record of test results
- a National Curriculum level of attainment for the beginning of the school year, with regular revisions at key points during the year
- an indication of which topics the pupil does well and which topics less well
- an ongoing assessment of effort.

Assessments are usually recorded in one of three ways. One way is to list pupils' performance on each piece of work as a mark, possibly scaled so that each assessment is recorded as a mark out of 10 or as a percentage. The second recording method is to use a grading scale from A to E for each piece of work. The third method is a variation on the traffic lights system for self-assessment: the teacher records a green mark for a piece of work that demonstrates full understanding, amber for partial understanding and red for little understanding.

Whatever system you use, you should be able to look along the records for each child and pick out individual strengths and weaknesses. This can only be done if you record what each mark is assessing. Overall your records should be useful; they should help you to spot trends, identify weaknesses of individuals or the whole group, help you to set targets for improvement, and monitor progress towards those targets.

REPORT WRITING

Schools are required by law to provide written reports to parents at least once per year. Producing well-informed, accurate and detailed information for parents is a major strain on teachers' time, but is a key feature of the school's public image as well as its public role. All the same, school inspectors report that parents often do not feel well informed about their child's progress. Parents generally rate being kept well informed as less effective than almost all other areas of school performance (Ofsted, 2003).

The quality of your reports will depend to some extent on the quality of your record keeping. You will be expected to provide parents with information about pupils' performance during the year (often using a summative assessment, based on an end of year examination). In addition to this you need to be more specific about individual strengths and weaknesses. For example, through analysing the examination performance, or by looking back at class records, you need to identify where each child has done well and where they have struggled or not fully understood the work. Your report writing should include comments such as:

> Joanne has found the work on trigonometry difficult, and would benefit from further work on calculating missing angles, and if necessary further discussion with me on the topic.

In addition, you will need to give an account of how the child can improve. This goes beyond the identification from the mathematics curriculum of a topic or two where performance has been weak. This refers to ways of working, ways that pupils can improve the way that they work in mathematics. At one level, this advice may include 'work harder' or 'make more effort with homework', but more specific advice is more helpful. Examples of advice of this kind may be:

> Hamid's mathematics would improve if he wrote out his ideas more clearly. As it is, he tends to try to do too many steps in his head, and this can lead to errors being made.

> Shelley should make more regular use of the number line in her arithmetical work, particularly when dealing with negative numbers.

> Karl needs to remember that he can work out all percentages by combining calculations of 10% and 1% of the number.

Sarcasm and attempts at humour are not acceptable. The days of comments such as 'Louise gets an A for everything she does – A for absent' are long gone. You need to find something positive to say about every pupil: either positive in terms of effort or attainment, or positive in terms of how to improve. Your report writing will be carefully monitored by senior staff in the school, and needs to contribute to the positive image that the school is aiming to project; weaknesses in spelling and grammar will be returned to you for correction.

EVIDENCE FROM THE RESEARCH

The effectiveness of AfL is firmly based in research evidence. The strength of the evidence is that it comes from a wide range of sources: different countries, different age groups and different subjects. Hence, it is generally accepted that good assessment practices help learning irrespective of these variables.

One example of the research involves a 1996 study of primary school pupils learning mathematics in Portugal, where the results indicate the effectiveness of self-assessment. Two groups on teachers, one trained in methods of self-assessment and willing to use self-assessment with their pupils, and another group of teachers of similar experience, but with a different course focus, taught their pupils. As part of their lessons, the experimental group used self-assessment on a daily basis; they were taught to understand their learning objectives and the assessment criteria, and assessed themselves on this basis. The researchers found (through pre-testing and post-testing) that the pupils using self-assessment made gains on average double those of the control group (Fernandes and Fontana, 1996).

In the USA, the performance of very young pupils taught by a group of teachers trained to use skills of observation to observe progress, together with regular diagnostic assessment and a review of the learning needs of individual pupils, was compared with a control group. Results in all of reading, mathematics and science were considerably greater in the experimental group (Bergan et al., 1991).

Black et al. (2003) report that in all they found 20 relevant studies. The studies showed the effectiveness of a set of common features of teaching, within very different learning environments, and with teachers who all had their own individual teaching styles. The practices that the studies report as effective for learning all involve strengthening the process of formative assessment, producing 'significant, and often substantial, learning gains' (ibid.: 9). Not all of the studies report that learning gains were more significant among the lowest attainers, but several did. In particular the features that seemed to be significant were:

- enhanced quality of feedback
- the active involvement of learners
- teachers using the results of assessment to adjust their teaching
- the ways in which the assessment affected the confidence and motivation of the learners.

It is these features that formed the basis for the Assessment for Learning initiative in English schools.

While Assessment for Learning stresses the use of feedback to help the learner improve, it is interesting to note that the feedback has to be of the right kind. Research shows that guidance on how to improve (scaffolding) is more effective than providing the complete solution (Day and Cordon, 1993). This means that showing pupils how their answers should look is not as good as advising them in more general terms how their answers could be better.

Research also provides evidence on teacher questioning. Observations show that on many occasions, the question is posed and, if no immediate answer is forthcoming, teachers ask someone else, provide some hint or answer the question themselves, rather than wait for the pupil to think out an answer. More interesting still is an analysis of the time between the pupil's response and the teacher's evaluation of that response. Evidence suggests that an immediate yes or no from the teacher is less effective than waiting a few seconds. Increasing the teacher response time to 3 seconds (but not more than 5 seconds) produces measurable increases in learning (Swift and Gooding, 1983; Tobin and Capie, 1980).

Point for reflection

Teachers' judgements on pupils 'are unavoidably based on a selection of what the pupil does', and subject to the teacher's own interpretation (Watson, 2001: 229). In your mathematics lessons, you will continually make informal assessments of pupils' ability. Sometimes you will find that your informal assessments are out of line with the results of tests and examinations. In such cases, what value can you place on the informal judgements? Is it fair to say that the pupil underachieves in examinations, or overachieves in class? You may wish to consider the basis for any informal assessments, whether those assessments have any validity, and what can be done to make informal judgements more accurate.

Further reading

Black, P., Harrison, C., Lee, C., Marshall, B. and Wiliam, D. (2003) *Assessment for Learning: Putting it into Practice*. Maidenhead: Open University Press.

In this book, the authors review the purposes behind Assessment for Learning. They paint a very positive picture of the benefits that an increased use of formative assessment can bring. They promote Assessment for Learning as a feasible aim for all teachers and something that involves a redistribution of effort rather than a whole host of extra work. The book provides examples of how individual teachers describe the impact of AfL on their classroom experiences, and gives advice to other teachers about how they can change their habits incrementally to provide a better learning experience for pupils.

Qualifications and Curriculum Authority (QCA) (2003) *Assessment for Learning: Using Assessment to Raise Achievement in Mathematics.* London: HMSO (or see the website below).

This publication has a specific focus on mathematics teaching at Key Stages 1, 2 and 3, so that some of the examples are from primary school mathematics, but the ideas discussed are relevant to the whole 11–16 age range. There is a helpful section on target setting, self-assessment and peer assessment, and advice on providing effective feedback. The section on effective questioning techniques expands on the examples that are quoted earlier in this chapter, to provide guidance on analysing pupils' responses, and using questions to assess understanding.

 ## *Useful websites*

Live links to these sites can be found on the companion website.

The following websites relate to national testing arrangements:
QCA site: http://www.qca.org.uk/ (regulatory authority for England and Wales)
CCEA site: http://www.ccea.org.uk/ (for Northern Ireland)
Individual examination boards give details about examination arrangements, past papers, marking policies and a range of support materials.
OCR site: http://www.ocr.org.uk/
Welsh Board: http://www.wjec.co.uk/
Edexcel site: http://www.edexcel.org.uk/home/
AQA site: http://www.aqa.org.uk/
The specific details about the AQA GCSE discussed in the chapter can be found at http://www.aqa.org.uk/qual/pdf/AQA-4306-W-SP-09.PDF.
The QCA publication *Assessment for Learning: Using Assessment to Raise Achievement in Mathematics* is available at the QCA website http://www.qca.org.uk/downloads/6311_using_assess_raise_acievement_maths.pdf
The Standards site has a wealth of materials on assessment for learning at http://www.standards.dfes.gov.uk/secondary/keystage3/all/respub/afl_ws. The address given here gives links to several downloads, designed for staff development training within schools. The subject-specific downloads are particularly good for reflecting on current practice, so you will find them most useful after you have been in school for several weeks. Example titles include 'Developing written feedback in specific subjects' and 'Developing peer and self-assessment in specific subjects', which include a section relating to practice in mathematics.

The Assessment Reform Group booklet *Assessment for Learning: Beyond the Black Box* is online at the QCA website http://www.qca.org.uk/downloads/beyond_black_box2.pdf. This 12-page pamphlet includes a review of evidence from research and from school inspections into good practice in assessment. It lists the key factors for improving learning, as well as warning of 'inhibiting factors' – assessment practices that can stand in the way of effective learning. The pamphlet concludes with a set of recommendations for action, many of which have fed through into the National Strategy initiative on Assessment for Learning.

The Assessment Reform Group's *Assessment for Learning: 10 Principles* are online at the Association for Achievement and Improvement through Assessment (AAIA) website http://www.aaia.org.uk/pdf/AFL_10principlesARG.pdf.

There is a tutorial on evaluating school performance, focusing on the use of RAISEonline data at http://www.standards.dfes.gov.uk/esp/

References

Assessment and Qualifications Alliance (AQA) (2007) *Mathematics 4306: Specification A 2009*. Online at the AQA website http://www.aqa.org.uk/qual/pdf/AQA-4306-W-SP-09.PDF (accessed 8 August 2007).

Assessment Reform Group (1999) *Assessment for Learning: Beyond the Black Box*. Online at the QCA website http://www.qca.org.uk/downloads/beyond_black_box2.pdf (accessed 8 August 2007).

Assessment Reform Group (2002) *Assessment for Learning: 10 Principles*. Online at the Association for Achievement and Improvement through Assessment (AAIA) website http://www.aaia.org.uk/pdf/AFL_10principlesARG.pdf (accessed 8 August 2007).

Bergan, J.R., Sladeczek, I.E., Schwarz, R.D. and Smith, A.N. (1991) 'Effects of a measurement and planning system on kindergartners' cognitive development and educational planning', *American Education Research Journal*, 28(3): 683–714.

Black, P. and Wiliam, D. (1998a) 'Assessment and classroom learning', *Assessment in Education: Principles Policy and Practice*, 5(1): 7–74.

Black, P. and Wiliam, D. (1998b) *Inside the Black Box*. London: King's College.

Black, P., Harrison, C., Lee, C., Marshall, B. and Wiliam, D. (2003) *Assessment for Learning: Putting it into Practice*. Maidenhead: Open University Press.

Day, J. and Cordon, L. (1993) 'Static and dynamic measures of ability: an experimental comparison', *Journal of Educational Psychology*, 85(1): 75–82.

Denvir, B. (1988) 'What are we assessing in mathematics and what are we assessing for?', in D. Pimm (ed.), *Mathematics, Teachers and Children*. London: Hodder and Stoughton.

Department for Education and Skills (DfES) (2004a) *14–19 Qualifications and Curriculum Reform: Final Report of the Working Group on 14–19 Reform*. London: Department for Education and Skills.

Department for Education and Skills (DfES) (2004b) Press release, 'National Curriculum Assessments of 14 year olds in England 2004 (provisional): Part One – Mathematics and Science'. Online at http://www.dfes.gov.uk/rsgateway/DB/SFR/s000491/SFR31-2004v2.pdf (accessed 7 August 2007).

Department for Education and Skills (DfES) (2004c) *Assessment for Learning: Guidance for Senior Leaders*. London: Department for Education and Skills.

Department for Education and Skills (DfES) (2005) 'Improving learning in mathematics: challenges and strategies', in the Standards Unit pack: *Improving Learning in Mathematics*. London: Department for Education and Skills.

Fernandes, M. and Fontana, D. (1996) 'Changes in control beliefs in Portuguese primary school pupils as a consequence of the employment of self-assessment strategies', *British Journal of Educational Psychology*, 66: 301–13.

Kirkup, C., Sizmur, J., Sturman, L. and Lewis, K. (2005) *Schools' Use of Data in Teaching and Learning*. (DfES Research Report 671.) London: Department for Education and Skills.

Mason, J. (2002) 'Minding your Qs and Rs: effective questioning and responding in the mathematics classroom', in L. Haggarty (ed.) *Aspects of Teaching Secondary Mathematics: Perspectives on Practice*. London: RoutledgeFalmer.

Office for Standards in Education (Ofsted) (2003) *Good Assessment in Secondary Schools*. London: Office for Standards in Education.

Office for Standards in Education (Ofsted) (2005) *The Annual Report of Her Majesty's Chief Inspector of Schools 2004/05*. London: Office for Standards in Education.

Qualification and Curriculum Authority (QCA) (2003) *Assessment for Learning: Using Assessment to Raise Achievement in Mathematics*. London: Qualifications and Curriculum Authority.

Secondary Curriculum and Assessment Authority (SCAA) (1997) *The Use of Calculators at Key Stages 1–3*. London: Secondary Curriculum and Assessment Authority.

Smith, A. (2004) *Making Mathematics Count: The Report of Professor Adrian Smith's Inquiry into Post-14 Mathematics Education*. (Smith Report.) London: HMSO.

Swift, J.N. and Gooding, C.R. (1983) 'Interaction of wait-time feedback and questioning instruction on middle school science teaching', *Journal of Research in Science Teaching*, 20: 721–30.

Tobin, K.G. and Capie, W. (1980). 'The effects of teacher wait-time and questioning quality on middle school science achievement', paper presented at the Annual Meeting of the *American Psychological Association*, Montreal, September.

Training and Development Agency for Schools (TDA) (2007) *Professional Standards for Teachers: Why sit still in your career?*. London: Training and Development Agency for Schools.

Watson, A. (2001) 'Making judgements about pupils' mathematics', in P. Gates (ed.), *Issues in Teaching Mathematics*. London: RoutledgeFalmer.

Watson, A. (2002) 'What does it mean to understand something and how do we know when it has happened?', in L. Haggarty (ed.), *Teaching Mathematics in Secondary Schools: A Reader*. London: RoutledgeFalmer.

Wiliam, D. (2002) 'Formative assessment in mathematics', in L. Haggarty (ed.), *Aspects of Teaching Secondary Mathematics: Perspectives on Practice*. London: RoutledgeFalmer.

7 | TEACHING DIFFERENT PUPILS

> ### This chapter:
>
> - examines the principle of inclusion in mathematics education, with particular reference to culture, gender and ethnicity
> - discusses different ways that mathematics teachers respond to different ability groups
> - shows how the role of the teaching assistant supports the teaching of mathematics
> - discusses the needs of the most able pupils
> - reviews the evidence relating to language and mathematics learning, with particular reference to the needs of pupils for whom English is an additional language
> - examines how mathematics teachers respond to special educational needs, with specific reference to dyslexia and dyscalculia.

INCLUSION

Inclusion is at the heart of the Every Child Matters agenda, and good schools put inclusion at the forefront of planning for improvement. It is a whole-school issue that involves ensuring that every pupil gets a fair deal, that barriers to learning are recognized and overcome, and that inclusive values and practice are promoted. Inclusion means catering for all, but does not mean treating all pupils the same. It means taking account of different backgrounds and different needs, and responding appropriately. The challenge for you in the classroom is to make learning more individual, more personalized. School inspectors have identified personalized learning as a key feature of raising achievement for different groups of pupils (Ofsted, 2006).

Inclusion refers to the aspiration in education that all pupils should have equal access to opportunities within school, but it is more than that. An inclusive school is one that recognizes and celebrates diversity. So it not sufficient to set up activities and say that they are open to all; it is necessary to examine the nature of the activities, and how different pupils might take an active part in them in different ways. No feature of race, class, gender or disability should present a barrier to participation in the curriculum and extra-curricular activities. By law, schools must take steps to improve the physical environment, and increase the extent to which disabled pupils have access to the curriculum. Schools are also required to evaluate the delivery of information, and if necessary improve it so that it is accessible to all. As an individual, you also have responsibilities. For example, by law you are required not simply to respond to situations of racism, but to promote actively good race relations.

The 1999 National Curriculum expounds three principles for inclusion: each pupil is entitled to be presented with suitable challenges; the curriculum should cater for diverse needs; and schools need to work to overcome any potential barriers to learning and assessment (DfEE, 1999a). You should ensure that your mathematics lessons are in line with these principles. Examples of how you can overcome barriers to learning in mathematics, include being aware that some pupils may require:

- help with number recall or processing presented information, to compensate for memory or vision difficulties
- access to tactile equipment for work on shape
- help with information presented orally (for example, requiring pupils to perform mental calculations), to compensate for hearing difficulties
- access to ICT to overcome physical difficulties with writing (DfEE, 1999a).

All mathematics departments (and hence individual teachers) have to analyse the achievement of different groups of pupils, and explain any differences. This applies particularly to test and examination results, but also to individual lessons. You should constantly assess whether any individual or any groups of pupils are being disadvantaged in your lessons.

Evidence of uneven achievement must be followed up. You will need to contribute to school or departmental policy initiatives designed to address the underachievement of particular groups.

CULTURE

In the classroom, you need to reflect on the extent to which the mathematics presented excludes certain groups. Contexts that you expect to be familiar to the pupils might be highly culture specific. There is no doubt that mathematics is a subject with a rich multicultural background. The 2007 revision of the

National Curriculum acknowledges that mathematics has 'a rich and fascinating history and has been developed across the world' (QCA, 2007: 141), and puts a greater emphasis than before on pupils learning about mathematics in its historical and cultural contexts. This has the potential to effect significant change in the mathematics classroom: if historical and cultural contexts are treated as key concepts, they must come through regularly in your teaching.

The Swann Report (DES, 1985) promoted a multicultural approach to education. Mathematics classrooms saw the introduction in some cases of mathematics from around the world, such as different number systems, Islamic patterns, and different calculation methods (such as, for example, the Egyptian method for multiplication). This attempted to demonstrate to the pupils that mathematics is a worldwide activity, but has been, at best, a bolt-on to the normal curriculum and, at worst, ignored altogether.

The view that mathematics is culture-free used to be commonplace. But although the mathematics developed in different cultures is similar, it is not identical. An example given by Bishop (1991) is of the angles of a triangle. It is clear that all mathematics, wherever developed, will conclude that the sum of the angles in a triangle will be the same as the angle of half a turn. But not everyone would use the same system of measurement in equating these two quantities. The use of 180° has a history behind it that will not be shared by all. On the other hand, mathematics is universal; it is a cultural activity that features in all civilizations in the same way as language and societal rules.

GENDER

The relative performance of boys and girls has been discussed for many years. Interestingly, differences are evident even in very young children. In 2007, inspectors found that by the end of the Foundation Stage (prior to starting Key Stage 1), girls had gained a clear advantage, reaching higher standards than boys in all areas of learning (Ofsted, 2007: 8). 'Girls applied themselves to table top activities more readily than boys, and were also keener to show their work and put their hands up in response to questions.' Boys also had weaker language skills; they spoke less confidently than girls.

Key Stage 2 and Key Stage 3 tests indicate differences in performance in English, but little difference in science or mathematics (2003 data, published in Ofsted 2004a; 2004b). At GCSE, the performance of boys and girls in mathematics is still similar, with the overall figures for 2005 showing that

- 52.5 per cent of boys have GCSE A* to C, with 12.9 per cent gaining grade A* or A
- 54.4 per cent of girls have GCSE A* to C, with 13.0 per cent gaining grade A* or A (Guardian, 2006a).

Interestingly, the performance of boys and girls in mathematics used to be quite uneven. In 1979, as reported by Cockcroft (1982)

- 24.5 per cent of boys had O level A to C, with 5.5 per cent gaining grade A
- 17.6 per cent of girls had O level A to C, with 2.6 per cent gaining grade A.

So, clearly, it used to be the case that boys outperformed girls in public examinations at age 16, certainly at the higher levels of attainment. In fact, it was not only the overall results that were higher for boys; boys outperformed girls in every mathematical topic area tested by the Assessment of Performance Unit in 1980 (Askew and Wiliam, 1995). By the mid-1990s, the gap in performance all but disappeared. In contrast, differences in gender performances are very pronounced in several other subjects. For example, in English, the figures for A* to C in 2005 are 67.9 per cent for girls and 53.9 per cent for boys.

Having looked at these facts and figures, you may think that there is no gender issue in mathematics, but this would be a mistake. It would be reasonable to assume that with boys and girls achieving similar results at GCSE, then take up at A level would reflect a similar gender balance. In fact the 2005 figures show that for every two girls opting to study A level mathematics, there are three boys (entries are 20,178 girls and 32,719 boys). For further mathematics, a subject traditionally chosen only by the most able mathematics students, the imbalance is much more marked, with two and a half times as many boys taking the subject as girls (Guardian, 2006b).

While uneven entry figures are a feature of almost all A level subjects, there is certainly a case to investigate why so many more boys than girls opt to take mathematics study beyond the compulsory years (a phenomenon that is evident in many countries). Research indicates that that there may be several reasons. Mendick (2005) concludes that the public image of the subject is sufficient to influence decisions, with girls equating mathematics to masculinity. Initiatives to increase the number of girls opting to study mathematics have had only limited success, and it may be that simple encouragement is not sufficient to effect changes in attitude, with societal attitudes tending to prevail. Girls' self-perception is that they are poor at mathematics, even when they are in the top set, with boys tending to overestimate their mathematical ability and girls tending to underestimate their mathematical ability (APU, 1981).

Interestingly, being told that the reason for poor performance is genetic may have a strong influence on self-image. An American study of university students (Dar-Nimrod and Heine, 2006) compared the performance in mathematics tests of women who were told that female underachievement in mathematics was down to genetic factors, and women who were told that social factors were responsible. Those who were told that genetic factors were a key determinant of performance scored much worse. This finding may have implications for children (boys or girls), whose parents speak of their own lack of mathematical ability, if such children grow up believing that poor mathematical ability is in their genes.

Another convincing argument for the differences in participation rates centres on the way that mathematics is presented in schools. Mathematics lessons with a lack of group work, discussion, co-operative learning, educative games and activities, may be particularly unattractive to girls. You may be able to investigate in one of your placement schools whether there are reduced language demands and social interaction in mathematics, compared with lessons in other subjects.

The contextual style of the question may also have an influence on the relative performance of boys and girls. Researching into science education, Gipps and Murphy (1994) report that girls are more likely to focus on the context of the experiment. In taking the context into account, girls sometimes fail to link in with the teacher's expectations for their solutions. Boys, on the other hand, have a tendency to ignore the context, to focus on the abstract science problem. It is reasonable to assume that these results transfer to the mathematics classroom, and may explain why more boys feel comfortable about their mathematical ability and therefore opt to study the subject at higher levels.

ETHNICITY

Recent evidence suggests that performance in mathematics is different across different ethnic groups. The mathematical achievement of different ethnic groups is affected by several different factors, including class, social standing and peer pressure. Since there can be no action without awareness and evidence, schools are required to analyse their examination results and to evaluate the performance of different ethnic groups in comparison to national averages. Where they identify an underachieving group, schools are expected (for example, by Ofsted inspectors) to first explain why, and then to draw up a plan to rectify the situation.

There is also evidence that intervention strategies are having a more positive impact with some ethnic groups than others. The Leverhulme Numeracy Research Project case study (reported in QCA, 2004) found that the biggest gains over the period 1998 to 2002 were made by Indian, black Caribbean and black British groups. In contrast, the black African group appeared to have made less progress than the average gains over the period concerned.

It is reasonable to argue (see Gates, 2002) that mathematics education fails to treat all pupils equitably, because the content of the curriculum reflects the bias of those who put it together. We therefore cannot achieve equality of opportunity while the mathematics that we present is fundamentally Eurocentric. Gates concludes that, since it fails to address this issue, the mathematics curriculum in

Britain is racist, and he challenges the curriculum from an anti-racist, rather than a multicultural, perspective. Anti-racist proponents advocate a greater integration of cultural aspects into the school curriculum, and a more active attitude to challenging pedagogy. There is some justification in the claim (Kassem, 2001) that the educational establishment has been slow to examine the nature of the curriculum or mathematical pedagogy from an anti-racist perspective, but with the 2007 curriculum review, there are signs that progress is being made.

DIFFERENTIATION

The most obvious aspect of differentiated provision that you will see is the use of setting by ability. Despite some limited evidence that ability groupings may not be the most effective for teaching mathematics (Boaler, 1997), the large majority of mathematics lessons are taught in such groups. It is interesting to note, however, that in many other countries grouping by ability takes place more within classes than between classes (Foxman, 1994).

You should appreciate that, although pupils are in ability sets, further differentiated provision is necessary. School inspectors have found that many mathematics teachers make little attempt to go beyond the use of setting in catering for the individual needs of pupils, particularly low-attaining pupils (Ofsted, 2006). You will need to identify additional strategies that you use to cater for different abilities within ability groups. The different strategies are grouped together under the two headings: differentiation by outcome and differentiation by task.

Differentiation by outcome means that all pupils undertake the same task. This is common in mathematics lessons where there is an investigative theme. For example, a common starting point for a piece of A level coursework may lead to pupils going off in several different directions with their mathematics, and the outcomes will clearly differ greatly in standard. Opportunities for this kind of differentiation exist in many lessons, but the task has to be carefully chosen so as to allow solutions at a range of levels.

Differentiation by task is straightforward. Within a teaching group, different abilities are catered for by providing different tasks at some stage during the lesson. Typically, this involves extension activities for the most able, and support materials for the least able. Often, extension activities consist of additional questions that are considered more difficult or broader in scope. In practice, you need to be clear that this is the case. There is nothing more demotivating for many able pupils than being given more to do, just because they have finished first; you need to demonstrate that you value the additional work that they are asked to do, by follow up questioning or discussion. It is important that these pupils see that the additional work is a planned, structured extension to the normal class work.

Here are some comments from experienced teachers about dealing with differentiation in their lessons:

Within every lesson you have a range of abilities. For example, in my Year 10 class I have pupils who are targeted a grade C and pupils who are targeted a grade F, so it is a massive range, very hard to deal with. I tend to set one main task within the lesson with an opportunity for an extension task for the pupils who complete it. For pupils who are weaker and are likely to find the main task difficult, I identify them in my plan as weaker pupils in the class and I will spend more time with them during independent working time checking that they understand.

If I have a lower ability group sometimes I will do writing frames or tables drawn out for them or axes already drawn so that the pupils focus on the skill that is being tested.

For the least able, drawing out a table or diagram is sometimes quite a task. At least for the first question, I will give out a blank table because I am testing whether they can find all the possibilities, not whether they can draw a table. On the other hand, I cannot ignore the need for them to develop basic skills; I just need to plan which lessons will address them, and which will not.

Support materials for the least able may be provided by back-up work, where the mathematics is presented in a different way, or by practical materials. Sometimes, specific support is available. For example, National Strategy materials include a support pack to help pupils to 'catch up' to level 4 during Year 7. Although the materials offer good support, they have often been insufficiently integrated into the standard curriculum (Ofsted, 2004c; 2006).

Low-attaining pupils, just as much as other pupils, respond well to the sort of active, discussion-based teaching approaches discussed in Chapter 5. Above all, they need to experience mathematics as something that makes sense. Low-attaining pupils may feel that their only route to success in mathematics is to try to remember what to do in different situations. They have this attitude because, based on previous experience, they do not expect to understand what they are doing in mathematics, but they know that sometimes they can obtain correct answers by following prescribed procedures. Haylock (1991) criticizes the large amount of time that pupils spend on routines and procedures, tasks that have little meaning for them. Even more than for other pupils, low attainers need to be convinced of the usefulness of mathematics, so wherever possible the activities should be presented in meaningful contexts.

One of the key drawbacks of setting is the effect that it has on the feelings of those in the bottom sets. By being placed in the bottom set, pupils are being told that they are among the least able in mathematics, a message that is certain to bring with it a knock to self-esteem and confidence (Larcombe, 1985; Sharp, 2004). Pupils who see themselves labelled as failures are difficult to motivate.

SPECIAL EDUCATIONAL NEEDS

Schools work to a code of practice in their provision for special educational needs (DfES, 2001a), which itself is set within the legal framework of the Special Educational Needs and Disability Act of 2001. Within the school, a special educational needs co-ordinator (SENCO) will have an overview of the school's provision, including monitoring all the pupils who receive individual support. The Professional Standards for QTS (TDA, 2007) require you to know and understand the role of the SENCO and of other colleagues with specific responsibilities for the progress of individual pupils. In addition, they require you to show that you can 'make effective personalised provision' (ibid.: 10) for pupils with a wide range of personal needs.

Schools are now more inclusive than was previously the case. Fewer pupils now attend special schools of various kinds, and where once a pupil would go to a special school to learn alongside pupils with similar needs, the pupil now attends a 'normal' school. As a result, schools cater for a wide range of abilities, and cater for pupils who have a wide range of individual special needs, whether physical, educational, emotional or behavioural. The key resource that is available to support the learning of these pupils is the teaching assistant.

The teaching assistant is a valuable part of many modern classrooms. When you start teaching, you are likely to find it difficult to organize your own contribution in the classroom, but your job is to do that and more. You need to organize the contribution of each teaching assistant in each lesson. This will involve joint planning before the lesson, as well as several 'quiet words' within the lesson to make sure that the learning is appropriate for every pupil in the group. Teaching assistants will usually be assigned to support one or two individuals within the class, but may have a more general support role. It can be expected that they will be familiar with the Individual Education Plans (IEPs) of the pupils whom they support.

One key contribution that teaching assistants make within mathematics lessons is in helping pupils to manage the transitions between different parts of the lesson. This can mean that at the start of the lesson, they get pupils organized to start work, and at the end of the lesson, they make sure that the pupils have noted down their homework. In oral work, they can encourage pupils to put up their hand (sometimes after the pupil has whispered the proposed answer, and checked that it is correct). In written work, teaching assistants help pupils to get started, helping them to read the question, and monitor the pupils' possibly tentative early steps in the work. Teaching assistants can also provide additional support through modelling solutions in more detail.

Teaching assistants also play an important role in helping pupils with poor organizational skills to take a more active part in the lesson. This may involve providing pupils with basic equipment, making sure that they have the correct page and task noted down, and possibly providing extra support materials such as a multiplication tables square or basic notes from earlier work.

There is some evidence that the use of teaching assistant support does not, in itself, ensure 'good quality intervention or adequate pupil progress' (Ofsted, 2006: 64). In fact, inspectors find that pupils in mainstream schools, supported by teaching assistants, are less likely to make good progress than those pupils who have access to specialist teaching. This would appear to be an indictment of the policy of moving more pupils into mainstream schools, but does not have to be so. It should rather be seen as an indication that the available resources in mainstream schools are not being used as effectively as they might be.

The 'Evidence from the research' section towards the end of this chapter goes into more detail about two particular types of special need – dyslexia and dyscalculia – with particular reference to learning mathematics.

GIFTED AND VERY ABLE PUPILS

Pupils with special gifts in mathematics are usually easy to identify. Typically, they grasp new ideas quickly, they work logically and accurately, and they can see and extend patterns easily. They are also likely to have strong communication skills, enabling them to justify their methods, and have a curiosity that asks, 'What would happen if … ?'

Where all the above features are evident, pupils may be capable of performing at a level well in advance of what is usual for their age. Other gifted pupils may be less easily identified. For example, they may have high levels of mathematical reasoning but cannot communicate their ideas well, or they may tackle questions in an original (and possibly obscure) way. The QCA guidance for mathematics teachers includes the following useful advice, stating that for these cases: 'formal testing alone is insufficient as a basis for identification. It is often helpful for teachers to provide enrichment and extension activities and to observe pupil responses to challenging activities' (QCA, 2002).

Dealing with the most able pupils can be very challenging. You will need your subject knowledge to have breadth and depth; you will need to be prepared to take risks, and respond to unexpected ideas from the pupils (Ofsted, 2001). There is evidence that able and gifted pupils are often insufficiently challenged (QCA, 2004), so you need to have suitable strategies available to ensure that the most able are achieving the best that they can. Extension activities, containing more difficult questions, often form part of the teacher's planning for the most able pupils in all classes. For the particularly gifted (the most able in the top set of the whole year group), extension activities are more interesting if they contain an element of enrichment.

Enrichment is an alternative to more difficult questions. Enrichment activities present questions that are not just more difficult versions of the same work, but are more general in nature. Let us consider a typical example from the topic of plotting co-ordinate points, and present two different versions of the same question:

Standard question. Plot the points (1, 2), (3, 1), (−1, −1) and (−3, 0). Join up the points to make a four sided shape. What is the name of your shape?

Enrichment question. Plot the points (1, 2), (3, 1) and (−3, 0). Plot a fourth point so that the four points form a parallelogram. How many different answers are there? Will there always be the same number of answers for any set of three points?

It is clear that the second version of the question is much more demanding, while still keeping within the same area of work as the rest of the class. The enrichment question promotes a much more general understanding of the problem.

Acceleration has often been used to cater for the needs of the most able pupils. Accelerated provision allows able pupils to progress through the school system in fewer years than is normal. Although frowned upon for many years, this approach is likely to become more common owing to increased flexibility in the examination system. The examination system allows schools to enter pupils for GCSE and the Key Stage 3 tests earlier than the 'normal' chronological age, and increasing numbers of schools are taking advantage of this opportunity. Anecdotal evidence suggests that acceleration in mathematics is more common than in other subjects.

Acceleration can be applied to whole groups of pupils, or it can apply to individuals. Where applied to individuals, care has to be taken with the social impact of moving a pupil away from his or her peers. This social impact has to be carefully balanced against any perceived educational benefit of accelerated learning. For example, in planning for the most able pupils, Koshy and Casey (1997) question the practice of simply importing work from higher age groups and giving it to younger children in order to accelerate their leaning. They conclude that accelerated learning 'involves more than accelerated content; it needs other factors such as student motivation, creativity and interest to be taken into account' (ibid.: 68).

An example of socially aware acceleration is given below. A secondary school needed to cater for the needs of a very able boy, with particular gifts in mathematics.

Tom arrived at secondary school having covered all the work on the GCSE mathematics syllabus at primary school. The school provided for him by arranging for him to study A level mathematics and physics alongside the 17-year-old students, but to attend other lessons with his peers. In consultation with Tom's parents, the school decided to try to maintain friendship groups within his own age group. After completing the A level course in Year 8, Tom's mathematics lessons were conducted on an individual basis. A personal tutor provided by the local authority visited the school regularly to work with him. His mathematics work in later school years focused on Open University modules.

Point for reflection

Reforms to the 14 – 19 curriculum in 2005 were prompted partly by evidence that existing courses were not sufficiently challenging for the most able pupils and young people (QCA, 2006). How can mathematics be made more challenging for the most able at a time when many claim that mathematics is already more difficult than other subjects at GCSE?

LANGUAGE IN MATHEMATICS EDUCATION

The Framework has brought the question of language in mathematics to the attention of every teacher, and it gives clear guidance about using the correct mathematical term, rather than a descriptive alternative (DfEE, 2001). All teachers are encouraged to use precise mathematical vocabulary, and to promote the use of mathematical vocabulary among pupils. For example, you should use the word 'denominator' rather than 'the bottom number in the fraction' or similar equivalent. One advantage of this approach is that usage will be consistent from teacher to teacher. If you use a paraphrase, there is no guarantee that your paraphrase will be the same as that used by another teacher, so any understanding gained with you may be offset by later problems when the pupil has a different teacher for mathematics.

It is clear that mathematics presents considerable language demands. These demands start with the need to understand simple vocabulary from outside mathematics, such as large, find or line. This basic vocabulary then needs to be built up so that the pupil can use this simple language interspersed with subject-specific words such as polygon and histogram. The National Strategy provides a helpful vocabulary checklist that indicates to teachers when pupils can expect to meet particular words.

The strategy provides a vocabulary list for Year 8, for example, that includes all the new words or mathematical terms that a pupil can expect to meet in Year 8 for the first time. The list is very extensive, including over a hundred new terms. For example, on the topic of shapes and angles alone, there are 18 new terms, including

- equidistant
- corresponding angles
- triangular prism
- tessellation.

These four terms alone give some indication of the language demands of the subject. The words are unfamiliar, multi-syllabled and highly specialized. In fact, they are so specialized that they give little opportunity for practice even in mathematics lessons, except where they form the focus of the lesson. It is worth spending some time looking through the vocabulary checklist; there may well be words on it that you yourself are not familiar with. Where you find unfamiliar words, you are advised to use a mathematical dictionary or follow the link, provided on the website, to the QCA mathematical Glossary pages.

Problems often occur because of the number of words whose usage in mathematics is in a different sense from their usage outside mathematics. Miles (1992) describes such words as 'deceptively familiar'. Some have completely different meanings outside mathematics, such as volume (loudness, in everyday usage) and mean (ungenerous). Other words have meanings in mathematics that have some resemblance to everyday usage, but the mathematical usage is far more specific. Examples of this kind are similar, range and difference. Where a word has multiple meanings, a pupil may feel familiar with the word, but use it incorrectly in its mathematical sense.

There is further guidance from the National Strategy (DfES, 2004) in the study materials *Literacy and Learning in Mathematics*, designed for self-study by teachers or as a focus for school-based professional development. As well as providing several examples of words that are used in different senses in mathematics and outside, the study materials suggest ways that mathematics teachers can develop general skills of literacy in their pupils. For example, it is helpful for teachers to be aware of the reading demands that mathematics texts pose. In addition to the normal language demands, reading in mathematics tends to take in a range of presentations; information may be in words, diagrams, tables, charts or mathematical expressions, or often a combination of these. In addition, reading in mathematics is not such a linear activity as in other subjects. Reading a mathematical question may involve moving backwards and forwards through the text, in order to extract the important information. Reading may also need to be frequently interrupted, while the pupil tackles an intermediate calculation or notes down some key information.

In the sample lesson, the teacher tries to develop mathematical language through use of the correct vocabulary and notation, through frequent rephrasing, and through refreshing the pupils' knowledge of previously-met terms. Note the following examples from parts 6 and 7 of the sample lesson, where the italicized items are all from the Framework vocabulary checklist for Key Stage 3 (DfEE, 2001). In the first example, the teacher takes the opportunity to remind the class what is meant by a prime number:

> That's right! You cannot get any more numbers into 13 and 25. There are no more
> *factors*. It isn't that we cannot *halve* them, because there might be a different
> *factor* that goes into them other than 2.
> What is special about the number 13 that helps me to know?
> Yes, it is a *prime* number, Jake, well done.
> What is special about *prime* numbers?
>
> *Jake*: Only one and it can go into it.
>
> Good. So if 13 doesn't go into 25 then we know there are no other *factors* that are
> *common* to them both.

In the same section, correct terminology and notation are encouraged. Daniel uses the phrase 45 out of 60 as his description of a probability, which leads to the following response:

> Or 45/60. Remember that we write it as a *fraction*. Now try to *cancel* that down to
> its *simplest form* – I'll let you try that yourselves. So what are the *factors* of 45 and
> 60, what numbers go into 45 and 60?

Mathematical notation is introduced in a natural, but planned way:

> For the *probability* that it is red, you can put *P(red)* =

It is not only difficult vocabulary that causes problems in reading mathematics; Shuard and Rothery (1984) report that at least as much difficulty is presented by the use of difficult syntax. In general, when setting word questions, it is advisable to use the present tense where possible, avoiding constructions that involve 'if', 'suppose' or 'given that', which can only be followed by fairly complex language constructions. It is also poor practice to present, in an introductory clause, information that needs to be used later on. Using two short sentences is usually preferable to one long sentence.

Point for reflection

Examine the word questions below. Consider each from the point of view of clarity of language, context, and vocabulary. All should be criticized in some way. Consider how you would reword the questions to make the language more accessible.

1. What is the difference between 14.3 and 3.8?
2. There is a certain number. If this number were 4 more than twice as large, it would be equal to 18. What is the number?
3. There are 10 birds in a tree. 2 get shot. How many birds are left in the tree?
4. John can eat a Big Mac in 5 minutes. How many could he eat in 2 hours?
5. Given that Wendy is 1.60 m tall, a bus is 5.50 m tall, and an elephant is 2.80 m tall, find the ratio of Wendy's height to the elephant's height, and the ratio of the elephant's height to the height of a bus.
6. A pharmaceutical company manufactures a drug called Fizmatum. Each 1.2 g pill contains active ingredients 5mg of Potassium Hypophosphate and 6.5 mg of Calcium Silicate. What proportion of the pill is made up of active ingredients?
7. As viewed from the batsman, the angle between the cover and extra cover fieldsmen is 28°. If each fielder is equidistant, 25 m, from the batsman, how far are the fielders apart?

When writing word questions, you also need to be aware of how certain features of the question act as cues to many readers. Interestingly, these cues may be numerical or verbal. The size of the numbers that are presented in a word problem affect the choice of number operation (Brown, 1981). For example, a problem that contains the numbers 3540 and 4201 is very likely to involve adding or subtracting the numbers. This is based on pupils' experiences of what they are usually asked to do in mathematics lessons. They often add or subtract numbers of this size, but rarely multiply or divide, so they take the size of the numbers as a cue, along with the other cues that may come through the context. Similarly, certain words may be taken as cues, possibly correctly, but possibly not. Consider the following example:

10 people share a sum of money. Each gets £48.60. How much is there in the sum of money?

The presence in this question of the word 'share' will make some pupils feel that they need to perform a division using the numbers given. This cue may be strong enough to outweigh the information provided by the context.

As well as specific language difficulties, mathematics has its own symbolic notation that is very much part of mathematical communication. Skemp's view (1982) is that the spoken language should be used for as long as possible, and the symbolic formulation avoided until very late in the learning process. In other words, spoken language is more effective in a situation where the learner is uncertain about the underlying concept. The symbolic representation should only be introduced when the concept is secure. On a more positive note, mathematical symbols can be very valuable in written communication, expressing ideas that are difficult to express verbally. Orton (1992) gives the simple example $(3 + 2) \times 4$, which is easily understood in writing, but is quite difficult to verbalize succinctly.

Researchers have generally given more attention to reading mathematics than to issues of pupils writing or speaking mathematics. Writing and speaking do, however, provide interesting areas for study. Pimm (1989) makes the point that written mathematics is 'not just spoken mathematics written down in words', and queries how pupils decide what they need to record and how they choose to record it. In spoken mathematics, pupils often lack confidence in verbalizing their ideas. This is illustrated in the number of 'hedge' words that pupils use when answering questions. Rowland (2002) transcribed several interviews with pupils and notes the frequency of words such as 'about', 'around', 'maybe', 'suppose' – words that serve to avoid saying something that is wrong.

Points for reflection

1. You are faced with a dilemma: you want the pupils to develop their mathematical language so that they can read and write accurately in the precise mathematical register, but you want them to feel that mathematics is accessible to all. It is argued that:

   > There is a tension between the wish to introduce pupils to conventional mathematical means of communication and the need to avoid the mystification and consequent anxiety or dislike of the subject that can be induced by using language that pupils are unfamiliar with. (Morgan, 2005: 156)

   Consider whether you feel that correct mathematical language can ever be a barrier to learning.

2. Pupils with poor language skills are at a disadvantage in mathematics, and tend to perform less well in public examinations. Consider the extent to which public examinations should avoid difficult mathematical language, and allow the assessment to focus more on using mathematics to solve problems. Consider also the possible consequence of examinations avoiding mathematical language: teachers will not feel the need to develop mathematical language skills, because they are not needed in the examination. To what extent is communication in mathematics fundamental to any study of the subject?

TEACHING PUPILS FOR WHOM ENGLISH IS AN ADDITIONAL LANGUAGE

The National Strategy provides some guidance for mathematics teachers on teaching pupils who have English as an additional language (EAL). A useful starting point to the discussion is a quote from the Framework. 'It is all too easy to underestimate what pupils can do mathematically simply because they are new learners of the English language. The expectation should be that they progress in their mathematical learning at the same rate as other pupils of their age' (DfEE, 2001: 35).

This is the essential challenge to mathematics teachers: to see through the language difficulties to the mathematical understanding, and to then teach the pupil according to ability. That is not to say that the language difficulties are ignored. Whatever level of mathematical ability, each child is entitled to the necessary support, most likely from specialist teaching assistants.

Evidence suggests that the numeracy strategy in primary schools has been of benefit to pupils from ethnic minorities. In particular, pupils at an early stage of language acquisition made larger gains in mathematical attainment at Key Stage 2 over the period 1998 to 2002 than those pupils characterized as 'English as a first/only language' (QCA, 2004). This may be because the different teaching styles encouraged by the strategy have helped pupils in their language acquisition. Whole-class teaching where pupils are taking part, interactive questioning, and discussion between pupils are all likely to be more helpful than an individualized learning programme, where the pupil is faced with the written word more than verbal communication.

It can be argued that mathematics is one subject where pupils with an uncertain grasp of the English language can display their true ability. The widespread understanding of the Arabic numerals in many areas of the world means that communication via numbers is often straightforward. Moreover, the universal nature of algebraic notation again provides an international language, so that pupils with little or no English may find that they can take a full part in the lesson. Such opportunities are not available in many other subjects.

On the website that accompanies this book, you will find an edited version of a mathematics lesson in Japan. You should watch the video as a simulation of what it is like to encounter a mathematics lesson where the language of delivery is unfamiliar. (This activity will not work for those readers who have a working knowledge of the Japanese language.) You may be surprised at how international the language of mathematics is. For example, even though the written Japanese language is made up of characters that are very different from the Roman script, triangles are still labelled with corners A, B, C and with sides a, b, c, and algebraic formulae are presented in exactly the format that is familiar from mathematics lessons in the UK. It is interesting to note that, in Japanese, fractions are read (and written) from bottom to top: the denominator followed by the numerator.

Another useful simulation activity that you can do is to try to use your mathematical skills to solve a written problem that is presented in an unfamiliar language. Undertaking this task will give you an insight into the frustrations that might be felt by able pupils, who are unable to show their ability in mathematics because of language barriers. This example is written in the Czech language.

> Z mista A vygel do mista B cyclista prumernou rychlosti 20 km/h. Za 45 munut vygel z A do B motocyclista prumernou rychlosti 44km/h. Oba do mista B dojeli soucasne. Urcete vzdalenost AB.
> (Example taken from DfES, 2002: 13)

It is suggested that you spend some time on this problem, making a serious attempt to come up with an answer. This generally proves to be a difficult task for trainees, who usually present a wide range of possible answers. Very few find the correct answer, 27.5 kilometres, often because they think that the question is asking for a time, rather than a distance. Try the question again, now that you know the correct answer, and try to decipher its meaning. (An explanation of the problem is provided on the website.)

Where the pupil's number system uses different symbols (which is the case for several languages in India, Pakistan and Bangladesh, for example), there are additional problems in early mathematics lessons. But you can be reassured by the fact that the number system that the pupil is familiar with is almost certainly using base 10, so a straight transcribing of symbols is possible. It is also worth noting that, although a language may be read from right to left, the numbers always appear with the tens digit to the left of the units digit.

You need to be well prepared for teaching pupils with English as an additional language. One key feature of preparation is to make sure that your own knowledge of the pupil's background is sound. In other words, a familiarity with different number scripts, and whether a home language is written from right to left are useful information for any teacher. But as well as a certain level of professional knowledge, you need to have access to a range of strategies for helping EAL pupils to learn mathematics.

The first, and most obvious, strategy is to use visual aids as much as possible. If a pupil is having difficulty following verbal explanations and discussions, then visual support is vital in strengthening the communication. So when talking about a triangle, it is useful to have a diagram of a triangle easily to hand. When asking for the result of a calculation, it is helpful to display the question alongside the verbal delivery.

Other strategies are also largely extensions of strategies that many good teachers use during their normal lessons. One strategy that is particularly important for EAL pupils is modelling the expected work. Being able to see a series of mathematical steps gives pupils a sense of security and a feeling that they can tackle the expected work. Group work also plays an important part in making EAL pupils feel part of the class. While they may not initially take an active part in any group discussion, they are able to hear the way that pupils discuss the problem, and watch the way that the other pupils respond to any practical task that they are doing. Group work also provides a more informal and secure environment for EAL pupils to begin to voice their views and to interact with other pupils.

The most useful strategy for helping EAL pupils is scaffolding. Again, scaffolding is used routinely in many mathematics lessons; what makes the difference for EAL pupils is recognition from the teacher that scaffolding may need extending and strengthening. Examples of scaffolding that might be helpful for EAL pupils are:

- showing every step in a mathematical argument
- using repetitive presentations of the same idea (avoiding any variation in the phrasing)
- presenting the pupil with partially completed solution.

Clearly a key aspect of preparation when EAL pupils are present in a class is to analyse the language demands of the lesson. Again what is expected for normal lessons is amplified in the case where EAL pupils are involved. Key words need to be displayed prominently, and real objects may be helpfully displayed alongside the word to make the meaning clear. Preparation for the lesson may involve obtaining a direct translation of certain key words into the pupil's native tongue or, if possible, spending a few minutes with the pupil before the lesson, pre-teaching the most important words.

When catering for EAL pupils, it is common to have some support in the form of a teaching assistant (TA). Again preparation is the key to making the most of this support. A good teacher will meet with the TA before the lesson and discuss the mathematical ideas and any additional help that is likely to be needed by the EAL pupils. It is helpful if the teaching assistant has some expertise in the pupil's first language, but this will not always be the case. Where it is, or where there is additional support from the local authority (LA), it is good practice to inform the parents as much as possible about what mathematics is to be taught. If parents know about the work to be covered, they can often provide support in the pupil's mother tongue both before and after the lesson.

Other strategies that are worth considering are listed below:

- Minimize written instructions on worksheets.
- Display vocabulary that is appropriate to the lesson.
- Underline key words where it may help:
  Find the <u>area</u> of a <u>square</u> of side <u>5 cm</u>.
- Where a list is used (for example, categories for a bar chart), start with the ones that are most likely to be familiar:

Dog, cat, ferret, mole is a better order than ferret, mole, cat, dog. In the second case the pupil is likely to take more time to understand that the list refers to types of animal.

- Avoid contexts that have a strong cultural link. Remember that while context can help some pupils to access the mathematics, it can also provide a barrier if the context is unfamiliar.

Supporting materials for mathematics teachers with EAL pupils are fairly limited in number. Ideas for use in multi-lingual classrooms, together with supporting resources are available from the Association of Teachers of Mathematics (ATM, 1993). Support for assessing pupils' ability is provided by the National Strategy assessment toolkit (DfES, 2003), which contains a wealth of visual aids, flash cards, and matching activities designed to help assess the level of ability of EAL pupils.

Point for reflection

It can be argued that EAL pupils enjoy mathematics lessons more than any other, because much of the content has a familiar ring. To what extent do you agree with this? Consider the types of experiences within mathematics lessons that are likely to make EAL pupils feel more comfortable, and the types of experiences that are likely to make them feel less comfortable. Choose one visual aid that you feel would be useful above all others in helping EAL pupils to make progress in your lesson.

EVIDENCE FROM THE RESEARCH

In this section, we concentrate on the research evidence surrounding two particular types of special needs that have important implications for teachers of mathematics – dyslexia and dyscalculia. These are both relatively common forms of special needs, and it is recommended that you understand both conditions, and how you might adapt your teaching to take account of these pupils' needs.

Dyslexia is a condition that affects pupils in a wide range of school subjects, but is associated more closely with the language-based subjects than with mathematics. There is little doubt, however, that dyslexia has specific links with mathematical performance that are worth trying to understand, especially as a high proportion of dyslexic pupils have problems with aspects of number work (Kay and Yeo, 2003). Secondary school pupils have usually already developed compensatory techniques that have helped with work at a simple level. When the work becomes more complex, these techniques may no longer be appropriate (Henderson, 1989), and may need discussing with a teacher or teaching assistant in a non-threatening situation (probably one-to-one). Henderson stresses the importance of building confidence, providing regular feedback and reassurance, and that teaching should be 'systematic, sequential and structured' (ibid.: 64).

Dyslexia may in some cases have consequences in mathematics that are more severe than those in English. For example, a word that has two letters interchanged is likely to be intelligible; a number with two digits interchanged gives no indication of whether a transcribing error might exist. Another possible area of difficulty concerns reading the decimal point. Some people use a comma to separate digits into sets of three, so that 4 000 is written as 4,000. Dyslexic pupils are more likely to confuse the comma with a decimal point (Henderson, 1992), so confusing 4,000 with 4.000. For this reason, if no other, you should avoid the use of the comma as a place value indicator; a space is the more common and correct alternative (see, for example, the National Numeracy Strategy – DfEE, 1999b).

As noted above, the language demands in mathematics are considerable and, not surprisingly, this poses particular problems for dyslexic pupils. In particular, dyslexic pupils experience difficulties with both the receptive (listening, reading and processing information) and with the expressive (talking and writing) sides of the communication process (Kay and Yeo, 2003). In order to alleviate these difficulties, you need to keep explanations brief and supported as much as possible by visual aids and practical equipment.

Other common characteristics of dyslexic pupils have an impact on progress in mathematics. For example, dyslexic pupils often experience long-term memory difficulties, which may affect their ability to recall number facts or procedures that they have met before. Weaknesses in working memory and sequencing can lead to poor performance on mental tasks and multi-step tasks (Yeo, 2002).

The use of visual patterns in mathematics is an effective way to overcome difficulties experienced by dyslexic pupils (Chinn and Ashcroft, 1992). In an interesting example of this, Johnson (2005) reports considerable success in a small-scale study on helping dyslexics to learn their multiplication tables. She found that, when pupils were presented with their seven times table arranged around the face of a clock (with the result of 3×7 in the '3' position, and 4×7 in the '4' position, for example) they were able to recall the results of the tables more effectively than when using methods that they had encountered previously. The facility to associate the results with a position on the clock face helped pupils by providing a visual image of the results.

There are two distinct learning styles associated with dyslexic pupils learning mathematics, referred to in the literature as 'grasshoppers' and 'inchworms'. Grasshoppers have strong visual skills; they like to look at the big picture, to solve the whole problem using intuitive methods. They may have plenty of original ideas, but tend to try out ideas impulsively. They are more likely to prefer oral work and mental methods of calculation, and may have difficulty writing down their ideas in any systematic, organized way.

Inchworms are pupils who prefer step-by-step approaches, and try to remember procedures that they have been shown. They are more comfortable trying to understand each step of a procedure than in understanding the overall approach. Studies suggest that inchworms are more common than grasshoppers among dyslexics (Chinn et al., 2001; Kay and Yeo, 2003), and you need to make particular provision for helping these pupils to build their confidence in tackling multi-step problems.

Dyscalculia, although much less researched than dyslexia, is a recognized condition that has been estimated to affect between 5 per cent and 8 per cent of the school population (Geary, 2004). Early definitions (for example, Farnham-Diggory, 1978; Rudel, 1988) describe dyscalculia simply as an inability to perform mathematical calculations. Hughes et al. (1994) identify dyscalculic as being unable to link the spatial aspect of numbers of objects with the equivalent symbolic representation. They describe 'the inability to co-ordinate the verbal and the spatial' as the most distinguishing characteristic of dyscalculia. More recently, the definition has been broadened to include an understanding of numbers and the number system, as well as calculations involving numbers. In their guidance for teachers on dyslexia and dyscalculia, the Department for Education and Skills in England present the following definition:

> Dyscalculia is a condition that affects the ability to acquire arithmetical skills. Dyscalculic learners may have difficulty understanding simple number concepts, lack an intuitive grasp of numbers, and have problems learning number facts and procedures. Even if they produce a correct answer or use a correct method, they may do so mechanically and without confidence.
> (DfES, 2001b: 2)

Dyscalculia can be temporary or can be long term. It can also be very specific to a particular area of mathematics, so a dyscalculic pupil may perform well overall on a mathematics test, but still have specific learning difficulties.

Responding appropriately to dyscalculia depends heavily on accurate and detailed diagnosis. Testing for the condition, and forming appropriate learning plans are still at an early stage, but the necessary support for teachers is beginning to appear. Work by Poustie (2001), Butterworth and Yeo (2004) and Hannell (2005) provides teachers with guidance about what the condition entails and what strategies to employ in the classroom.

Your response to dyscalculic pupils should recognize that they have particular needs. Supporting visual materials, such as number lines and place value apparatus should be made available. In addition, you should understand that dyscalculic pupils may often be dyslexic as well, and have a range of language difficulties that inhibit mathematical learning. These language difficulties may mean that they lack the inner language that most pupils use to internalize their learning. As a result, it is more important than ever to make connections between mathematical ideas, to make sure that new learning fits in with and builds on existing structures, and to present new mathematics in a range of contexts (Hannell, 2005).

Further reading

Sharp, B. (2004) *Meeting SEN in the Curriculum – Maths.* London: David Fulton.

This is part of a series that aims to give teachers practical support, illustrated by specific examples. In this book, Brian Sharp discusses general issues to do with special needs in mainstream schools, including the statutory Framework. He describes a wide range of special needs, reviews the common terminology, and describes how departments write their special needs policies. The chapters on inclusion and the use of teaching assistants are particularly helpful. The book ends with eight case studies of special needs pupils, giving a useful insight into how policies and practices impact upon individuals.

Shuard, H. and Rothery, A. (1984) *Children Reading Mathematics.* London: John Murray.

Although now many years old, this collection of research into the language demands of mathematics remains full of insight and good advice. The authors discuss the problems of communicating mathematically in terms of vocabulary, syntax and graphical presentations, and illustrate their ideas throughout with examples from pupils' work. As suggested in the title, the emphasis is on reading mathematics more than speaking and listening, and there is no section on issues relating to non-native speakers of English, but overall, you will find this is a very readable and informative review of mathematical texts and readability.

Department for Education and Skills (DfES) (2003) *Assessment in Mathematics Toolkit to Support Pupils for Whom English is an Additional Language.* London: Department for Education and Skills.

Although it focuses more on the assessment of pupils than teaching them, this pack provides a wealth of ideas for presentations. All the materials are presented in large, clear print and contain graded activities that help to match the pupil with an appropriate National Curriculum level. It is not a series of lesson plans, but requires imagination on the part of the teacher as to how the materials can best support the learning of individual pupils. It is more of a resource for 'dipping into' than using wholesale, but is worth a place on the shelf in any mathematics workroom. The pack comes in loose-leaf form, with an accompanying CD, which includes all the materials in electronic form. The pack is available free on the Teachernet website, http://publications.teachernet.gov.uk, with a link available on the website accompanying this book.

 Useful websites

Live links to these sites can be found on the companion website.

For mathematics and inclusion, there is a useful document on the Standards site at http://www.standards.dfes.gov.uk/primary/publications/mathematics/itt_maths_and_incl usion/nns_itt_math_inclusion060503.pdf

Although this is information aimed at teaching mathematics in primary schools, it contains a wealth of useful information and advice.

http://www.teachernet.gov.uk/supportpack/case.aspx?cs=814

This site includes a video to illustrate how EAL pupils are integrated into a Year 9 mathematics lesson.

http://www.teachers.tv/video/5466

This is a video that shows one school's personalized learning policy being applied with a low ability GCSE mathematics class.

References

Askew, M. and Wiliam, D. (1995) *Recent Research in Mathematics Education 5–16*. London: HMSO.

Assessment of Performance Unit (APU) (1981) *Mathematical Development, Secondary Survey Report No. 2*. London: HMSO.

Association of Teachers of Mathematics (ATM) (1993) *Talking Maths, Talking Languages*. Derby: Association of Teachers of Mathematics.

Bishop, A. (1991) 'Mathematics education in its cultural context', in M. Harris (ed.), *Schools Mathematics and Work*. London: Falmer.

Boaler, J. (1997) *Experiencing School Mathematics: Teaching Styles, Sex and Setting*. Buckingham: Open University Press.

Brown, M. (1981) 'Number operations', in K. Hart (ed.), *Children's Understanding of Mathematics: 11–16*. London: John Murray.

Butterworth, B. and Yeo, D. (2004) *Dyscalculia Guidance*. London: David Fulton.

Chinn, S.J. and Ashcroft, J.R. (1992) 'The use of patterns', in T.R. Miles and E. Miles (eds), *Dyslexia and Mathematics*. London: Routledge.

Chinn, S., McDonough, D., van Elswijk, R., Harmsen, H., Kay, J., McPhilips, T., Power, A. and Skidmore, L. (2001) 'Classroom studies into cognitive style in mathematics for pupils with dyslexia in special education in the Netherlands, Ireland and the UK', *British Journal of Special Education*, 28(2): 80–5.

Cockcroft, W.H. (1982) *Mathematics Counts*. London: HMSO.

Dar-Nimrod, I. and Heine S.J. (2006) 'Exposure to scientific theories affects women's math performance', *Science*, 314: 435.

Department of Education and Science (DES) (1985) *Education for All*. (Swann Report.) London: Department of Education and Science.

Department for Education and Employment (DfEE) (1999a) *The National Curriculum for England: Mathematics*. London: HMSO.

Department for Education and Employment (DfEE) (1999b) *The National Numeracy Strategy: Framework for Teaching Mathematics from Reception to Year 6*. London: Department for Education and Employment.

Department for Education and Employment (DfEE) (2001) *Key Stage 3 National Strategy. Framework for Teaching Mathematics: Years 7, 8 and 9*. London: Department for Education and Employment.

Department for Education and Skills (DfES) (2001a) *Special Educational Needs: Code of Practice*. London: Department for Education and Skills.

Department for Education and Skills (DfES) (2001b) *Guidance to Support Pupils with Dyslexia and Dyscalculia*. London: Department for Education and Skills.

Department for Education and Skills (DfES) (2002) *Access and Engagement in Mathematics: Teaching Pupils for Whom English is an Additional Language*. London: Department for Education and Skills.

Department for Education and Skills (DfES) (2003) *Assessment in Mathematics Toolkit to Support Pupils for Whom English Is an Additional Language*. London: Department for Education and Skills.

Department for Education and Skills (DfES) (2004) *Literacy and Learning in Mathematics*. London: Department for Education and Skills.

Farnham-Diggory, S. (1978) *Learning Disability*. Cambridge, MA: Harvard University Press.

Foxman, D. (1994) 'The Second International Assessment of Educational Progress (IAEP2)', *British Congress on Mathematical Education: Research Papers*. Leeds: Centre for Studies in Science and Mathematics Education, University of Leeds.

Gates, P. (2002) 'Issues of equity in mathematics education', in L. Haggarty (ed.), *Teaching Mathematics in Secondary Schools: A Reader*. London: RoutledgeFalmer.

Geary, D.C. (2004) 'Mathematics and learning disabilities', *Journal of learning disabilities*, 37: 4–15.

Gipps, C. and Murphy, P. (1994) *A Fair Test? Assessment, Achievement and Equity*. Buckingham: Open University Press.

Guardian (2006a) *GCSE Results by Subject and Gender*. Online at the Guardian website, http://education.guardian.co.uk/gcses/table/0,,1556318,00.html (accessed 6 August 2007).

Guardian (2006b) *A Level Results by subject 2005*. Online at the Guardian website, http://education.guardian.co.uk/alevel/page/0,,1551646,00.html (accessed 6 August 2007).

Hannell, G. (2005) *Dyscalculia: Action Plans for Successful Learning in Mathematics*. London: David Fulton.

Haylock, D. (1991) *Teaching Mathematics to Low Attainers 8–12*. London: Paul Chapman Publishing.

Henderson, A. (1989) *Maths and Dyslexics*. Llandudno: St David's College.

Henderson, A. (1992) 'Difficulties at the secondary stage', in T.R. Miles and E. Miles (eds), *Dyslexia and Mathematics*. London: Routledge.

Hughes, S., Kolstad, R. and Briggs, L.D. (1994) 'Dyscalculia and mathematics achievement', *Journal of Instructional Psychology*, 21(1): 64–7.

Johnson, P. (2005) 'Will a multi-sensory device called Clock Tables© help dyslexic and children with dyslexic tendencies to improve their mental recall of multiplication facts?', unpublished research report, Edge Hill University, Ormskirk.

Kassem, D. (2001) 'Ethnicity and mathematics education' in P. Gates (ed.), *Issues in Teaching Mathematics*. London: RoutledgeFalmer.

Kay, J. and Yeo, D. (2003) *Dyslexia and Maths*. London: David Fulton.

Koshy, V. and Casey, R. (1997) 'Curriculum provision for higher-ability pupils', *Support for Learning*, 12(2): 66–9.

Larcombe, T. (1985) *Mathematical Learning Difficulties in the Secondary School: Pupil Needs and Teacher Roles*. Milton Keynes: Open University Press.

Lisbon, Portugal: The Programme Committee of the 18th PME Conference. 2–112.

Mendick, H. (2005) 'Mathematical stories: why do more boys than girls choose to study mathematics at AS-level in England?', *British Journal of Sociology of Education*, 26(2): 235–51.

Miles, E. (1992) 'Reading and writing in mathematics', in T.R. Miles and E. Miles (eds), *Dyslexia and Mathematics*. London: Routledge.

Morgan, C. (2005) 'Communicating mathematically', in S. Johnston-Wilder, P. Johnston-Wilder, D. Pimm and J. Westwell (eds), *Learning to Teach Mathematics in the Secondary School*. Oxford: Routledge.

Office for Standards in Education (Ofsted) (2001) *Providing for Gifted and Talented Pupils: An Evaluation of Excellence in Cities and Other Grant-Funded Programmes*. London: Office for Standards in Education.

Office for Standards in Education (Ofsted) (2004a) *National Summary Data for Primary Schools*. Online at http://www.ofsted.gov.uk/assets/3443.pdf (accessed 3 July 2007).

Office for Standards in Education (Ofsted) (2004b) *National Summary Data for Secondary Schools*. Online at http://www.ofsted.gov.uk/assets/3500.pdf (accessed 3 July 2007).

Office for Standards in Education (Ofsted) (2004c) *The Key Stage 3 Strategy: Evaluation of the Third Year*. London: Office for Standards in Education.

Office for Standards in Education (Ofsted) (2006) *The Annual Report of Her Majesty's Chief Inspector of Schools 2005/06*. London: Office for Standards in Education.

Office for Standards in Education (Ofsted) (2007) *The Foundation Stage: A Survey of 144 Settings*. London: Office for Standards in Education.

Orton, A. (1992) *Learning Mathematics: Issues, Theory and Classroom Practice*. London: Cassell.

Pimm, D. (1989) *Speaking Mathematically: Communication in Mathematics Classrooms*. London: Routledge.

Poustie, J. (2001) *Mathematics Solutions: An Introduction to Dyscalculia: How to Teach Children and Adults Who Have Specific Learning Difficulties in Mathematics Pt. B (Finding the Key to Specific Learning Difficulties)*. Taunton: Next Generation.

Qualifications and Curriculum Authority (QCA) (2002) *Guidance on Teaching the Gifted and Talented*. Online at http://www.nc.uk.net/gt/mathematics/index.htm (accessed September 2007).

Qualifications and Curriculum Authority (QCA) (2004) *Mathematics: 2002/3 Annual Report on Curriculum and Assessment*. Online at http://www.qca.org.uk/7404.html (accessed 10 June 2007).

Qualifications and Curriculum Authority (QCA) (2006) *The 11–19 Reform Programme*. Online at http://www.qca.org.uk/qca_4071.aspx (accessed 1 September 2007).

Rowland, T. (2002) 'Language issues in mathematics', in L. Haggarty (ed.), *Aspects of Teaching Secondary Mathematics: Perspectives on Practice*. London: RoutledgeFalmer.

Rudel, R.G. (1988) *Assessment of Developmental Learning Disorders: A Neuropsychological Approach*. New York: Basic Books.

Sharp, B. (2004) *Meeting SEN in the Curriculum – Maths*. London: David Fulton.

Shuard, H. and Rothery, A. (1984) *Children Reading Mathematics*. London: John Murray.

Skemp, R. (1982) 'Communicating mathematics: surface structures and deep structures', *Visible Language*, 16(3): 281–8.

Stellenbosch, South Africa: The Programme Committee of the 22nd PME Conference.

Training and Development Agency for Schools (TDA) (2007) *Professional Standards for Teachers: Why Sit Still in your Career?*. London: Training and Development Agency for Schools.

Yeo, D. (2002) *Dyslexia, Dyspraxia and Mathematics*. London: Whurr.

8 TEACHING DIFFERENT TOPICS

This chapter:

- reviews mental methods of calculation
- summarizes how the standard written algorithms for calculation are built up through informal methods
- addresses issues in the teaching of fractions and decimals
- shows how arithmetical ideas are generalized in algebra, and discusses why pupils find some aspects of algebra difficult
- reviews ways of teaching geometrical ideas
- reviews some of the difficulties in teaching measures
- discusses issues in the teaching of probability and statistics
- argues that the process aspects of mathematics need to be taught and assessed systematically in order to help pupils develop transferable skills.

NUMBER

One of the important things to learn as a potential mathematics teacher is that the way you learnt to do some mathematics many years ago is probably only one of several possible methods. Consequently, you need to broaden your knowledge about all the different methods that are available so that you can make a professional judgement about which method to use. The starkest example of this is in basic calculation methods: addition, subtraction, multiplication and division of whole numbers. Here are simple pieces of mathematics that you have learnt many years ago, but now you need to look at them with new eyes. There is much to learn before you are ready to provide full support to the range of pupils that you will meet.

The first distinction that you need to make is between the way you want to develop the pupils' mental methods, written methods and calculator methods. A key principle is that pupils at all ages should be encouraged to make sensible decisions about when each might be appropriate.

MENTAL METHODS

Mental methods are important in the understanding of calculations. Pupils in the early years of school, before they start with written methods, are taught to use mental methods with small numbers. Mental methods are used to emphasize the relationships between the operations. For example, pupils performing $16 + 5$ need to understand that if they subtract 5 from their answer, they get back to 16. With more difficult calculations, mental methods illustrate the flexibility of calculation strategies. In the case of mental addition, consider the number of (sensible) ways that you could choose to calculate $59 + 47$:

- $50 + 40 + 9 + 7$
- $59 + 40 + 7$
- $59 + 7 + 40$
- $59 + 1 + 46$

This list is clearly not exhaustive, and you can probably think of several alternatives that could be added. What is interesting is that 'front-end' methods tend to be more efficient in mental calculation. This means dealing with the biggest part of the numbers first (the tens digits in the example above), and contrasts with most of the standard written algorithms, which start with the units digits. The second general characteristic of efficient mental methods is that they retain the place value of the digits, partitioning 59 into 50 and 9 rather than 5 and 9. While it is possible to perform mental calculations as mental pictures of the standard written methods, this tends to be inefficient – the effort required is large and the probability of obtaining the correct result is small, compared with other methods.

Sometimes, particular numbers in the question suggest particular methods for mental calculation. One example is when adding two numbers that are close together ('near doubles') such as $39 + 38$. In these cases, in addition to the methods listed above, there is also the method of doubling 39 and subtracting 1 (or doubling 38 and adding 1). Another example of a special case is when multiplying. While the standard mental method for multiplying 24 by 6 would be to calculate six twenties and add on six fours, an alternative for multiplying 24 by 8 would be to double, double and double again.

Confidence with mental methods leads to a general confidence with numbers. The aim is for pupils to have a feel for numbers, and this can be promoted through structured practice in progressively more difficult mental skills. Where pupils have an inflexible approach to calculation, they tend to ignore mental methods. This can lead to entirely inappropriate methods, such as using a calculator to work out 24×2 or using a written method for calculating 2000–1.

Whatever age the pupils are, mental methods will be slow to develop without specific teacher intervention. Pupils who lack efficient strategies will only acquire those strategies through discussion and a structured programme of support. One standard activity that is useful for developing mental skills is the 'think of a number' type, where you can easily tailor the required operations to a particular sort of calculation and to the abilities of the group.

WRITTEN METHODS

You probably perform the four operations by applying the algorithms that you have been taught, but you may not have given any thought as to why the algorithms work. As the teacher, you need to make sure that you do understand why they work. Phrases that you may have used for many years, like 'carry one', 'borrow ten', or 'add a nought', need to be deconstructed. Finally, you need to take time to learn about the way that number is introduced in the primary school, so that you have some understanding of the pupils' prior experience.

The first thing that you need to understand about number work in primary schools is that the standard algorithms are taught much later than you may remember learning them yourself. This is so that pupils can build up a feeling for number before learning a set of steps that in themselves do not help understanding. The emphasis early on is for pupils to use mental methods and informal written methods. Only when they are ready to move on are they introduced to the formal written methods of calculation. The informal methods are not intended to replace formal methods; formal methods have the advantage of being quick and efficient. The National Strategy aims for the great majority of pupils to finish Key Stage 2 with an efficient method of written calculation for each operation, which they can use with confidence and understanding (DfES, 2007). As a secondary school teacher, you will need the skills to take less able pupils back to a stage that they are happy with. For these pupils, the stage that they understand may be the informal stage.

One thing that the informal methods have in common is that they tend to be written horizontally rather than vertically, and they retain the value of the numbers at all times. This means that in their early years, pupils are more familiar with 46 + 25 than they are with the column layout:

$$\begin{array}{r} 46 \\ + \underline{25} \\ \hline \end{array}$$

It also means that the methods that they use never refer to the 46 as being made up of a four and a six; it is always referred to as being a forty and a six. Compare this with the standard written algorithms, which routinely 'digitize' the numbers, giving the impression that numbers are a collection of digits, rather than a number that uses a place value system.

For addition, a great deal of early work is related to the number line, and to the partitioning of the numbers. Consider our addition question 46 + 25. Pupils are taught to use an expanded written method that uses a partitioning of one or both numbers. For example, a partitioning that might be useful is 40 + 6 + 20 + 5 (as could be used in mental calculation). Alternatively, a partitioning of the second number that makes use of a 'bridge' number may be easier to calculate. Thus 46 + 25 could be calculated as 46 + 4 + 21, using the value 50 as the bridge. On the number line this is represented by Figure 8.1.

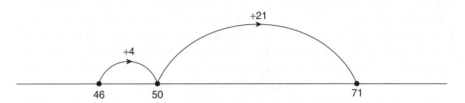

Figure 8.1   46 + 25 by bridging

Of course, Figure 8.1 could be broken down further to show an extra step going from 50 to 70 (adding 20) and then from 70 to 71 (adding 1). Note that, although this may seem like very trivial work, it can be applied in more advanced work. Where pupils have a secure understanding of informal methods, they are able to apply them to more difficult numbers, such as decimals.

Subtraction is characterized by the two concepts of counting on and taking away. The two concepts give rise to different representations on the number line. As with addition, the taking away method often bridges through a multiple of ten (Figure 8.2), and looks similar to Figure 8.1, but working from the high number to the low number. The counting on method uses the number line differently. The example 84 − 27 would be represented by putting both 27 and 84 on the number line, and counting on in convenient jumps.

The expanded written methods are similar to those for addition. For example, the calculation 56 − 29 can be 56 − 20 − 9, or it can be 50 + 6 − 20 − 9, which then is transformed to 40 + 16 − 20 − 9 = 20 + 7 = 27.

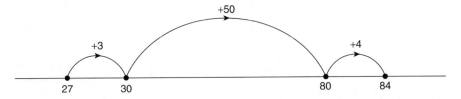

Figure 8.2 84 − 27 by counting on

The move towards a more formal written method for subtraction is made using an expanded layout, where 56 − 29 is written as

50 + 6
−20 + 9,

which then transforms to

40 + 16
−20 + 9,

This expanded layout is then eventually refined into the abbreviated version that will be familiar to you. Make sure that you fit in with the language used in primary schools, and avoid referring to individual digits (and hence removing their place value). In the calculation,

56
−25,
 31

you should articulate the process as 'six take away five' and then 'fifty take away twenty' (not 'five take away two'). (In a similar way, when adding, you should 'carry ten' or 'carry one hundred', rather than 'carry one'.)

Multiplication is first introduced as repeated addition. Unfortunately, some pupils never get beyond this limited interpretation of what multiplication means. These pupils tend to calculate 26 x 12 by writing out 26 twelve times and adding up. But multiplication is more than just repeated addition. Repeated addition cannot explain a scaling up by a non-integer scale factor, or any multiplication of two non-integer values.

The most common expanded method of multiplication involves drawing a grid (Figure 8.3). The illustration here is a fairly difficult example (one that would need long multiplication), but the same principle is used for simple examples as well, with a gradual build up to calculations such as this. The calculation 67 × 23 is written as

x	20	3
60		
7		

Figure 8.3 67 × 23 by the grid method

Within the grid, pupils enter the results of multiplying 60 by 20, 7 by 20, 60 by 3, and 7 by 3. They then add the results to give the answer. The grid method is so common that you are sure to encounter secondary school pupils who use it. It is your professional decision whether and when you encourage these pupils to move on to a more efficient method.

The link to the standard long multiplication layout is achieved by using the expanded layout:

```
   67
 × 23
 1200    60 × 20
  140     7 × 20
  180    60 × 3
   21     7 × 3
 1541
```

Only when pupils are comfortable with this expanded layout are they introduced to the shortened, standard, layout for long multiplication.

There are two standard written algorithms for performing division calculations. The most common is the short division method, but the long division method, which sets out the steps more fully, is also in common use. The most numerate people switch happily between the two methods, depending on the size of the numbers involved. You need to become familiar with both layouts, because the pupils you teach may be using either method, and you need to understand any errors that they make. You also need to think about how the standard division algorithm works.

Consider the calculation 522 ÷ 6. Before reading on, it is suggested that you take a pen and paper and write out your solution to this. Then think through how you could explain the steps that you have carried out. By this, I do not mean can you explain what processes you have applied, but whether you can explain your steps mathematically. This will probably be harder than you expect.

In trying to make the algorithm make sense, again we avoid treating the number 522 as a collection of digits, 5, 2, and 2. We retain all place values throughout any explanation. One explanation of how the algorithm works is as follows:

522 can be partitioned as 520 + 2, but 520 is not a multiple of 6. We look for a multiple of ten (less than 520) that six will go into exactly. The number to choose is 480, so we re-partition 520 + 2 as 480 + 42. The division now follows easily: dividing 480 by 6 and dividing 42 by 6 to get 80 + 7, and an answer of 87.

This process is summarized in the expanded layout given below.

$$80 + 7$$
$$6\overline{)522} = 6\overline{)520} + 2 = 6\overline{)480 + 42}$$

When pupils are comfortable with this expanded layout, they can be introduced to the more efficient layout of short division. In this way, the short division method is explained mathematically before pupils attempt to apply the standard algorithm to whole sets of questions.

There is another written method for division that you need to be familiar with. This is the method known as chunking – a method that is in common use in primary schools, and one that you will certainly see in your work with secondary school pupils. Chunking is an extension of the idea of division as repeated subtraction, as in vocalizing 522 ÷ 6 as 'how many sixes are there in 522?'. The layout for chunking looks like this:

$$6\overline{)522}$$

360	6 × 60
162	
120	6 × 20
42	
42	6 × 7
0	

60 + 20 + 7 = 87

As you can see, the chunking method requires the repeated subtraction of multiples of 6. The efficiency of the method depends on the size of the multiples that you select; the layout given above would look different depending on the size of the 'chunk' that you chose to subtract at any stage. In general, subtracting large chunks is more efficient than subtracting small chunks. The chunking method does not link in well with the partitioning method that leads to short or long division; it is simply an alternative informal method that helps pupils to understand what division means.

We have discussed written methods for each of the four standard operations. All the work follows the same progression, summarized by the following steps:

- the foundations for written work are provided by extensive mental work, initially with small numbers, and building up a knowledge of number relationships
- informal written methods, possibly based on jottings, are gradually refined into more compact and efficient methods
- expanded written methods (based on expanded versions of the standard algorithms)
- standard written methods
- extension to larger numbers.

The role of the calculator is much reduced in this framework. Recommendations from the National Strategy (DfEE, 1999a) are that the calculator should be introduced only in Year 5, once pupils are familiar with mental methods and written methods. In the secondary school, you should try to retain the emphasis on mental methods, providing regular opportunities for pupils to recall number facts and apply them in varied situations. You should also promote the links between adding and subtracting, multiplication and division, stressing the notion of inverse operations, doing and undoing, which helps to lay the foundations for algebra.

Point for reflection

Take time to practise the methods described here, so that they become familiar to you. Check that you can verbalize why a particular algorithm works by trying to explain it to a fellow trainee.

A calculator can be used in many more ways than performing a calculation. The drawbacks of using a calculator are perhaps obvious, but consider the positive aspects of using a calculator, particularly as a tool for learning.

FRACTIONS, DECIMALS AND PERCENTAGES

Work on decimals also benefits from an approach that stresses the size of the numbers more than learning routines. This includes mental work, where pupils are encouraged to respond to addition and subtraction questions such as

$3.1 + 0.1$, $3.0 - 0.1$, $4.9 + 0.01$, $5 - 0.5$, $6 - 0.01$,

and general 'size of numbers' questions, such as

Give me a number between 3 and 4
Give me a number half way between 6 and 7

Give me a number between 6.1 and 6.2
Show the number 1.65 on a number line
Estimate 2.5×4.01
What is the approximate answer to $71.8 \div 8.9$?

In multiplication and division too, the emphasis on pupils understanding the routines that they employ should be retained. Many adults recall being taught to multiply two decimal numbers by applying a routine:

- Ignore the decimal point.
- Multiply the numbers.
- Count the number of decimal digits in the question.
- Count in that number of places from the right in the answer, and put the decimal point back in.

The procedure clearly produces the correct answer, but it does not teach any mathematics. Pupils who learn to follow the procedure are no more knowledgeable about number than they were previously. The routine is divorced from all other mathematics that has been learnt elsewhere, so to apply it correctly, you need to remember it exactly. Teaching this procedure is not recommended!

A more mathematical approach is to write out the steps in a logical way. One alternative is to use the grid method for multiplication, which might be appropriate for some groups of pupils. The more formal standard alternative is to manipulate the numbers. For example, 2.3×0.2 can be written:

$$\begin{aligned} 2.3 \times 0.2 &= (23 \div 10) \times (2 \div 10) \\ &= 23 \times 2 \div 100 \\ &= 46 \div 100 \\ &= 0.46 \end{aligned}$$

This approach uses steps that can be justified mathematically, and its success depends on understanding rather than memory. A similar approach is usually used for division of decimals. For example, the calculation $2.48 \div 0.4$ is expressed as:

$$2.48 \div 0.4 = \frac{2.48}{0.4} = \frac{2.48 \times 10}{0.4 \times 10} = \frac{24.8}{4} = 6.2$$

Fractions often cause difficulties, possibly because they can be used to represent different things. For example, sometimes a fraction is a part of a

Table 8.1 Progression in using fractions

Level	
3	Use simple fractions that are several parts of a whole. Recognize when two simple fractions are equivalent
4	Recognize approximate fractions of a whole
5	Calculate fractional parts of quantities and measurements
6	Evaluate one number as a fraction of another. Add and subtract fractions. Multiply an integer by a fraction; divide an integer by a fraction
7	Multiply a fraction by a fraction; divide a fraction by a fraction
8	Substitute fractions into algebraic formulae

Source: adapted from DfEE 1999b; 2001

whole (a quarter of a cake) and sometimes it is part of a set (a quarter of the people). Sometimes it is simply a number – a position on the number line. Progression in learning about fractions is summarized in Table 8.1 (levels are approximate, and may depend on the complexity of the calculation).

The equivalence of fractions, decimals and percentages should be emphasized whenever possible. For example, when teaching calculating a fraction of a quantity, it is good to teach it alongside calculating a percentage of a quantity. The two pieces of mathematics are entirely equivalent, and need to be presented as such if pupils are to grasp the point.

Another useful activity relating to fractions is to ask pupils to match up different ways of representing the same quantity, so emphasizing the links between the different representations. The Sharing Cakes activity below illustrates the idea; the cards shown are an abbreviated version of an activity on the Maths4Life website. In the full version, there are 12 different fractions, each represented in four different ways; our abbreviated version shows the flavour of the activity, but shows just four of the fractions.

SHARING CAKES

The activity includes 4 sets of cards (Set A to Set D), all of which have to be cut up and matched. On the diagram cards (Set C), pupils indicate each fraction by shading parts of whole cakes, or by drawing dividing lines between the cakes on the sets of cakes.

Set A

5 cakes shared between 4 people	12 cakes shared between 4 people
1 cake shared between 2 people	1 cake shared between 3 people

Set B

$12 \div 4$	$5 \div 4$
$1 \div 2$	$1 \div 3$

Set C

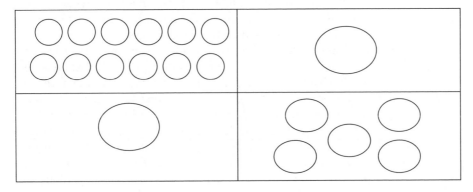

Set D

$\frac{1}{2}$	$1\frac{1}{4}$
$\frac{1}{3}$	3

ALGEBRA

Algebra poses its own problems, but should be linked with number work wherever possible. For example, $a + a + a + a = 4a$ is easily linked with $5 + 5 + 5 + 5 = 4 \times 5$. Similarly, the result of multiplying 4 by 6 and then adding 1 is different from adding 1 to 4, then multiplying by 6; this corresponds with the difference between the algebraic expressions $6x+1$ and $6(x+1)$. The second important principle in teaching algebra is to present algebra as something that is useful and powerful, rather than obscure and pointless. This means selecting activities that generate a need for algebra, so that the algebra is used as a tool. It also means reducing the time spent practising algebraic skills out of context.

Looking at patterns in a range of contexts provides an important introduction to algebra. One simple context is finding, extending and then generalizing patterns in number sequences. Number sequences that are arithmetic progressions (such as 9, 13, 17, 21, 25, …) are easy to continue for the next few terms, but it is a much harder question to find the hundredth term or the thousandth term. This gives a simple context for the introduction of algebra; algebra is clearly helpful in giving an expression for the nth term, which can then be used to answer the problem set. Another rich source of patterns is a number square, where the relationships between numbers can be expressed algebraically. For example, for any position on the number square x, the number underneath it is always $x + 10$, and the number to its left is always $x - 1$. Some quite advanced algebraic ideas can be introduced through activities based on the number square.

Skills of solving equations need to be built up quite systematically. A key teaching principle in this build up is to provide opportunities for pupils to express generality (identified in the National Strategy guidance – DfES, 2004). Pupils are more likely to understand the meaning of algebraic expressions if they have experience of generating some for themselves, rather than seeing algebra as an external feature, imposed upon them from outside. As Mason (2002: 118) says, 'doing someone else's algebra … is greatly facilitated and motivated by generating one's own algebra first'. Pupils' experience of building up expressions also helps them to understand the process of undoing that is so important in solving equations.

The ability to solve equations depends heavily on pupils feeling 'at home' with algebra. If each step is uncertain, then pupils' uncertainty about what they are doing simply builds up as they work through a multi-step solution. This facility with algebraic expressions can be built up through encouraging pupils to express algebraic expressions and relationships in as many ways as they can (DfES, 2004), and identifying where expressions are equivalent. One aspect of this, the equivalence of the relationships

$$a + b = c, \; c = a + b, \; c - a = b, \; b = c - a, \; a = c - b, \; c - b = a,$$

is easier to achieve if the pupils have done similar work when dealing with numbers (for example the equivalence of $10 = 6 + 4$, and $10 - 6 = 4$). Pupils are more likely to understand the most efficient operation to perform on an equation if they have experienced all sorts of different transformations, some of which lead to simpler statements and some of which do not lead to any simplification at all. For example, the equation $3x + 1 = 10$ can be rewritten in a huge number of ways. $3x + 2 = 11$; $4x + 1 = 10 + x$; $3x - 2 = 7$ are all valid, and pupils should be encouraged to explore these formulations before encountering the fact that $3x = 9$ is the most useful formulation.

Simultaneous equations offer a range of different solution methods. To the 'normal' two methods of substitution and elimination can be added solution by inspection, graphical solutions and solutions using matrices. As part of their experience of algebra, all pupils should first experience solving simultaneous equations using common-sense methods (for example, by identifying values of x and y that make the two equations $x + y = 30$, and $x - y = 2$). When they are confident in this, you can introduce the elimination method, with possible extensions to the method of substitution for the most able pupils (see Chambers, 2007; French, 2005; Jagger, 2005).

When teaching pupils to simplify algebraic expressions by collecting like terms, you need to avoid a common pitfall. This pitfall is known as fruit salad algebra, and comes about through the following explanation:

We need to add together the two expressions $5a + 4b$ and $6a + 2b$.
Think of the first expression as representing 5 apples and 4 bananas, and the second expression as representing 6 apples and 2 bananas.
Apples and bananas are different things, so we have to add them up separately.
If we add up what we have, then we have 11 apples and 6 bananas. That is $11a + 6b$.

You have probably heard explanations along those lines. The reason that you should avoid it is because reading $4b$ as 'four bananas' suggests that b is simply a label, whereas in fact it represents a number. In algebra, b can stand for the number of bananas, the weight of a banana, the cost of one banana, or several other things, but it is not just b for bananas. Apart from being incorrect, if you teach that you have to add the apples and the bananas separately, then you run into difficulties in explaining the meaning of ab or a^2.

The manipulation of algebraic terms is often thought of as a dull activity, with pupils working through long exercises of similar questions. It does not have to be so. There are several published activities that present pupils with the opportunities to manipulate algebra as part of a puzzle or piece of group work. One example is the pyramid presentation, where pupils fill in the missing boxes by adding together the two expressions immediately above. An example of this is shown in Figure 8.4.

Fill in the missing expressions:

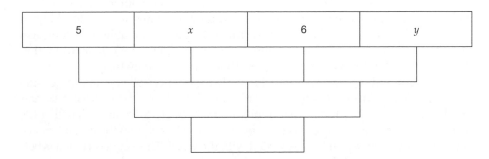

Figure 8.4 Pyramid presentation for algebra

In this case, the entries in the second row should be $5 + x$, $x + 6$, $6 + y$. The third row should read $2x + 11$ and $x + y + 12$, and the final entry should be $3x + y + 23$. This is a relatively simple example; much more difficult examples can be generated by giving starting information in boxes other than the top row.

A second type of activity involves matching equivalent expressions, for example in a dominoes activity. One example of this is where each domino contains an expression in factorized form, and a different expression in expanded form. The task (usually in groups) is to lay out the dominoes in a line, matching the equivalent expressions on adjacent dominoes. An excellent piece of software, called Tarsia, helps you to create the dominoes for this sort of activity. It is available on a CD from the Standards Unit, or through following the link on the website for this book.

Another example that helps pupils to become more comfortable with algebraic expression is to write a simple expression in many different ways. This is an open-ended activity, so it may be wise to introduce a limit of, say, 10 different ways of writing an expression such as $3n$. To the obvious $3 \times n$ and $n + n + n$ can be added such expressions as $4n - n$, $3n + 6 - 6$, $6n/2$, with enormous scope for different answers.

Research suggests that pupils find work on algebra easier if they are finding the value of a letter, where the letter represents a specific value (Küchemann, 1981). They find it more difficult to work with algebraic expressions where the letter represents a generalized number (for example, in manipulating algebraic expressions). In a similar way, pupils are sometimes uncomfortable with leaving an algebraic expression as the solution to an equation (Tall and Thomas, 1991). This results in the equation $x + a = 12$ being much more difficult than $x + 4 = 12$, although the structures are clearly identical. This difficulty is caused by what is seen as a lack of closure; pupils expect to be able to give a numerical answer, and cannot do so in cases such as these.

Hart (1981) associates difficulties with algebra with stages of cognitive development; if pupils cannot understand algebra, it is because they are not ready. Macgregor and Stacey (1997) provide evidence that this may not be the whole picture. They report that pupils' errors in algebra can often be characterized in one of three ways: intuition and guessing, analogies with other ways that symbols are used, and false generalizations that may be rooted in poor teaching or poor teaching materials. For example, many pupils are unable to distinguish between letters used as labels to represent a person (person A), an abbreviation (the shorthand m for metres), or a quantity (a number of metres).

Macgregor and Stacey also argue that early experiences of algebra can provide opportunities for incorrect generalizations that can be difficult to overcome in later work. Specifically, they report that pupils are more likely to retain a view that the letter is an abbreviated word if the teacher (or book) has chosen the initial letter of a word to represent a number associated with the word. This suggests that it is better to represent the number of pence or the number of cars as x rather than p or c.

GEOMETRY

Geometry is field of mathematics that offers enormous potential for bringing the subject alive. The visual nature of geometry, its rich history and culturally diverse background, and its links with art and design, all provide opportunities to make geometry lessons interesting and stimulating. The potential for exploring mathematical ideas is enormous.

There has been concern about the position of geometry in the school curriculum. The report *Teaching and Learning Geometry 11–19* (Royal Society, 2001) affirmed the importance of geometry as a branch of mathematics, and warned against what was seen as an increasing marginalization of the subject. As a result, between 1998 and 2007, geometrical reasoning played a slightly increased role in revisions of the National Curriculum.

It is generally accepted that pupils' appreciation of geometry develops from global recognition of the whole shape to the more analytical understanding of properties and relationships (Bell et al., 1983). In other words, pupils can identify a triangle before they can explain what makes it a triangle.

A commonly quoted theory of the development of geometrical understanding is the van Hiele model. In the van Hiele model, pupils progress through stages:

Pupils identify shapes by considering the whole picture. They can identify a square, but cannot say why it is a square.

Pupils begin to identify particular properties of shapes. They know that a square has four equal sides.

Pupils can combine properties of shapes to give precise definitions, and relate shapes to other shapes. They know that what makes a shape a square is the fact that it has four equal sides and four right angles, or that it is a four-sided shape with four lines of symmetry. They know that a square is a special kind of rectangle.

Pupils apply formal deductive arguments (for example in proof).

Within the van Hiele structure, language plays an important part, and for this reason (and others) the structure can never be seen as an entirely one-way route. Although the levels describe development, they are helpful to the teacher only in the sense that they show a general direction for the learning. An understanding of the levels may be helpful in identifying how a pupil has taken a step backwards before moving forwards, but it is difficult to organize teaching that is located entirely within one of the levels, and therefore it is difficult to manage the progression.

For an overview of geometry, it is useful to hold on to three central themes that run through the curriculum. These three themes are invariance, symmetry and transformation. Invariance is an important principle of geometrical investigation; we can find that an angle drawn in a semicircle measures 90°, but the interesting fact is that it remains 90° wherever on the circumference we locate the third vertex. Symmetry is central to the study of shapes, and has important applications in science. It helps us to classify shapes, understand their properties and describe them in simple terms. Transformation is the key to the study of how shapes change when we operate on them. It has important links with algebra in the idea of inverse operations, and strong links with art and design (for example, frieze patterns).

Figure 8.5 Simple tessellation of rectangles

An interesting application of transformation is in the topic of tessellations. For example, let us consider a very simple tessellation of rectangles (Figure 8.5).

We know that the basic shape, the rectangle, fits the tessellation. What is more interesting is that we can transform the rectangle in such a way as to guarantee that the new shape will also form a tessellation (Figure 8.6).

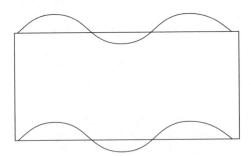

Figure 8.6 Distortion to two sides

The top side of the rectangle has been transformed into a wiggly line, and then this transformation has been copied onto the bottom side of the rectangle.

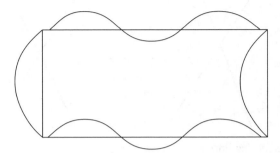

Figure 8.7 Distortion to all four sides

Doing something similar to the left and right of the rectangle, we obtain the shape in Figure 8.7. (The original sides of the rectangle have been left in for clarity.) Although not very artistic, the resultant shape is one that will fit together to form a tessellation, and with some artistic ingenuity, could be made to look more attractive. For some impressive examples of the artistic application of tessellations, see work by Seymour and Britton (1989) and Ernst (1985), which discuss, among other things, the work of the artist M.C. Escher, and demonstrate some of the creative aspects of geometry.

One useful approach to the development of geometrical reasoning is to use visualizations, mental images of mathematical situations, and encourage pupils to make links between their private images and the symbolism of a mathematical diagram. Examples of this approach are provided by the Open University (1992a) and the National Strategy guidance (DfES, 2002). Visualization activities help to strengthen the hierarchy of ideas that pupils encounter in their geometrical work. The idea is that pupils develop a 'chain of reasoning', where they build up their understanding using images and language. In visualization tasks, pupils are encouraged to form mental images of diagrams, and to transform them mentally. By using mental images, pupils analyse features of their geometrical 'pictures', identifying particular properties. They also are encouraged to use language to describe what they can see.

Another feature of this approach is to put emphasis on building up geometrical diagrams from smaller components. Again, we encourage pupils to focus on parts of a diagram, rather than the whole picture. They see the angles made by an intersecting pair of lines, and then see how this element

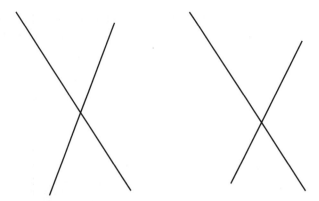

Figure 8.8 Intersecting lines as two diagrams

of the diagram joins with other elements to form the full diagram. This is the opposite way round from presenting the whole diagram, and trying to pick out the important features. For example, in dealing with corresponding angles, the approach is to show two sets of intersecting lines (Figure 8.8).

The two intersections are then moved (easily demonstrated on a computer screen), and combined to form a single diagram (Figure 8.9). Corresponding angles can be identified. The discussion then focuses on when these corresponding angles will be equal. It is hoped that pupils will see that the two crossing lines need to be parallel.

The focus of this approach is to help pupils to acquire the skills of analysing information that is presented geometrically. Through experience of building up the diagram, pupils are more able to see how a diagram needs breaking down to identify important features. Compare this with the approach to algebra described above, where we claimed that pupils would be more able to solve equations if they had experience of writing (building up) their own algebraic expressions first.

You need to consider two other features of pupils' learning in geometry. The first is that orientation and other general surface features can mean more to pupils than you might expect. Because their introduction to naming shapes often associates a single representation of a shape with the name of the shape, some pupils find it difficult to accept that a different-looking shape has the same name (Kerslake, 1979). Pupils find difficulty identifying the shapes in Figure 8.10, the first two because of the orientation, and the third because of its 'unusual' appearance.

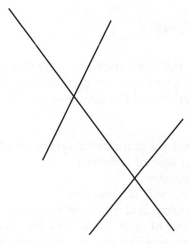

Figure 8.9   Towards a definition of corresponding angles

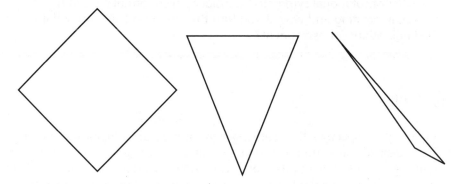

Figure 8.10   Shapes that pupils find more difficult to identify

The second difficulty is that we require pupils to understand our conventions in diagrams (Open University, 1992b). For example, when we draw a triangle, we often want pupils to understand that it is a representative of all triangles. We want pupils to understand generality from a particular example. The way that dynamic geometry software can present pupils with a continuously changing diagram is extremely helpful here.

Point for reflection

Consider ways that you can make your pupils more creative in their geometrical work. As you do so, try the following task for yourself. (You are given the clue that two of the questions cannot be done.)

Draw a shape that has:

1. No lines of symmetry and rotational symmetry of order 2.
2. Six sides, and two lines of symmetry.
3. Three lines of symmetry.
4. Six sides, and three lines of symmetry.
5. Two lines of symmetry, and rotational symmetry of order 4.
6. Rotational symmetry of order 3, but no lines of symmetry.
7. Three lines of symmetry, but no rotational symmetry.
8. Rotational symmetry of order 4, but no lines of symmetry.

Consider whether the task was more difficult than being given some shapes and being asked to draw in the lines of symmetry and to identify the order of rotational symmetry. Consider which formulation of the task is more interesting and why. If you turn the task round like this, what are the implications for assessment?

MEASURES

The curriculum specifies the metric system of measures, including the more difficult ideas of compound measures such as speed or density, and the imperial units in common use. Pupils should learn how the metric measures relate to each other, and how they relate to the common imperial units. It is also important to give pupils a feel for measures, so that they can use appropriate units and estimate accurately. To do this effectively, you should develop a range of benchmarks that you can use to help pupils with comparisons. For example, pupils should understand that a tonne is 1000 kg, and that this is approximately the mass of a small car. A few facts and figures at your fingertips (such as the mass of a paperclip, or the height of a door) can make a lesson on measures much more effective.

One of the difficulties in teaching measures is the large range of different measures that are in common use. Although schools have concentrated on teaching metric measures for over 40 years, society in the UK has never seemed entirely comfortable with metric measures, and many people still think of their height in feet and inches, and their weight in stones and pounds. The choice of which measure to use can be surprisingly difficult. When a large squid was seen close to the British Isles in February 2007, British newspapers had to choose how to report its weight in terms that would mean something to their readers. This choice led to them reporting its weight variously as 450 kg, 71 stone, 990 lb, nearly half a ton and nearly half a tonne (Miles, 2007).

STATISTICS

Statistics occupies an unusual position in the mathematics curriculum. It is regarded by some as a subject in its own right (and exists as a separate GCSE subject). Moreover, many skills in statistics are used (and taught) in other subjects; for example, data presentation is needed in geography, and the interpretation of tables and charts is needed in several subjects. The particular strengths of teaching statistics are:

- the cross-curricular nature of mathematics is strengthened
- it is easy to provide examples where statistics are used in contexts outside of school
- the handling data cycle (planning, collecting data, processing the data, interpreting the results) closely links with mathematical problem-solving skills.

Statistics is the least objective of the branches of mathematics, in that collecting and interpreting data is usually subject to personal preferences. Because of this, it is important to realize that pupils will bring to their study of statistics opinions and intuitive assumptions that may not coincide with what you expect. Shaughnessy (1992) discusses this from the viewpoint of the teacher, indicating how teachers bring to the lesson their own experience and attitudes. As a result, some feel uncomfortable in comparison with their security in the impersonal rules of arithmetic or theorems of geometry.

The study of probability requires that pupils understand theoretical probability based on equally likely outcomes. It also requires that they understand that experiments can give estimates of that theoretical probability, based on the relative frequency of each outcome. Theory tells us that this relative frequency will tend towards the probability as the number of trials gets very large. This is quite a difficult idea, but one that is fundamental to the link between theory and experiment.

Pupils' notions of probability are interesting. Some believe that throwing a six with a single die is less likely than throwing other numbers (Amir and Williams, 1994). Others believe that random events should have outcomes that appear random (Shaughnessy, 1992). An example from the national lottery illustrates the point. Theory tell us that any set of six numbers is equally likely to turn up, but far more people choose 'randomly' spaced numbers than numbers that form a clear pattern. In fact a discussion of how likely it is to get an outcome of 1, 2, 3, 4, 5, 6 is an interesting way to illustrate how unlikely it is to win.

The structure of the National Curriculum suggests that understanding probability is based on an intuitive understanding of the terms 'chance' and 'fair'. Interestingly, pupils' perceptions of probability are found to depend on pupils' belief system more than any other factor (Amir and Williams, 1994). Pupils' belief in the laws of probability is affected by whether they believe in an overriding structure to life and being, or if they believe in superstition. As a result, in planning your lessons, you should take into account the likely range in the pupils' cultural and spiritual backgrounds, which contribute to a subjective view of probability and chance.

Jones et al. (1997) propose a framework for assessing the understanding of probability, based on the four constructs: sample space, probability of an event, probability comparisons and conditional probability. They identify four levels of understanding of each construct. For example, in considering pupils' understanding of conditional probability, the following descriptors are provided (summarized and paraphrased):

Level 1   When an outcome has occurred, the pupil overgeneralizes and assumes that it will always occur, or possibly that it will not occur again

Level 2   The pupil begins to realize that the previous outcome may affect the next result in a non-replacement situation

Level 3   The pupil can calculate probabilities in a non-replacement situation

Level 4   The pupil has a deep understanding, including being able to distinguish between dependent and independent events.

The framework for probability is not as widely known as the van Hiele levels in geometry, but it provides a similarly useful structure for describing the progression in pupils' understanding.

The focus of statistical enquiry gives you plenty of scope for choice. As mentioned above, statistical enquiry offers opportunities for cross-curricular work that are often not available in other mathematical areas. The first factor to consider in choosing a focus for work in statistics is whether the topic is interesting. This might seem an obvious thing to say, but it is surprising how often a statistical lesson focuses on a banal investigation or, worse, becomes a lesson on how to draw a bar chart. It is important to plan lessons so that all data collection has a clear purpose; any survey should be designed to find something out – what is the most popular, whether two factors are connected, what average values can be used, or how much variation there is in the results. A particularly good source of data (and planning for lessons) is the Census at School project, which has examples of data on a range of issues that are of interest to pupils. There are opportunities to contribute data from your own school as well as access data from schools in other countries.

As well as being interesting, statistical enquiries should focus on questions where we genuinely do not know the answer. For example, a survey into the most popular football team is likely to confirm what most pupils know anyway. In addition, you need to think about the likely responses very carefully, since too many different responses can lead to data that is meaningless and very difficult to analyse. Finally, you need to consider issues of sensitivity, so details about family backgrounds or pupils' weights, for example, are best avoided.

Point for reflection

The place of statistics in the mathematics curriculum was challenged in the conclusions of Adrian Smith's report into post-14 mathematics education (Smith, 2004), which recommended that the QCA undertake a review of where statistics teaching should be located. This review has not led to any change – statistics teaching remains part of the mathematics curriculum – but it has raised an interesting question about whether statistics belongs within mathematics or outside.

Given that GCSE statistics (which has considerable overlap with GCSE mathematics) has been available for many years, consider the advantages of taking statistics out of the mathematics curriculum, and making it entirely a subject in its own right. If the study of statistics became a separate subject at Key Stage 4, reflect on whether it needs to be compulsory for all, whether it should be an option or whether it should be subsumed within the citizenship curriculum. With statistics retained within mathematics, as at present, is the current weighting of approximately 20 per cent of the assessment correct?

MATHEMATICAL PROCESSES

Developing mathematical thinking remains a challenge to all teachers. Mason et al. (1982: 183) refer to mathematical thinking as a process that enables pupils to tackle increasingly complex ideas, through 'specialising, generalising, conjecturing and convincing'. The National Curriculum (QCA, 2007a; 2007b) acknowledges that mathematics is more than just a set of contents, and refers to a set of 'key processes', general mathematical skills that help pupils to apply their knowledge to solve problems and communicate the results. As mentioned in Chapter 2, the programmes of study summarize these processes as:

- representing
- analysing
- interpreting and evaluating
- communicating and reflecting.

Developing these processes lies at the heart of learning mathematics, and teaching that focuses on 'critical thinking and reasoning' makes a significant contribution to high achievement in mathematics (Ofsted, 2006). Research evidence suggests in particular that pupils from educationally disadvantaged backgrounds benefit from a more thinking-oriented curriculum, in terms of both engagement and achievement (Boaler, 1998; Tanner and Jones, 1995). Mathematical processes underpin all the 'content' aspects of the subject, and need developing just as much as specific skills in algebra or skills of mental arithmetic. Their presence in the National Curriculum should be sufficient to discourage teachers from 'teaching for the exam'.

A key weakness of mathematical education is pupils' inability to transfer their knowledge to new situations (Ofsted, 2005). Schools where pupils do demonstrate the ability to transfer their knowledge systematically teach and monitor pupils' progress in the process aspects of mathematics. Problem-solving skills can only develop if the pupils have the opportunity to tackle extended problems and investigative work, and if pupils then exercise a degree of autonomy about how they tackle the work.

Developing the process skills (described by De Geest et al., 2003, as 'guiding learners into mathematical cultural practices') takes planning, and usually includes one or more of the following:

- A list of possible ways to tackle a problem, thus providing scaffolding for the pupils as they think through a problem. These prompts help pupils to structure their problem solving, and in particular structure the way that they communicate their results to others.
- A task where the need for one particular key process is demonstrated. For example, a problem may appear very difficult to solve until simpler cases of the problem are investigated and understood.
- A teaching approach that introduces a problem, and gives pupils a short time to discuss the problem in groups, and plan possible strategies. The teacher then leads the whole class in a discussion of possible approaches, comparing the ideas of different groups, before asking the pupils to tackle the problem in earnest. Tanner and Jones's research (reported in Tanner and Jones, 2000) indicates the success of this teaching strategy.
- A degree of personal reflection is encouraged. This not only requires pupils to assess their own learning, but also asks them to reflect on how they have successfully solved a problem. Through doing this, pupils are able to articulate mathematical approaches that they have used.

The literature contains a wealth of examples of interesting investigational tasks in mathematics (see, for example, Bell et al., 1992; Chambers, 1991a; 1991b; Smile, 2002). If you have never worked on a mathematical investigation, or you are not clear what is meant by developing mathematical ways of working, then consider the following task on the topic of Happy Numbers.

> Pick any number. Square the digits and add together. Repeat, writing down the results at each stage to form a sequence.
>   A starting number that generates a sequence ending in 1 is called a Happy Number. Investigate Happy Numbers.

An extension to the Happy Numbers task is to change the rule from squaring the digits and adding to cubing the digits and adding. Do any numbers generate a sequence that ends in 1?

Point for reflection

For the Happy Numbers task and its extension, think about how you tackled the problem. What mathematical processes did you use? Consider how you could manage tasks such as this in the classroom. What additional demands might this sort of activity place on you in your preparation? Reflect on how you might assess pupils' performance on a task such as this.

EVIDENCE FROM THE RESEARCH

In this chapter, the evidence from the research has been subsumed into the individual sections.

Further reading

Nickson, M. (2000) *Teaching and Learning Mathematics: A Teacher's Guide to Recent Research and its Application.* London: Cassell.

This is an excellent review of research evidence, based on classroom studies. Written for teachers, the book gives the theoretical background to a topic, summarizes relevant research studies and then presents the implications for teaching. The evidence is presented in four sections: number, geometry, statistics and algebra. Within each section, the research is summarized in a roughly chronological way, enabling the reader to pick out the evidence that is particularly relevant to, say, the secondary school pupil. The final chapter discusses general issues relating to classroom research – the nature of research, its value in challenging teachers, and its role in helping pupils to learn.

Prestage, S. and Perks, P. (2001) *Adapting and Extending Secondary Mathematics Activities: New Tasks for Old.* London: David Fulton.

This books focuses on classroom tasks. In particular, it examines how 'standard' tasks can be changed so that they are more challenging and are more effective learning experiences. Sometimes the change can involve the way the problem is presented, with several alternatives offered to the standard list of questions on an exercise. The authors also discuss the availability of new resources, along with the way that resources can change the way that we teach a range of mathematical topics. Overall, the book is a collection of ideas; in reading it, you are sure to pick up some new ideas that you will want to try out.

Tanner, H., Jones, S. and Davies, A. (2002) *Developing Numeracy in the Secondary School.* London: David Fulton.

Despite its title, this book is not solely focused on number work, but covers the whole mathematics curriculum. There is a useful discussion of recent initiatives in mathematics education, together with a review of what constitutes good practice in the classroom. Following that, the authors provide separate practical guides to teaching in number, algebra, geometry and statistics, including a summary of likely misconceptions.

Useful websites

Live links to these sites can be found on the companion website.

Guidance for primary school teachers on how to deliver a structured approach to developing calculation skills, and very helpful for you in understanding pupils' prior experience http://www.standards.dfes.gov.uk/primaryframeworks/mathematics/Papers/Calculation/

The Royal Society website has a www.royalsoc.ac.uk, and its subsidiary the Advisory Committee on Mathematics Education http://www.royalsoc.ac.uk/acme/ contain useful responses to topical issues in mathematics education, together with reports of working groups.

The website www.censusatschool.ntu.ac.uk allows you to register and gain access to a wealth of data from all over the UK, and from several countries around the world.

The Maths4Life website http://www.maths4life.org is aimed at young adult learners, but contains several resources that are useful for your teaching in schools.

References

Amir, G. and Williams, J. (1994) 'The influence of children's culture on their probabilistic thinking', *Proceedings of the 18th International Conference for the Psychology of Mathematics Education*. Vol. 2: 24–31.

Bell, A., Costello, J. and Küchemann, D. (1983) *A Review of Research in Mathematical Education: Part A Research on Learning and Teaching*. Windsor: NFER-Nelson.

Bell, S., Brown, P. and Buckley, S. (1992) *'Hole Numbers' and other practical investigations*. Cambridge: Cambridge University Press.

Boaler, J. (1998) 'Beyond "street mathematics": the challenge of situated cognition', in A. Olivier and K. Newstead (eds), *Proceedings of the 22nd Conference of the International Group for the Psychology of Mathematics Education*, 2–112.

Chambers, P. (1991a) 'Rolling n-gons', *Mathematics in School*, 20(1): 8–11.

Chambers, P. (1991b) 'Rolling n-gons 2', *Mathematics in School*, 20(4): 2–4.

Chambers, P. (2007) 'Solving simultaneous equations intuitively', *Mathematics in School*, 36(1): 30–1.

De Geest, E., Prestage, S. and Watson, A. (2003) 'Thinking in ordinary lessons: what happened when nine teachers believed their failing students could think mathematically', paper presented to the Psychology of Mathematical Education Conference 27, Hawaii, 13–18 July.

Department for Education and Employment (DfEE) (1999a) *The National Numeracy Strategy: Framework for Teaching Mathematics from Reception to Year 6*. London: Department for Education and Employment.

Department for Education and Employment (DfEE) (1999b) *The National Curriculum for England: Mathematics*. London: HMSO.

Department for Education and Employment (DfEE) (2001) *Key Stage 3 National Strategy: Framework for Teaching Mathematics Years 7, 8 and 9*. London: Department for Education and Employment.

Department for Education and Skills (DfES) (2002) *Interacting with Mathematics in Key Stage 3: Year 9 Geometrical Reasoning Mini-pack*. London: Department for Education and Skills.

Department for Education and Skills (DfES) (2004) *Interacting with Mathematics in Key Stage 3: Constructing and Solving Linear Equations*. London: Department for Education and Skills.

Department for Education and Skills (DfES) (2007) *Guidance Paper – Calculation*. Online at the Standards website http://www.standards.dfes.gov.uk/primaryframeworks/ mathematics/Papers/Calculation/ (accessed 10 July 2007).

Ernst, B. (1985) *The Magic Mirror of M. C. Escher*. Diss: Tarquin Publications.

French, D. (2005) 'More comments on the teaching of simultaneous equations', *Mathematics in School*, 34(5): 30–1.

Hart, K.M. (1981) *Children's Understanding of Mathematics 11–16*. London: John Murray.

Jagger, J. (2005) 'A comment on the teaching of simultaneous equations', *Mathematics in School*, 34(1): 32–3.

Jones, G.A., Langrall, C.W., Thornton, C.A. and Mogill, A.T. (1997) 'A framework for assessing and nurturing young children's thinking in probability', *Educational Studies in Mathematics*, 32: 101–25.

Kerslake, D. (1979) 'Visual mathematics', *Mathematics in School*, 8(2): 34–5.

Küchemann, D. (1981) 'Algebra', in K.M. Hart (ed.), *Children's Understanding of Mathematics 11–16*. London: John Murray.

Macgregor, M. and Stacey, K. (1997) 'Students' understanding of algebraic notation: 11–15', *Educational Studies in Mathematics*, 33(1): 1–19.

Mason, J. (2002) 'Generalisation and algebra: exploiting children's powers', in L. Haggarty (ed.), *Aspects of Teaching Secondary Mathematics: Perspectives on Practice*. London: RoutledgeFalmer.

Mason, J., Burton, L. and Stacey, K. (1982) *Thinking Mathematically*. London: Addison Wesley.

Miles, J. (2007) 'Letters', Guardian, 27 February.

Office for Standards in Education (Ofsted) (2005) *The Annual Report of Her Majesty's Chief Inspector of Schools 2004/5: Mathematics in Secondary Schools*. London: Office for Standards in Education.

Office for Standards in Education (Ofsted) (2006) *Evaluating Mathematics Provision for 14–19 Year Olds*. London: Office for Standards in Education.

Open University (1992a) *Learning and Teaching Shape and Space*. Milton Keynes, Buckinghamshire: Open University.

Open University (1992b) *Mathematics: Symbols and Meanings*. Milton Keynes, Buckinghamshire: Open University.

Qualifications and Curriculum Authority (QCA) (2007a) 'Mathematics Programme of Study: Key Stage 3'. Available for download at http://www.qca.org.uk/qca_12216.aspx (accessed 23 August 2007).

Qualifications and Curriculum Authority (QCA) (2007b) 'Mathematics Programme of Study: Key Stage 4'. Available for download at http://www.qca.org.uk/qca_12217.aspx (accessed August 2007).

Royal Society (2001) *Teaching and Learning Geometry 11–19*. Online at http://www.royal-soc.ac.uk/document.asp?id=1420 (accessed 9 August 2007).

Seymour, D. and Britton, J. (1989) *Introduction to Tessellations*. Palo Alto, CA: Dale Seymour Publications.

Shaughnessy, J.M. (1992) 'Research in probability and statistics: reflections and directions', in D.A. Grouws (ed.), *Handbook on Research in the Teaching and Learning of Mathematics*. New York: Macmillan.

Smile (2002) *Mathematics Reasoning: Activities for Developing Thinking Skills*. London: RKBC Smile Mathematics.

Smith, A. (2004) *Making Mathematics Count: The Report of Professor Adrian Smith's Inquiry into Post-14 Mathematics Education*. London: HMSO.

Tall, D. and Thomas, M. (1991) 'Encouraging versatile thinking in algebra using the computer', *Educational Studies in Mathematics*, 22: 191–228.

Tanner, H. and Jones, S. (1995) 'Teaching mathematical thinking skills to accelerate cognitive development', in L. Meira and D. Carraher (eds), *Proceedings of the 19th International Conference for the Psychology of Mathematics Education*, Recife: Universidade Federal de Pernambuco.

Tanner, H. and Jones, S. (2000) *Becoming a Successful Teacher of Mathematics*. London: RoutledgeFalmer.

ICT IN MATHEMATICS TEACHING

This chapter:

- considers the background to the use of ICT in mathematics teaching
- discusses issues relating to pedagogy and ICT
- examines the use of computer suites and individual computers
- discusses how teachers use data projection facilities
- examines how the interactive whiteboard can lead to changed practice in the classroom
- speculates whether ICT can help mathematics to be seen as a more creative subject.

BACKGROUND

Innovation in teaching mathematics is a constant and recurring aspect of teachers' lives. Standing still is never an option. This is recognized in the standards for QTS, where, as part of your professional attributes, you need to demonstrate a 'creative and constructively critical' approach toward innovation (TDA, 2007: 8). In recent years, much innovation has centred around ICT, and its increasing use in mathematics lessons. By 2004, 80 per cent of mathematics departments were using ICT in their teaching on occasions, but only one department in six used ICT often (QCA, 2004). These figures are likely to have significantly increased since then.

One of the major drivers for educational change is the needs of employers (discussed in Chapter 1), which focus more on mathematical approaches than particular content. Skills such as making and testing hypotheses, gathering and analysing data, testing and validating models, and the ability to communicate in concise and precise ways are highly valued (Oldknow and Taylor, 1999).

Unless these demands change, it is easy to see that ICT will continue to have a key role in schools, because the effective use of ICT can contribute to the development of all these skills.

Information and communications technology in the classroom can perform a large number of different functions. Some of these relate directly to helping pupils learn mathematics; others help indirectly by allowing access to larger data sets or performing fast analysis of data that would, without a computer, take a long time. A third function is the more general one of contributing to the pupils' general ICT capability, and hence to their ability to use computers to organize, analyse and present information. Consider the ways that computer use in mathematics can contribute to pupils' learning. Use of the computer can:

- contribute to developing further pupils' ICT capability
- provide quick feedback on answers and ideas, avoiding the situation where pupils wait for the teacher to provide feedback
- increase the pace of the lesson by allowing quick switches between different displays, and giving instant responses to large numbers of questions
- improve the quality of the display, so that pupils see, for example, a perfect diagram, rather than a hand-drawn one that may contain inaccuracies
- allow pupils to explore different ideas to 'see what happens', for example when investigating the effect of different constants in an algebraic graph
- model mathematical ideas
- explore mathematical patterns and relationships
- test hypotheses, adapt and retry
- sift, sort and analyse data quickly and easily
- facilitate work with large sets of data, including real data.

Using a bit of imagination, you can use ICT to strengthen connections between different mathematical ideas, and to promote cross-curricular links. It is important to note that even when ICT makes a major contribution to the lesson, your role as the teacher remains paramount (Becta, 2004). You cannot assume that the technology will run the lesson for you! It is only with your intervention that the ICT can be used to demonstrate, explain and question, to stimulate discussion and to invite predictions and interpretations.

You should consider, in your planning and evaluation, two important issues relating to ICT. The first is whether the ICT is adding value to the lesson; in other words, has the learning been enhanced by the use of ICT, or could the same learning have been achieved more efficiently without the use of ICT? Second, consider whether you have chosen the most appropriate form of ICT. These two points feature in the National Strategy guidance (DfES, 2004), and it is absolutely crucial that you keep them in mind when reflecting on your use of ICT. As well as answering those two questions, another helpful way for you to evaluate the use of ICT is to ask pupils during the plenary. You can ask pupils, as part of their reflection on the lesson, to articulate how the ICT has contributed to their learning.

The availability of resources through technology has increased enormously. The National Grid for Learning (NGfL) has had a significant impact, but there is now such a vast number of resources that teachers are in danger of wasting time looking for the most effective materials. The Internet is too large for it to be neatly co-ordinated!

PEDAGOGICAL ISSUES

Evidence supports the use of ICT as a learning tool, but its use in mathematics is less effective than in other subjects (Ofsted, 2004). Nevertheless, inspectors identified ICT as having a significantly positive effect on standards and achievement in mathematics in over a third of the schools visited. The most effective use of ICT is often when it is used flexibly, not necessarily by all pupils, as a supporting resource. What is important is to integrate the results of using ICT into the mathematics work that is being learnt (Goldstein, 2001), so that pupils see ICT as a facilitating tool rather than an end in itself.

Some ICT usage is functional, rather than pedagogical (Oldknow and Taylor, 2003). When used in this way, the ICT performs a simple function, such as calculating the mean of a set of numbers, investigating the effect of changing a variable using a spreadsheet or displaying data in the form of a chart. In these cases, the ICT saves time by allowing exploration of more situations, or presenting results in an attractive form. Such uses do not in themselves contribute to the pupils' understanding of mathematics, except indirectly by allowing more time to be spent on more interesting or valuable things.

Innovative use of technology in mathematics has not always developed. One example is the use of programming. The Framework lists as one of the 'main uses of ICT in mathematics in Key Stage 3, Programming languages, such as Logo or Basic, and the programming capabilities of graphical calculators' (DfEE, 2001: 25).

Whatever the educational merits of programming, and there are many, the use of programming has declined rather than increased as more technological options have become available. In the 1990s, many mathematicians promoted the use of the computer language Logo, as a vehicle for rich mathematical learning. Logo's simple structure and powerful scope have enormous potential to put pupils in control of their learning. Research into its effectiveness was strongly positive (a review of the available research is provided by Jones, 2005), and many teachers wholeheartedly embraced its potential, but others never really took to it. For reasons that are unclear, it does not feature prominently in the National Strategy and appears to be used less now than in the 1990s. Although Hyde (2004) expressed surprise that only 73 per cent of her teacher respondents reported using Logo, I believe that the figure of 73 per cent is a great overestimate of the current situation. It is now rare to see Logo being used in mathematics lessons.

Given the difficulties of access associated with computer suites, some teachers anticipated that graphical calculators would have a big impact. Graphical calculators are small (and cheap) enough for every pupil to have one, can be used in powerful ways, and can be used flexibly. The evidence, however, is that they are underused (Ofsted, 2004). Current trends suggest that graphical calculators will continue to be underused, because of the initial difficulties in becoming familiar with their features, which present a barrier to both teachers and pupils. However useful graphical calculators are, they are different from standard computers in the way they operate, and this unfamiliarity has led to fewer teachers choosing to use them in lessons. Similarly, it seems that only a small number of enthusiasts will ever fully exploit the programming capabilities of these calculators.

It remains to be seen whether replacing graphical calculators with wireless laptops will bring about more widespread change in practice. The major benefit from the teacher's point of view is that laptops use a familiar operating system, so there are no new skills associated with using them. At present the issue of security means that the set of laptops has to be kept securely locked away, and giving them out and taking them in, together with logging on and off can take an unsatisfactorily long time. Provided that the reliability and security can be assured, it is likely that sets of laptops will be used routinely in mathematics lessons in the near future. The breakthrough in usage is likely to come when pupils bring to all lessons their own laptop, which is switched on and logged in to the school network at all times.

Overall, school inspectors report that the use of ICT in mathematics is a 'relatively weak and underdeveloped' aspect of provision, with 'an unacceptably wide variation' between schools (Ofsted, 2004). The best use of ICT is when it helps pupils to explore mathematical ideas, investigate the effects of changes, and try alternative approaches. Consider this example of a mathematics lesson, where the main objective was for pupils to be able to draw in a line of best fit:

> The ICT played a significant part in the lesson. The prepared graphs were helpful in giving high quality illustrations of correlated data, and the computer enabled quick and easy switching from one diagram to another. The use of a

wireless mouse meant that the teacher was not fixed to one spot, and could add more life to his delivery and management of the whole-class discussion. (Ofsted, 2004: 7)

In this lesson, the ICT has made a clear positive contribution to pupils' learning. It does not detract from the main purpose of the lesson; rather it enhances pupils' engagement with the key mathematical ideas.

COMPUTER SUITES

One use of ICT is by the pupils themselves. This is very much dominated by the available facilities in the department or school, which may include a dedicated computer suite. In the 1990s, a computer suite was the pride and joy of every secondary school, but its value to mathematics teachers has remained limited. There are two issues that influence its effectiveness: availability and separateness. We discuss each in turn.

Teachers often cite the problem of access to computer suites as a barrier to using ICT within mathematics (Hyde, 2004). Some departments have easy access to a dedicated ICT suite with a set of 30 computers, and can book the use of the room with a small amount of forward planning. In other schools, the ICT suites are whole-school facilities, which have to satisfy demands from right across the school. Following additional government funding from 2001 onwards, many schools invested heavily in computer suites that could be booked by departments for occasional lessons. Concurrent changes in the National Curriculum, however, required more use of the computer suites for dedicated ICT lessons, and other curriculum subjects found that, although the school had many more computers than previously, their access to them was reduced.

The second difficulty for subject teachers using computer suites is the separate, remote nature of the room. The room itself is unfamiliar; it is not where pupils usually learn their mathematics. It is also typically filled with 30 desktop computers, which are also unfamiliar in mathematics lessons. As a result, pupils tend to see the lesson as separate from their normal mathematics lessons, and teachers have to work hard to convince the pupils that it is a mathematics lesson, and not a lesson 'on the computers'. Without specific input from the teacher, pupils have difficulty appreciating the connection between their computer activities and the mathematics curriculum (Goldstein, 2001).

Computer suites present one additional difficulty. The physical layout of the room makes flexible working difficult, and yet flexible working is what is needed so often in mathematics. Much of mathematics requires a few minutes of work on the computer, then some written work or activity, and then maybe a return to test further ideas on the computer. It is difficult to retain this flexibility of approach when working in a computer suite because of the lack of working space.

In a computer suite, pupils see the computer as the main focus of the lesson, instead of the mathematics. Only when the computer becomes just another resource in the classroom will it cease to be the focus of attention. Pupils will get full value out of using a computer themselves when the computers become a resource to support learning that can be used for 2 minutes at a time if necessary and appropriate. Pupils will be on the way to being truly autonomous learners when they themselves decide when to use the computer, what software they need to access, and evaluate whether the computer has helped in what they are trying to find out.

INDIVIDUAL COMPUTERS

A second way for pupils to use ICT is within or adjacent to their normal classroom. This has the obvious advantage of being easier to organize, and is more flexible, in that it does not have to be planned in advance; it can be responsive to need as the need arises. This form of use may involve a small number of computers situated along a bench at the side of the room, or in an open area within the mathematics department.

This type of layout lends itself to pupils breaking off to perform some research or to answer a particular question. This scenario brings its own difficulties: for example, what happens when six pupils want access to a computer, and there is only one available? This simply puts extra demands on the teacher's managerial skills.

One type of software that is worth discussing is the integrated learning system, where pupils respond to a set of computer-generated questions. This operates on a one pupil to one computer basis, so the management often requires pupils to be assigned to a computer, either inside the classroom or outside, in rotation. Sometimes groups of pupils move to work on a small group of computers for a limited time within the lesson, before returning to the lesson when they have finished their turn at the computers.

The integrated learning system (ILS) presents pupils with a series of questions. In response to their answers, the computer selects a programme of related teaching with accompanying questions that are designed to focus on the learning needs of the individual pupil. The programme presents progressively more difficult questions, and gives pupils a progressive assessment. The individual nature of the work in this context is both its strength and its weakness. The advantage is that the work is tailored to the needs of the individual, but the drawback is that the work can be isolating, lacking in interaction, and dull. Where integrated learning systems are used, they are often employed as a back-up to the normal mathematics lessons, an additional facility rather than a replacement for the normal learning activities.

Integrated learning systems are designed to be flexible, and to respond to pupils' individual needs, but they can also be seen as highly inflexible. However much the programme provides flexibility, it remains a programme, and is therefore limited by its writers. Critics refer to this use of computers as rigid and mechanistic, far removed from the philosophy that computers should be tools for learning that are within the control of pupils (Ainley, 2001).

Point for reflection

There is often an assumption among trainees that the use of ICT in teaching is always good. Think about the ways that ICT can be used with individual pupils or with small groups, some of which have been described above, and reflect on when such a lesson might be ineffective. Consider such issues as:

- the opportunity for pupils to discuss their work
- pupils' focus on the mathematics
- pupils recording their work
- differentiation
- the length of time that the activity might hold the pupils' attention.

DATA PROJECTION

An alternative use of ICT is to have available in the mathematics classroom a computer that is linked to a data projector. The data projector, which can also accept other input sources such as video and DVD, transfers the monitor display onto a large screen at the front of the classroom. One obvious benefit of using ICT in this way is to save time. For example, it is possible to display the lesson objectives very quickly if they are already prepared on the computer and projected onto the screen. Writing the same things on the board by hand takes time that can be used more productively for teaching.

In a similar way the display can present brief notes or key facts about the topic, show the new vocabulary that is needed and give a brief recap of previous work. Using the display board in this way is simple, needs minimal training, but can still contribute to an improved lesson. Comments from teachers given here illustrate the sort of simple contribution that the display board can make to the lesson:

> I use the projector in most lessons, sometimes for just projecting the worksheet up or for a couple of prepared slides.
>
> I always use the screen to project the lesson's objectives, and then return to the page at the end of the lesson.
>
> If I have got a lot of notes I might put them on a slide and have them ready to display. The projector is useful especially if you cannot turn your back on a class while you are writing on a board.
>
> Rather than spending a lot of time writing on the board, I make sure that the notes are already up there on the display. It saves teaching time.

It is certainly possible to use ICT inappropriately, when it can have a negative effect on standards and achievement. There is a danger that the use of display technology can lead to passive learning, with pupils 'becoming passive recipients of on-screen presentations' (DfES, 2007: 5). One way that teachers sometimes misuse ICT is in believing that a PowerPoint presentation will always provide a good start to a lesson. While PowerPoint does provide a good visual impact, it can be used mechanistically, and fail to engage pupils. The prepared slides can be very constraining. They provide a script, and encourage questions that can only have one correct answer, the one that is to be revealed on the next slide. Any unexpected response to the question, although correct, may be seen as inferior, because it does not match exactly the way it is presented on the next slide. The danger is that pupils are 'funnelled through a pre-determined learning path' (Tanner and Jones, 2007), with little scope for discussion or original ideas.

Some comments from teachers illustrate this point:

> I don't like PowerPoint presentations in mathematics. You cannot be as responsive to the way things are going if you are relying totally on a presentation; you cannot respond to things that are happening in the room.
>
> I only ever use slide presentations to supplement what I am doing on the board. That way, I am dictating the pace of the lesson, rather than the PowerPoint. I tend to use slides only for the key elements, and always write on the board a lot as well.
>
> If you rely totally on a ready-prepared presentation, it takes the spontaneity out of the lesson, and the way you can respond to problems that come up.
>
> If you are interacting as you are going along, you are much more in tune with the way that the children are thinking. When pupils ask questions, you have to respond straight away. It is much harder to respond if you are relying on something that you have already prepared, because you cannot change it there and then.
>
> You cannot divert off to something else because you are very reliant on the slides that you have prepared. I am not a huge fan.

PowerPoint is not, in itself, good or bad; it is simply a way of presenting information. You can use it successfully as part of an interactive teaching session, but you need to provide something extra to bring the lesson to life. The success of the lesson depends on the way that you manage the interaction with the pupils alongside the screen images.

USE OF THE INTERACTIVE BOARD

A major extension of the use of data projectors is to project the image onto an interactive whiteboard (IWB). The interactive board is touch-sensitive, and icons on the board respond to touch in the same way that computer screen icons respond to clicks of the mouse. Interactive whiteboards are increasingly common in mathematics classrooms, and are having a big impact on the way that mathematics is presented.

It takes some time to become conversant with the full range of interactive facilities, and before you use an IWB, you are certain to need some time to explore on your own. You can also draw great benefit from having guidance from an experienced user, who can save you time by directing your explorations. Clearly your confidence will grow with time, but you are urged to proceed slowly; check at every stage that the new technology is having a positive effect on your teaching.

Many simple features of the IWB can add interest to your lessons. There is an on-screen timer that you can use to set short-term targets within the lesson; there are rulers and protractors that can measure lengths and angles on screen; and there are cover and reveal facilities that can be used to predict and check results.

You can use an IWB with your own prepared resources, with resources bought in by the school or with resources available on the Internet. All three possibilities offer opportunities and drawbacks. The clear drawback of producing your own material is the time that is needed to do the job well. You need the ICT skills in the first place and then the time to put together a usable teaching resource. The advantage is that you know the material thoroughly, you can tailor it to the needs of the class that you are teaching, and you can include elements of your own style.

With resources that you have not made yourself, the reverse is true. Using a pre-prepared resource saves preparation time, but loses the personal touch. There is a danger that you will not be fully familiar with all the features of the materials when you first use them, and lose the slickness that goes with using materials that you know really well. But more than anything, you lose an element of control; you are locked into someone else's lesson plan. The examples given might not suit your particular class, or the progression of ideas might not suit the pace at which you wish to work.

The big positive about the IWB is that it provides a quality image, with far more opportunities for dynamic presentation than were available previously.

The attractiveness of the presentation is clearly a positive feature that you will wish to exploit. And although the teacher is still a key feature in its use, there are also opportunities for pupils to explore ideas in a class setting. Pupils can demonstrate their ideas visually using the board, and this may be very helpful for pupils who have difficulty using language to communicate their ideas.

> A bright, colourful, dynamic device at the focus of the classroom provides opportunities for greater attention levels and more sustained engagement between pupils and the mathematics. IWBs offer the potential for play and autonomous learning to occur in a public domain in which mathematical features can be managed by the pupils as well as the teacher.
> (Tanner and Jones, 2007: 40)

In this way, the IWB resource is a focus for discussion, and allows pupils and teachers to focus on key points. There are powerful arguments for urging teachers to use not only the presentational qualities of the IWB, but also the opportunities it offers to make the learning more interactive, in ways that are not otherwise possible.

Several IWB lessons rely on specialist software. The IWB is particularly effective in illustrating geometrical ideas. Whereas a traditionally drawn diagram is static, the IWB allows for diagrams that are dynamic. For example, a triangle can have one vertex 'picked up' and moved around the screen. The computer can demonstrate that as the triangle and the angles change, the angle sum remains 180°.

> Investigating geometrical relationships by dragging points directly on the screen makes for a much more powerful demonstration than would the same exercise carried out via a 'remote' laptop. Pupils can focus on the teacher and the action on the IWB at the same time, and the teacher can make a much greater use of non-verbal communication (including gestures and hand waving) to indicate what is going on.
> (DfES, 2007: 7)

In this way, geometry loses its image of being abstract and formal; it begins to resemble more an experimental science, where pupils explore and investigate (Noss, 2001). Dynamic geometry software has been available for many years, but its use has increased greatly with the introduction of IWBs.

Teaching about algebraic graphs has also been greatly enhanced by the use of specialist software and, again, the IWB has helped teachers to make more use of the software. At a simple level, pupils can come to the board and draw where they think that a particular graph will go, and explain their reasoning. The computer can then reveal the exact position of the graph. The facility for changing a single variable and drawing a succession of graphs quickly and easily is another powerful learning tool.

The amount of available software is huge, and can appear daunting. Experienced teachers tend to concentrate on two or three key applications, and then develop their repertoire gradually. As a baseline, you should try to master some generic software that can be used in several areas of mathematics, such as a geometry package, a graph plotter and a spreadsheet, and then gradually add to that your favourite dedicated pieces of software, each designed to enhance the teaching of a specific mathematical topic.

Here are some examples of teachers talking about their use of the interactive board. Many are in their first or second year of using an IWB, but it is interesting to note that the responses are universally positive.

The interactive board is the only ICT in the classroom. It is particularly useful for teaching graphs and geometry and measures: plotting graphs, showing rotations, enlargements. I also use lots of little interactive programmes.

One particularly good interactive programme relates to finding the area of a circle, when pupils know how to find the circumference. I use a programme that shows a circle being cut up into as many sectors as you want. You can increase the number of sectors whenever you want. It then shows the sectors being laid out to form what looks like a parallelogram. This helps pupils to deduce a formula to find the area. To do that without the computer at the front would mean a lot of time cutting and sticking when, visually, the computer display is so much clearer.

The IWB is very useful for the transformation of graphs. You can see how graphs transform at a click of a button.

Autograph has been great. The pupils use Autograph to find the mean and median, and draw box plots and diagrams. They can investigate the effect of grouping the data. The software helps me to assess whether pupils know why they are using a particular analysis or a particular display.

The computer helps pupils to check their ideas quickly.

I like all the geometry software, Cabri, etc. In our department, we all use that a lot.

The IWB is a popular resource, and it can provide new opportunities in the mathematics classroom, but the teacher remains the key factor in pupils' learning. The key to effective learning lies in how well the teacher can establish linkages between the screen representations, the activity that pupils do at their desks and their internal representations of the mathematics. The National Strategy guidance (DfES, 2007) puts this succinctly in terms of a triangle of interactions. The strength of the interactions depends on the skill of the teacher.

A note of caution is provided by Miller and Glover (2006). Their case study involving repeat visits to six schools in the first year of IWB use suggests that the full impact of the IWB is not realized when it has been introduced without suitable training. Interestingly, they note that training needs are not limited to the technology, but also encompass features of teaching and learning.

OTHER ICT EQUIPMENT

I wish to discuss briefly two other pieces of ICT equipment that are available to mathematics departments, but are only in limited use. The first is a piece of equipment that has been around for a long time, called a motor sensor. This is a small electronic device that can be connected to a computer (and display screen) that helps pupils to explore the linkages between movement and the graphs that describe movement. The sensor is a small box that faces one way. When a pupil moves in front of the sensor, the distance between the pupil and the sensor is mapped onto a distance–time graph.

The device makes it easier to investigate relationships between physical motion and mathematical graphs in a way that other equipment cannot match. For example, the teacher can present a distance-time graph, and challenge the pupil to move in such a way relative to the sensor as to produce that graph. This approach leads to a multitude of suggestions from the rest of the class, and leads to lively discussions. To learn more about the motor sensor, you can read accounts by Mercer and French (1994) that describe how pupils can use the motor sensor to explore the difficult ideas of interpreting graphs.

A second piece of equipment that is at an early stage of introduction is the personal response device. This is a small, hand-held device that is distributed to each pupil. The device enables pupils to select one of up to four possible answers to a question on the computer screen. The main advantage of the device is that it enables all pupils to give a response to any given question, not just those who are more confident. Pupils who may be reluctant to voice their answers because they may be unable to explain their thinking are able to take part as much as their more articulate peers. It is also particularly useful in a large group, where it is difficult to make every pupil feel involved.

When a vote has taken place, the class results are shown on the screen, so it is clear to all how many pupils voted for each of the four answers. What is not given is any identification of who voted in any particular way. This enables pupils to get immediate feedback and to compare their answers with answers given by others. It also, importantly, provides the teacher with information about the full class, and is a very useful assessment tool.

The device can be used for self-assessment in a variation on the 'traffic lights' system. In this version, pupils press button A if they have fully understood the topic, B if they have partially understood and C if they have not understood at all. A more reflective use is where pupils are presented with a question, and all have to give an immediate, intuitive response to that question. The class is then given five minutes to discuss the question in groups and a revised response is invited.

Personal response devices are quite expensive pieces of equipment, because a class set is needed for them to be effective, but they do have a lot of potential for helping pupils to increase their personal contribution to a lesson, and for teachers to gain instant assessment of pupils' learning.

The debate about how much technology should influence the mathematics curriculum has been around since calculators were first introduced, and continues today. It is certainly possible to argue that various mathematical skills that have been thought to be important for many years become less important with the increased availability of ICT. One example is the whole field of algebraic manipulation. For centuries, mathematicians have needed competence with algebra in order to work at any advanced level. Now, the algebraic manipulation can be done by a computer algebra system (CAS), which can be easily available and widespread, so it can be argued that there is less need to do the manipulation by hand, or even to know how to do the manipulation.

Point for reflection

Reflect on the last paragraph above, and think how you can argue that knowing how to manipulate algebraic terms is a fundamental mathematical skill needed by all who study the subject to a higher level, however much technology is available.

Think forward to 10 years from now. Consider how important you think that it will be for pupils to be able to perform the following mathematical skills:

- calculate a percentage of a quantity
- measure an angle
- simplify sums of like terms in algebra
- solve linear and quadratic equations.

You should consider whether the skill is needed as a 'life skill', or in other fields of learning. Are there any other elements of the current curriculum that you feel can be given reduced importance in an increasingly technological world?

CREATIVITY IN MATHEMATICS

Clearly, creativity is a word that is more easily associated with art, design and writing than it is with mathematics, but that is not by any means the full picture. The 1999 National Curriculum illustrates this in describing mathematics as a creative subject, which can promote moments of pleasure and wonder (DfEE, 1999). Since then, creativity has enjoyed a higher profile, and is now an element in the National Curriculum that is common to all subjects, including mathematics. Creativity is a transferable skill that pupils can develop in their school subjects but can then apply outside school. Creativity is valued in many workplaces, and is a key feature of many leisure pursuits. In the 2007 National Curriculum for mathematics, the word creativity is listed as one of the key concepts. Creativity in mathematics is characterized by pupils:

- combining understanding, experiences, imagination and reasoning to construct new knowledge

- using existing mathematical knowledge to create solutions to unfamiliar problems
- posing questions and developing convincing arguments
  (QCA, 2007).

Information and communications technology can provide an important environment for promoting creativity. Although it is not an inevitable consequence of an ICT-rich curriculum, an open and enquiring atmosphere where a variety of resources are available is exactly the environment where creativity can thrive. For example, ICT can change a pupil's attitude to taking risks and worries about being wrong, because of the way that it provides quick and simple feedback. In offering alternative approaches, ICT can also stimulate a more imaginative treatment of a problem (Brown and Wright, 2002).

In this sense, it can be seen that creativity in mathematics is not particularly innovative. What is new is the use of the word 'creativity' in connection with mathematics. This connection can only help to weaken the view that mathematics is a closed subject, discovered by other people, and simply there to be learnt. It is to be hoped that, by putting the word 'creativity' prominently in the National Curriculum, mathematics can develop a stronger reputation as a creative subject.

EVIDENCE FROM THE RESEARCH

Teachers frequently refer to the use of ICT as providing an important motivator in their lessons. Pupils like using computers and calculators. For example, Howard (1993) reports the positive effects of undertaking an ICT-based project with boys having emotional and behavioural difficulties. Not only did the pupils engage with their work for longer than normal, their self-esteem also rose noticeably through producing work that they were pleased with. Improved motivation and self-esteem are reported elsewhere in the literature (for example, Knight et al., 2005; Smith, 2004).

The computer can be seen as providing an additional mediator between the mathematics and the learner. Mason (2004) compares the way that learners form mental images and the images that are available on external screens. The external screen can provide a powerful help in forming mental images. Of course it does not guarantee that the mental images formed by the learners are correct, but it does make the mathematics more visible and less abstract. There is less need for visualization, because the mathematics is modelled on the screen.

Very often research into the use of ICT has indicated the difficulty of separating the effects of the ICT itself from the effects of the changed pedagogy employed by the teacher. Moreover, the effectiveness of the software can depend crucially on the way that it is used. Healy and Hoyles (2001) report that pupils' understanding of proof did not develop automatically through using dynamic geometry software, but depended on well-designed tasks, and an environment that valued conjecture and reasoning. When these conditions were present, there were clear learning gains.

Positive effects of ICT are sometimes not immediate. For example, Laborde (2001) reports that using a dynamic geometry package showed very limited short-term gains in understanding, but that its use over an extended time had beneficial effects.

Miller and Glover (2006: 3) undertook a sponsored research project with the aim of ascertaining 'the potential for interactive whiteboard use to contribute to improvements in teaching and learning in mathematics, to increase pupils' engagement in the subject and so help to raise standards'. Although the project operated in a small number of schools, a large number of lessons were seen and a number of clear conclusions were drawn. Where IWBs are used, the lesson usually follows a lively pace, and the generally stimulating atmosphere helps to minimize any behaviour problems. Positive effects are also reported when the IWB becomes a routine part of lessons. Where the IWB is used as a medium for discussion and explanation, pupils become more involved and greater interaction is stimulated. In addition, where teachers plan their lessons with the use of the IWB in mind, they tend to structure the lesson well, leading to a more systematic approach to the learning process.

In an experiment into the use of the IWB to teach shape, Merrett and Edwards (2005) found that pupils liked the clear and comprehensible shapes provided by the software, especially the ease with which they could move lines, shapes and text. They report that the IWB is a good medium for generating class discussions, comparing the outcomes favourably with a similar lesson where the pupils worked on laptops with very limited interaction.

They report improvement in the pupils' thinking skills and confidence, with pupils asking more probing questions and being more prepared to think for themselves.

Knight et al. (2005) report a positive effect on pupils' motivation, and suggest that this motivation can be sustained over a period of two years, suggesting the IWB is not only seen as having novelty value. They did find, however, that where the required conceptual level was high, the IWB itself was not sufficient to maintain a high level of interest. In these cases, the liveliness of the teacher becomes more important. The most important finding of this study appears to be the report that revisiting prior learning was a key feature of using the IWB that contributes to pupils' learning. Because the IWB stores the results of previous work, all previously recorded experiences can be recalled quickly and easily. It helped the pupils to have a secure base from which to build their new learning.

Overall, the research shows that the use of an IWB does make a difference to the pupils' classroom experience, and the effects are undoubtedly positive.

 Further reading

Oldknow, A. and Taylor, R. (2003) *Teaching Mathematics Using ICT*. London: Continuum.

Inevitably, all books date, and this is particularly true for books relating to ICT. This remains, however, the most comprehensive coverage of the subject, and is accompanied by a CD-ROM containing free versions of some of the key software, together with ideas for use and supporting articles. There are suggestions for ICT use in number, algebra, geometry and statistics, as well as some cross-curricular ideas and a look into the future. The book is designed to support you in learning more about ICT, not just through reading the text, but also through the use of occasional practical exercises for you to try.

Edwards, J. and Wright, D. (2005) *Integrating ICT into the Mathematics Classroom*. Leicester: Association of Teachers of Mathematics.

This book is a collection of articles that appeared in the ATM journal *Micromath* over a period of five years. The book starts with a section on general issues, including evidence from the research and practical advice about using ICT in mathematics teaching. The book then covers a range of topics with collections of articles on particular types of software: dynamic geometry, Logo and graph plotting, spreadsheets, graphical calculators, interactive whiteboards and the Internet. In such a collection of articles, you are certain to find some stimulating comments, as well as extensive practical advice on classroom practice.

 *Useful websites*

Live links to these sites can be found on the companion website.

The 2004 Ofsted report into the use of ICT in mathematics teaching is at http://www.ofsted.gov.uk/assets/3646.pdf

The National Curriculum in Action website http://www.ncaction.org.uk/subjects/maths/ict-lrn.htm contains discussion of the way that ICT can be used in mathematics lessons, together with supporting examples.

Within the Standards website, you will find a set of mathematics lesson materials. Following this link, you will find a series of lesson plans and resources designed to show how ICT can support the learning of mathematics. http://www.standards.dfes.gov.uk/secondary/keystage3/all/respub/ma_ict

Also within the Standards website, the publication *Integrating ICT into Mathematics in Key Stage 3* is a valuable set of advice on how and when to use ICT effectively. http://www.standards.dfes.gov.uk/secondary/keystage3/all/respub/ma_integrate_ict

The Teachernet website at http://www.teachernet.gov.uk/teachingandlearning/subjects/maths/ includes advice on how to integrate ICT into your teaching.

A 2003 review of research into the use of ICT in mathematics teaching is available on the Becta website http://partners.becta.org.uk/page_documents/research/wtrs_maths.pdf

Advice on the use of web-based materials in secondary mathematics lessons is available for download at http://publications.becta.org.uk/display.cfm?resID=25875&page=1835

The article entitled 'ICT and mathematics: a guide to learning and teaching mathematics 11–19', is the report of a Mathematical Association working group, prepared in 2002. It is at http://www.crme.soton.ac.uk/publications/kjpubs/ICT_and_Mathematics.pdf

References

Ainley, J. (2001) 'Adjusting to the newcomer: roles for the computer in mathematics classrooms', in P. Gates (ed.), *Issues in Mathematics Teaching*. London: RoutledgeFalmer.

British Educational Communications and Technology Agency (Becta) (2004) *Using Web-based Resources in Secondary Mathematics*. Coventry: British Educational Communications and Technology Agency.

Brown, G. and Wright, D. (2002) 'ICT used to promote pupils' creativity across the curriculum: report from the mathematics group', *Micromath*, 18(2): 19–20.

Department for Education and Employment (DfEE) (1999) *Mathematics Key Stages 1–4: The National Curriculum for England*. London: Department for Education and Employment.

Department for Education and Employment (DfEE) (2001) *Key Stage 3 National Strategy, Framework for Teaching Mathematics Years 7, 8 and 9*. London: Department for Education and Employment.

Department for Education and Skills (DfES) (2004) *ICT across the Curriculum: ICT in Mathematics*. London: Department for Education and Skills.

Department for Education and Skills (DfES) (2007) *Using Interactive Whiteboards to Enrich the Teaching of Mathematics*. London: Department for Education and Skills.

Goldstein, R. (2001) 'Integrating computers into the teaching of mathematics', in L. Haggarty (ed.), *Teaching Mathematics in Secondary Schools: A Reader*. London: RoutledgeFalmer.

Healy, L. and Hoyles, C. (2001) 'Software tools for geometrical problem solving: potential and pitfalls', *International Journal of Computers for Mathematical Learning*, 6(3): 235–56.

Howard, B. (1993) 'Building self-esteem', *Micromath*, 9(2): 12.

Hyde, R. (2004) 'What do mathematics teachers say about the impact of ICT on pupils learning mathematics?', *Micromath*, 20(2): 11–13.

Jones, K. (2005) 'Using Logo in the teaching and learning of mathematics: a research bibliography', *Micromath*, 21(3): 34–6.

Knight, P., Pennant, J. and Piggott, J. (2005) 'The power of the interactive whiteboard', *Micromath*, 21(2): 11–15.

Laborde, C. (2001) 'Integration of technology in the design of geometry tasks with Cabri-geometry', *International Journal of Computers for Mathematical Learning*, 6(3): 283–317.

Mason, J. (2004) 'Mediating mathematical thinking with e-screens', *Micromath*, 20(1): 4–8.

Mercer, A. and French, D. (1994) 'Two lessons with the motion sensor', *Micromath*, 10(2): 13.

Merrett, S. and Edwards, J. (2005) 'Enhancing mathematical thinking with an interactive whiteboard', *Micromath*, 21(3): 9–12.

Miller, D. and Glover, D. (2006) *Interactive Whiteboard Evaluation for the Secondary National Strategy: Developing the Use of Interactive Whiteboards in Mathematics*. Keele: Keele University School of Criminology, Education, Sociology and Social Work.

Noss, R. (2001) 'Mathematics in the digital technology age', in L. Haggarty (ed.), *Teaching Mathematics in Secondary Schools: A Reader*. London: RoutledgeFalmer.

Office for Standards in Education (Ofsted) (2004) *2004 Report: ICT in Schools – the Impact of Government Initiatives. Secondary Mathematics*. London: Office for Standards in Education.

Oldknow, A. and Taylor, R. (1999) *Engaging Mathematics*. London: Technology Colleges Trust.

Oldknow, A. and Taylor, R. (2003) *Teaching Mathematics Using ICT*. London: Continuum.

Qualifications and Curriculum Authority (QCA) (2004) *Mathematics: 2002/3 Annual Report on Curriculum and Assessment*. Online at http://www.qca.org.uk/down loads/7404_ma_ann_rpt_2002-03.pdf

Qualifications (QCA) (2007) 'Mathematics Programme of Study: Key Stage 3'. Available for download at http://www.qca.org.uk/qca_12216.aspx (accessed 23 August 2007).

Smith, A. (2004) *Making Mathematics Count: The Report of Professor Adrian Smith's Inquiry into Post-14 Mathematics Education*. London: Department for Education and Skills.

Tanner, H. and Jones, S. (2007) 'How interactive is your whiteboard?', *Mathematics Teaching incorporating Micromath* 200, January.

Training and Development Agency for Schools (TDA) (2007) *Professional Standards for Teachers: Why Sit Still in your Career?* London: Training and Development Agency for Schools.

10 CONTINUING PROFESSIONAL DEVELOPMENT

> ## This chapter:
>
> - examines how to evaluate your lessons on teaching practice
> - gives examples of how experienced teachers evaluate their lessons, together with Ofsted criteria for judging lessons
> - discusses the need for a continued commitment to professional development throughout your career
> - summarizes the support that is available from local advisory services
> - reviews the processes for the Career Entry and Development Profile, and the induction year
> - outlines the role of the two professional associations for mathematics teachers
> - summarizes the criteria for assessment at master's level
> - discusses possible opportunities for involvement in research and further study.

During training, your lessons are observed by teachers and tutors, who provide feedback about how effective your lesson has been. Receiving feedback is a key feature of all training programmes, but as the course progresses, you should take more responsibility for evaluating your own performance. The skills of self-evaluation that you develop during your training course need to be applied and developed throughout your teaching career. The QTS standards include requirements that you should:

- reflect on and improve your practice, and take responsibility for identifying and meeting your professional needs
  (TDA, 2007a).

In addition, you need to demonstrate a positive attitude to receiving advice, and a positive attitude to change. Having fixed views is considered a weakness,

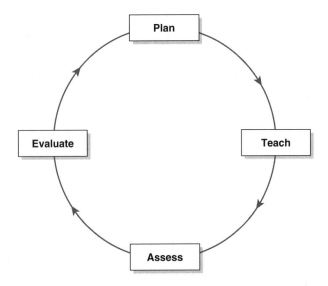

Figure 10.1 Planning and evaluation cycle

and marks you down as a potentially difficult colleague. Specifically, you should demonstrate during training that you can:

- act upon advice and feedback and be open to coaching and mentoring
- respond positively to innovation when benefits are identified, and adapt your practice accordingly (TDA, 2007a).

In this chapter, we shall start by looking at ways of evaluating lessons. Initially, we shall focus on the sort of evaluations that you need to do as part of your training, then we shall give examples of how experienced teachers evaluate their lessons. Quotes from experienced teachers illustrate how they use their skills of evaluation to improve their teaching.

Chapter 3 was all about how to plan a lesson (and a series of lessons), but omitted any detailed discussion of the relationship between planning and evaluation. The planning and evaluation cycle is an important part of improving as a teacher. In summary the planning and evaluation cycle consists of the stages shown in Figure 10.1.

The cycle works in a clockwise direction, starting with plan and teach. The assessment that goes on during the lesson is helpful in telling you how much the pupils have learnt. You can then evaluate the lesson. Your evaluation then helps you to plan the next lesson that you do.

During training, you are expected to produce written lesson evaluations, which look in some detail at the effectiveness of the lesson. A few sentences describing what happened in the lesson will not be acceptable; comments should be evaluative rather than descriptive. In order to help with your evaluations, it is recommended that you set up a template that gives a series of prompts or questions. These prompts give you a focus for the evaluation.

One way to approach evaluation is to separate out your comments into just two headings: the *quality of teaching* and the *quality of learning*. Under the 'quality of teaching' heading, you should comment on the things that you, the teacher, did well and not so well. You might comment on how well you planned the lesson, how well you organized the classroom activities and how well you built productive relationships with the pupils. Under the 'quality of learning' heading, you should comment on whether the pupils have met the lesson objectives. You may be able to note down which objectives were met by all the class and which were met by only some of the class. You may even be able to pin-point individual pupils who have not attained a particular objective, so that you can follow up the work with these pupils in a future lesson.

An alternative to the two simple headings *quality of teaching* and *quality of learning* is to use a longer list of prompts. The following list gives one example of how this can be presented.

- *Did the pupils achieve the objectives? Who did and who didn't?* This is similar to the evaluation of learning discussed above.
- *What would I do differently next time?* This is a key evaluation question to ask yourself. Given that your lesson has not been perfect, you need to analyse why it was not perfect, and how you could have made it better.
- *What went wrong and why?* This is a slightly different way of asking what you would do differently, but should focus your attention on the fact that you, the teacher, have a big influence on what happens. If the pupils have not worked well, it is not their fault. You need to think how you could have changed the pace, the relationships, the planning or other aspects of the lesson to make it better.
- *What went well and why?* In your early days, it is very easy to think about all the things that have gone wrong in a lesson. You need to be positive as well! Even in a lesson that you are unhappy with, you should be able to identify features of the lesson that you think went well. You should then try to make the link between your actions (possibly good planning, or setting targets) and the impact that they have had.
- *Did the assessment give me feedback on the learning?* This question helps you to focus on your in-class assessment. At the end of the lesson, you are likely to have gained an impression of how much the pupils have learnt. You need to consider how you have come to that view. What assessment did you undertake during the lesson? Should you have done more?

- *Were the pupils given good feedback on their work?* It is also worth reflecting on whether the pupils left the room knowing whether their work is correct or not, and whether you gave constructive advice.
- *Do I have any additional information on pupil attainment?* You may need to update your written records for the class after the lesson.
- *How can this lesson be followed up?* You may need to follow up the mathematical difficulties encountered by one or two individuals. You may need to follow up the fact that some pupils have not done their homework. This heading can be used for making notes for next lesson.
- *Were there any unexpected pupil misconceptions or errors?* This question focuses specifically on the mathematical learning. If there have been unanticipated difficulties with understanding, then it is worth making a note of them for future reference. Think again about how your lesson could be changed in the light of these mathematical difficulties.
- *What targets should I set myself?* You may reflect that you need to give more attention to a particular aspect of your teaching next lesson. If you identify a weakness, you should set personal targets for next lesson.
- *Which of the standards were addressed during the lesson?* It is likely that, as you progress through your training, you are asked to gather evidence against each of the standards for QTS. You can help yourself with the indexing of this evidence if you link your performance in individual lessons with the standards.

Of course, these are not the only possible headings for an effective evaluation. There are many other possible prompts that will help you to focus effectively on how well the lesson went, how it can be improved and how your teaching had an effect on the pupils' learning. Tanner and Jones (2000) suggest that the key focus should be on possible improvements. If you were to teach the lesson again, you need to know how you would change it and why. Tanner and Jones suggest four suitable areas of focus for an evaluation template:

- The effectiveness of your planning — lesson structure, choice of activities;
- Your teaching skills — explaining, questioning, discussing;
- The extent to which the pupils achieved the learning objectives;
- The pupils' behaviour and your class management skills.
  (Tanner and Jones, 2000: 68)

On the next few pages, there are three actual examples of trainees' lesson evaluations. Each uses a slightly different format for the evaluation, but each of these templates provides a useful framework to work within. Electronic versions of these evaluations are available on the website, so you can easily save them and adapt as you wish. The website also includes several other examples of lesson evaluations.

LESSON EVALUATION

Year 7		Set 2	Number in class 30
Date Tuesday 23rd January	Period 4	Room 5	

Were the learning objectives met?

Yes: Pupils were able to use both a number line and a calculator to find the difference between numbers, involving negative numbers.

Quality of learning that took place:

The lesson was less tight than the one yesterday. Most pupils worked well, but some were off task, talking. I will move Darren or Sharon next lesson if the work level does not improve. Pupils were happy using the number line to find the difference, and I could see that they were getting the answers correct, so we moved on very quickly to the calculator use. Quite a few pupils got onto the extension worksheet and showed that they could calculate differences in a range of contexts.

Quality of teaching that took place:

Not as good as the last few lessons. This was because when I was doing the input, the pupils were already able to do part of the work I had planned to cover. I was thrown by this and found it hard to pick up the threads of the lesson again. In my planning I need to try to predict where pupils will find work easy or struggle, and plan alternatives accordingly. This will cut down the number of problems I could have in the classroom as I will be prepared for them in advance.

I saw most of the pupils' work throughout the lesson, but my timing was a little off: I didn't have enough time for a proper plenary at the end, and I had to delay reading out the answers until next lesson. I had also planned to give marked work back, but I ran out of time.

Good feature: I used some weather temperatures I had gathered from the Internet before the lesson and projected it onto the screen, incorporating some geography, ICT and knowledge of the world into the lesson.

Control of class:

My control of the class was quite good. I didn't allow pupils to talk when I was talking, but I still need to work in my whole class awareness throughout the lesson.

Issues with work covered:

I started off with work that was too easy but the extension sheet was at the right level to stretch pupils.

Issues with SEN or G&T pupils:

I need to plan separate activities for Bertha as she has already covered this work.

Evaluation

Standards Addressed
3.3.7
3.3.3
3.1.1

Teaching

The introduction to the main activity did not go too well. I did not really take enough time to explain to the pupils what the area is, and this was due to me being annoyed with some pupils for not listening during the starter activity. Pupils worked well through the estimating area worksheet, however, some of them did not hear me tell them to count the squares as they circle them, therefore this task took longer than planned. Unfortunately I did not complete the planned plenary for this lesson, this was due to me dealing with pupils who had not completed their homework at the beginning of the lesson.

Learning (have the objectives been met?)

I feel that only some pupils would be able to give a definition of area and that most would be able to confidently identify units to measure area therefore I do not feel that all pupils have met this learning objective. Pupils were able to find the area of simple shapes by counting squares. There was not enough time to look at area by multiplying: therefore I do not feel that this learning objective was met. I hope to cover this learning objective in tomorrow's lesson.

Assessment

Assessment of the pupils' knowledge of area took place during the introduction to the starter activity. Each pupil had to hold up a card to demonstrate which unit they felt would be appropriate to measure the area of various items, and because each pupil had to hold the appropriate card in the air it allowed me to assess who got it right/wrong.

Classroom Management

During this lesson the class did not behave very well, and I had to stop the starter activity and tell all pupils to sit down as they were being too noisy. During the lesson I had to raise my voice numerous times, telling the pupils to stop constantly calling out. This worked for a while. Overall the pupils did not behave well this lesson and at the end of the lesson I told them this and said I would be expecting better behaviour tomorrow.

Targets

- To ensure I only help pupils who put their hands up (do not allow them to shout out Miss)
- To ensure all pupils are quiet before I continue talking

Evaluation: 09.01–7X3

Were the learning objectives met?

Yes, many pupils came up to the board to plot points in all four quadrants. All pupils already knew the *x* and *y* axis.

During the lesson most pupils successfully completed the plotting points in all four quadrants.

Some pupils need some help in drawing their axes.

Quality of the learning that took place?

Very Good/Good/Satisfactory/less than satisfactory

Not all pupils fully engaged with the lesson. James was particularly unco-operative; he refused to come up to the board and did very little work. I will have to come up with a way to deal with pupils who do not complete up to a certain question.

I think the concepts were understood by the pupils, but the drawing of the axes took longer than expected, and not enough work was completed.

Quality of teaching that took place?

Very Good/Good/Satisfactory/Less than satisfactory

Pupils enjoyed the treasure hunt. I should have drawn the axes from scratch rather than having them already on the flipchart. Modelling how to draw the axes may have made it easier for the pupils to copy. I overestimated their ability to draw straight lines with a ruler and mark the values evenly. I did stop the lesson and re-explain that the distance between 0 and 1, 1 and 2, and −2 and −3 must be the same, but I should have insisted on all pens down while I explained this. Many pupils continued to draw their axes incorrectly.

During the explanation of the different levels certain pupils were very excited to do 'harder' work and I used this to encourage them to try hard. Beth really understood the levels probably due to her extra maths lesson and she was very keen to understand and do the work.

Issues of classroom management

Behaviour management was poor today. Too many pupils got away with too many things. Still too much talking back to me especially Neil; possibly move him next lesson and reprimand him early on, and give him a clear target. Pupils are arriving late and dishing out equipment is taking up a lot of time. I need to think of some new entry procedures and be more forceful with bad behaviour.

(Continued)

Issues with the work covered

Most pupils fully understood the concepts but struggled drawing out the axes.

Issues with SEN or G&T Students

The homework involves spelling words with co-ordinates; this should help to improve literacy and writing. All pupils should be able to complete the homework as the axes are already drawn and it is just the reading of co-ordinates that is needed. Beth was very excited to do level 5 work and it encouraged her to try harder so I will try to incorporate this into more of my lessons.

Key Points to improve for next lesson

Positive reinforcement; use raffle tickets in the lesson. Don't be slow to move pupils who are misbehaving. Use names on the board policy. Improve the start of the lesson. Insist all pens and pencils down if I have to stop a lesson to re-explain something.

EVALUATION OF LESSONS LATER IN YOUR CAREER

Once you have completed your training, you are unlikely to write out formal evaluations of your lessons in the type of format described above. What you are expected to do, however, is to use professional reflection to informally evaluate your lessons, to review your performance and to take responsibility for improving your teaching. The effort that you put into lesson evaluations, and the support that you receive, should help you to develop the necessary skills so that you can continue to improve your teaching, both with and without the continued support of colleagues. The following illustrations come from interviews with experienced teachers.

A successful lesson for me is when I know the pupils are going out of the classroom and they have achieved the objectives that we set at the beginning of the lesson. I aim to measure whether they have achieved them or not through my assessment in the lesson. I find that the plenary is really useful for that: asking the questions at the end, and giving them the opportunity to reflect.

I evaluate my lessons almost straight away rather than going away to think about it. It tends to be a mental note as I am going through: that didn't work, don't do that again; that works really well; or those elements of the lesson didn't fit together very well.

I go away and analyse later. I analyse what has happened and I go through what I taught, and then I make lots of mental notes.

At home, I will make notes in my planner or write on the back of my planning forms directly for the next day or maybe for the next year when the topic comes round again. The notes will trigger straight away, 'I'm not going to do it like last time' or 'what I did last year really worked'.

I think that evaluation is something that gets easier as you go along, because you get over-critical of yourself initially and then as you go along you get a bit easier on yourself. But you also have more options and know when something doesn't work, and you are not scared to try something different.

If something doesn't work perfectly I say to myself, 'Well, that didn't work, but it is not the end of the world. It's not because I'm a bad teacher; it's just that today it didn't work, and tomorrow I'll try a different approach'.

When I evaluate my lessons, it mostly results in me changing the tasks, and sometimes the length of time that I spend expecting the pupils to do things.

If I change anything through evaluating the lesson it tends to be the difficulty of the task. If I pitch the lesson too high or too low, then I note it down. If the work is too easy, the pupils get bored, and then that is when you can start having behavioural problems in the lesson. That can also happen if it is too difficult as well.

I do evaluate a lot, but I don't do it formally. I don't sit down and write an evaluation of my lessons, but I always think about how successful they have been, and make notes for future reference.

One particularly good opportunity for using evaluations to improve your teaching occurs when you teach two parallel classes.

In Year 9 I have two classes, a Set 1 and a Set 3 and they are following the same scheme of work. The Set 1 group are generally ahead of the Set 3 group, and I evaluate the lessons with Set 1 and use that to help me plan my Set 3 lessons. So, for example, if an unexpected misconception has arisen in the lesson, I will plan to address that misconception in the Set 3 lesson. I might say 'some people might think this' or 'can you spot a mistake that people might make here' or 'why do you think some people do this?' If my timing in my lesson has not been quite right then obviously I can adjust that accordingly. Sometimes an example that I use may not work well, and so I think of a different one for next time.

OFSTED INSPECTIONS

Ofsted inspections are an established part of school life, and provide another, external, means of evaluation of your teaching. Since 2005, all inspections are undertaken in partnership with the school, with the school's self-assessment providing the starting point for the work of the inspection team. The majority of inspections have a whole-school focus and do not contain, as used to be the case, a specific report into the quality of the mathematics department. The quality of teaching and learning across the school, however, remains one important focus for the inspection. This is only one of many judgements made by the inspection team, but is probably the one that will affect you most directly as a newly qualified teacher (NQT) or in your early years of teaching. As a result, you need to be aware of the criteria that Ofsted inspectors use to judge lessons.

Inspectors tend to view parts of lessons – possibly 20 to 30 minutes. They give a judgement on a four-point scale: outstanding, good, satisfactory or inadequate. Criteria for the four grades are:

Outstanding (1)	Teaching is at least good in all major respects and is exemplary in significant elements. As a result, learners thrive and make exceptionally good progress.
Good (2)	Learners make good progress and show good attitudes to their work, as a result of effective teaching. The teachers' good subject knowledge lends confidence to their teaching styles, which engage all groups of learners and encourage them to work well independently. Classes are managed effectively. Learners respond to appropriate challenges. Based upon thorough and accurate assessment that informs learners how to improve, work is closely tailored to the full range of learners' needs, so that all can succeed including those with learning difficulties and/or disabilities. Learners are guided to assess their work themselves. Teaching assistants and other classroom helpers, and resources, are well deployed to support learning. Good relationships support parents/carers in helping learners to succeed.
Satisfactory (3)	Teaching is inadequate in no major respect, and may be good in some respects, enabling learners to enjoy their education and make the progress that should be expected of them.
Inadequate (4)	Learners generally, or particular groups of them, do not make adequate progress because the teaching is unsatisfactory. Learners do not enjoy their work. Behaviour is often poor and is managed inadequately.

Teachers' knowledge of the curriculum and the course requirements are inadequate, and the level of challenge is often wrongly pitched. The methods used do not sufficiently engage and encourage the different groups of learners. Not enough independent learning takes place or learners are excessively passive. Assessment is not frequent or accurate enough to monitor learners' progress, so teachers do not have a clear enough understanding of learners' needs. Learners do not know how to improve. Teaching assistants, resources, and parents/carers are inadequately utilised to support learners.
(Ofsted, 2006b: 11, 12).

Inspectors look for the quality of teaching and evaluate its impact on learning. As can be seen from the above criteria, they look for the way pupils respond in the classroom, whether they enjoy the work, and whether they engage actively with the lesson. If you are observed, even for just part of a lesson, then you can expect some feedback from the inspector.

The majority of headteachers believe that inspection leads to better schools (NFER, 2006a). You will find that self-evaluation is a key part of the inspection process, and headteachers use the inspection process to improve the school's self-evaluation skills in dialogue with the inspection team. Inspections often confirm the school's priorities for improvement, and 90 per cent of headteachers are content with their inspection reports (Ofsted, 2006a), a remarkably high proportion in what remains an area of some controversy.

PROFESSIONAL DEVELOPMENT WITHIN THE SCHOOL/DEPARTMENT

Professional development is a two-way process, with obligations on both the teacher and the school. 'All teachers should have a professional responsibility to be engaged in effective, sustained and relevant professional development throughout their careers' (TDA, 2007a: 2). In addition, teachers are entitled to expect that their professional development will be facilitated in the school where they work. At the beginning of the chapter, we gave three extracts from the Professional Standards for QTS relating to professional development for trainees. In fact the same requirements apply to teachers throughout their careers. At all points of assessment (for example, at the end of the induction year, or for promotion to advanced skills teacher) teachers need to demonstrate:

- an ability to evaluate their own performance
- a commitment to improve
- a constructive attitude to innovation
- a willingness to act on advice
- an openness to coaching and mentoring
  (TDA, 2007a).

During your training, you will need to monitor your progress against the Professional Standards for QTS, and will assess yourself and your further training needs regularly. You are likely to find that your confidence grows as your time in school goes on, as will your professional skills. Most commonly, the professional skills that trainees feel they develop most in the early months of their training are their ability to structure a lesson and their class management skills (Chambers, 2007). To a lesser extent, they develop their time management, learn how to relate to pupils and learn how to pitch the lesson at the right level. Your own reflection needs to identify strengths and weaknesses; your progress depends on you engaging regularly in professional discussion with your mentor about your development needs.

In your early days of teaching, you will benefit enormously if you are in a department with a strong team ethic, a department where different teachers share ideas and share professional reflection. This support from colleagues is often particularly valued when it works on an informal level. Again some quotes from mathematics teachers in different departments illustrate the idea:

> We have a strong department and we share ideas and resources. If something didn't work or something worked really well, we talk about it. We show each other our good ideas.
>
> There's a lot of give and take in this department. I use lots of ideas that have come from other people, but also I share what I have. For example, I learnt how to use the software package Cabri, and then we arranged some sessions where I showed everyone else how to use Cabri. So it just enriches everybody's teaching; we share a lot and that really helps.
>
> In our department, if you have got something that you have struggled to teach, then it is normal to ask if anybody has got any good ideas for that topic. Invariably somebody has, and the rest of us pick their brains.

Other support from within the school is rather more formally organized through departmental meetings, performance review and pre-arranged programmes of peer observation.

Each year we have a professional development meeting with the head of department. We have to set ourselves targets: one based on results, one based on our teaching and learning, and one that can be based on anything. Later in the year, our Head of Department comes and observes us teaching. At the end of the year, we have another meeting to see whether we have reached our targets, and our targets might be revised.

At the end of each year, we are sent a questionnaire and we record anything that we need training on. Based on the results, the Head of Department puts together a programme for training. We have very little external training; very few people come in from outside. Most of our professional development training is internal, from the mathematics department, and from other departments as well.

We do a programme of peer lesson observations, where we go in and observe each other's lessons. We use a school pro forma to record the observations. There is a big tick-list that we use to identify teaching styles, evaluate cross-curricular themes, comment on the use of ICT, and other things.

We are observed under Ofsted framework, so we are given descriptors for what is an outstanding lesson, a good lesson, a satisfactory lesson and an unsatisfactory lesson. When colleagues watch a lesson, they give a grade for the lesson, and also identify areas for improvement. It does help staff development.

Before peer observation, you can pick on something specific, something that you realise that you should improve, and ask the observer to comment on that aspect of your work.

We do peer observation each year. We have an observation form that is developed from the school's teaching and learning policy, so we all look for things like

- does the lesson have a hook at the beginning?
- is there appropriate differentiation in the lesson?
- are the pupils given the opportunity to have peer assessment?

The person watching the lesson is looking for those things, and afterwards we have feedback, and they go through the areas of focus with us.

I think a lot staff find plenaries very difficult. Many mathematics teachers are used to finishing the lesson checking the answers and that's it, that's the plenary. So we have had whole-school in-service sessions and voluntary training sessions on plenaries.

Something that we have done recently is to pair up to film lessons. Following those lessons we have looked through the school's teaching and learning policy, and in pairs we have evaluated the lesson. We have looked at what our strengths are, and if there are any areas for development, we have thought about training needs.

We use peer observation to focus on something specific in our lessons that we might want to improve on. That is a very general thing across all subjects.

The culture of self-evaluation means that developing teaching and learning is an ongoing priority in many schools. As a result, schemes of peer observation are commonplace, and tend to be highly valued by teachers.

SUPPORT FROM THE LOCAL AUTHORITY ADVISORY SERVICE

Many schools also have access to support from the local authority (LA) advisory service. Among other things, staff in the advisory service co-ordinate training across schools, and provide additional support for major new initiatives. The authority also provides additional support for all newly qualified teachers. Here are some examples of the way that mathematics teachers have interacted with their local authority advisory staff:

> Our Numeracy Advisor comes in and supports on a range of issues. The last time she came in was to talk to the department about using self-assessment in our lessons.
>
> I remember particularly the support from the LA when I was newly qualified. The advisor came in and watched some of my lessons.
>
> In the past, I have asked the LA advisor to come into my lessons to support my plenaries and starters.
>
> We have had a whole-school focus recently on the children who are underachieving in Year 9. As part of that, we were all observed by the LA during the autumn term, and we all got lesson feedback.

The quality and effectiveness of LA support to schools is under frequent review. National Foundation for Educational Research (NFER) survey data suggests that the aspects of LA support that secondary headteachers value most highly are

- providing them with data
- helping with the self-evaluation process.

Headteachers feel that LAs are less effective in providing training, supporting individual subjects or helping schools to share good practice (NFER, 2006b). Ofsted are supportive of LAs providing support for schools, but they have been unable to find any consistently demonstrable link between good LA support and improved standards in schools (Ofsted, 2001).

Many local authorities have set up facilities to make it easier for teachers to access web-based materials. In the case of mathematics specifically, several authorities provide a dedicated website, with links to a whole range of teaching materials. Some examples are given at the end of the chapter (and on the website for this book). Your own local authority may well run a site for sharing good ideas in mathematics teaching. You may be able to submit your own contributions if you have original material that you think will be of use to others.

CAREER ENTRY AND DEVELOPMENT PROFILE

At the end of your training, you are required to complete a Career Entry and Development Profile (CEDP). This document is designed to help bridge the gap between your training and your first year in teaching, and you should use it to reflect on your professional development at key times during the beginning of your career (TDA, 2007a; 2007b). In completing the CEDP, you will provide summary details about your training programme, and highlight any distinctive aspects of your training. More importantly, the CEDP provides an opportunity for you to reflect on your strengths and weaknesses as you make the transition into teaching. The operation of CEDP is arranged around three 'transition points':

- at the end of the ITT programme, when the CEDP is first drafted under the supervision of your training provider
- at the beginning of the induction year, when it is reviewed by the induction tutor, and a programme of support planned
- at the end of the induction year, when any targets that you have set for the year are reviewed and assessed.

The CEDP is designed to help the school co-ordinate your induction, professional development and performance management, and provide you with a good start to your career.

The CEDP asks you to focus on four questions:

1. At this stage, which aspect(s) of teaching you do you find most interesting and rewarding?
2. As you approach the award of QTS, what do you consider to be your main strengths and achievements as a teacher?
3. In which aspects of teaching would you value further experience in the future?
4. As you look ahead to your career in teaching, you may be thinking about your longer-term professional aspirations and goals. Do you have any thoughts at this stage about how you would like to see your career develop?

Although the CEDP is designed to be chiefly of benefit to you, the user, the main audience for the CEDP is the teacher in charge of newly qualified teachers at your first school, known as the induction tutor. This teacher will want to know something about your background, and the CEDP provides this information. Your response to question 3 is likely to be of particular interest to the induction tutor. This will form the basis of discussion, and should involve a focus on how the school can support you in your professional development in the areas that you have highlighted. You will be able to make suggestions on how you think this can be done. The induction tutor may discuss whether the support can be provided in school or whether you may need to attend further training outside school.

The CEDP is therefore very important for you. It gives you the chance to submit a written request for support in specific areas, so it is worth you spending time thinking about where you would welcome support most. For some ideas about possible areas for further development, you may find the following list helpful:

- The range of your experience:
    a wider range of work at Key Stage 4
    work with pupils with special needs
    experience preparing pupils for external exams
    working with particular groups of pupils (SEN, G&T, EAL, and so on).
- Assessment skills:
    assessing against attainment levels
    assessing the process aspects of mathematics.
- ICT knowledge and its use in the classroom. You may be interested in a particular programme to broaden your expertise.
- Writing reports, communicating with parents.
- Target-setting. You may need some support on how to predict GCSE grades, or how to set appropriate targets for individual pupils.
- Your role in the school:
    the role of the form tutor
    teaching PSHE
    citizenship education in the school.
- Extra-curricular activities.

THE INDUCTION YEAR

Schools work within a statutory framework for the induction year, and their provision for NQTs and the support they provide are monitored by local authorities. During your induction year you will have a slightly reduced timetable, but you will still be teaching more, with less non-teaching time, than you did in your training. The school will recognize your training needs, as identified on your CEDP, and will design an individual programme of support for you. Most likely this will include you observing other teachers, visiting other schools and taking part in formal training. At the end of your induction year, you are assessed against the Induction Standards, similar to, but rather more demanding than, the Standards for QTS.

You will be observed teaching, once in the first four weeks at the school, and then again at intervals of between six and eight weeks. The observations will be followed by discussions about your teaching. You have a more formal review of your progress at the end of each term.

PROFESSIONAL ASSOCIATIONS

The National Centre for Excellence in the Teaching of Mathematics (NCETM) is a relatively new organization, having been set up partly in response to recommendations in the Smith Report (Smith, 2004). The organization has a national profile, but also operates on a regional level. At a regional level, the NCETM organizes workshop sessions for local teachers, and meetings for sharing information about new initiatives. At a national level, the organization aims to provide a focus for improving teaching and learning, to raise the professional standing of mathematics teachers. The NCETM website has several features that are useful for people training to be mathematics teachers. One feature in particular that you will find useful is the exemplification of the Professional Standards for QTS, where each of the standards has been contextualized for mathematics teaching. Another interesting feature is the 'Mathemapedia', designed to mirror the style of the web-based encyclopedia, Wikipedia, but with mathematical content.

There are two well-established professional associations for teachers of mathematics that you should note: the Mathematical Association (MA) and the Association of Teachers of Mathematics (ATM). Each provides a network for mathematics teachers and educators to share ideas and discuss innovations. They also represent the profession, by providing representation on the General Teaching Council, the Training and Development Agency for schools, and similar national bodies of note. There is a charge for membership, but each organization has special introductory rates for newly qualified teachers. Each organization holds an annual conference (this has sometimes been held jointly) with keynote speakers, research reports and working groups. They also publish books, pamphlets, discussion papers and specialist teaching materials, and have local associations whose members meet together on a regular basis. Above all, the two associations provide opportunities for you to keep up to date with new initiatives and recent developments in mathematics teaching, something that will be important throughout

Table 10.1 Mathematical Association Publications

Title	Issues per year	Description
Equals	3	Focuses on mathematics and special educational needs
MA News	3	A free newsletter sent to all members
The Mathematical Gazette	3	The original magazine of the association, now focusing on the 15–20 age range
Mathematical Pie	3	A small pamphlet of puzzles and challenges, aimed at the 10–14 age range
Mathematics in School	5	Aimed at primary and secondary teachers. Mainly articles on teaching methods and reports of research projects
Primary Mathematics	3	Aimed at primary school teachers
Symmetry Plus	3	A magazine aimed at readers in the 10–18 age range. Contains articles, puzzles and competitions.

your career. The website for this book provides links to both the MA and the ATM websites.

The MA publishes seven regular magazines to support mathematics teachers (Table 10.1). Not all members receive all publications. Different membership packages entitle you to different combinations of the above journals.

The ATM publishes one bi-monthly journal called *Mathematics Teaching* (*MT*), which contains a wealth of articles by teachers and mathematics educators. Some articles are accounts of interesting classroom activities; others express views or contribute to debates.

You will find plenty of useful and interesting articles in these magazines, and there is no reason why you should not become a contributor yourself at some stage.

MASTER'S LEVEL CREDITS

It may be that your training course gives you the chance to gain credits that count towards a master's level qualification. At master's level (M level) you will need to show an ability to critically evaluate, to review existing research and to synthesize arguments. For example, criteria for success at M level may include

- comprehensive knowledge of the topic
- evidence of wide reading, together with the ability to synthesize a coherent argument, including consideration of opposing views

- an ability to support arguments with convincing evidence, accurately referenced
- critical reflection on your own classroom practice
- provision of evidence from your own research, comparing it with evidence from the literature
- independent thought.

In many training courses, one of the assessments will involve you in carrying out a small-scale research project in school. This will require you to collect evidence in a systematic way, and to present your evidence in the context of the existing research. The focus for this project is likely to be your own choice, but you may wish to use the following list of ideas to help you to choose. You could choose to concentrate on:

- analysing the effects of specific formative assessment techniques on pupils' learning in mathematics
- evaluating the impact of a particular initiative on gifted and talented pupils
- analysing common errors in a particular mathematical topic
- comparing two different teaching approaches
- evaluating a mathematical software package or teaching pack
- comparing boys' performance to girls' performance in a particular area of mathematics
- evaluating a series of innovative lessons
- investigating the short-term effects of intervention strategies (such as booster units) on pupils' learning in mathematics
- analysing how specific behaviour management techniques promote learning in mathematics
- evaluating strategies aimed at enabling pupils with special needs to make progress in mathematics.

Three case studies of trainees' research projects are included below. It is hoped that these will give some guide as to the methodology to employ in this kind of project.

Case study 1 – Tina

Tina chose to study pupils' understanding of percentages at Key Stage 3. After giving an introduction that explained why she was interested in the topic, she gave an extensive review of the existing literature on percentages. The literature review compared the findings of different research projects, summarizing common pupil errors and misconceptions. She then designed a test on the topic of percentages, including some questions that were calculations, some that were in word form, and some that required an interpretation of data presented in tabular or graphical form.

She gave the test to a class of Year 9 pupils, marked and analysed the results. She then planned a series of lessons on percentages, making sure that she gave particular attention to the type of questions that gave most difficulty in the test. After the teaching, the pupils took the same test again.

Tina's analysis found that:

- even in the post-test, pupils used calculation methods that were different from those she had taught
- a major source of difficulty was in converting the percentage to a decimal or fraction.

Tina then tried to explain her findings, and referred to other related research. She finally summarized the strengths and weaknesses of her findings, and how she planned to use her findings in her future teaching.

Case study 2 – Shakira

Shakira chose to compare the effectiveness of two different teaching styles. In particular she wanted to investigate whether the way that a topic is first introduced has an effect on the subsequent learning. She chose to introduce Pythagoras' theorem (a new piece of mathematics to all the pupils involved) in two completely different ways. She randomly split a Year 8 class into two groups of 14 pupils, and arranged with the class teacher that for one week she would teach Pythagoras' theorem to one of the groups, and then teach it to the other group the following week using a different approach.

The write-up describes Shakira's approach to each of the two groups in some detail. Through applying a post-test, Shakira was able to analyse which group had learnt more from the lessons and draw conclusions about effective teaching styles. She also commented on her observations that one type of teaching led to a more positive classroom atmosphere. She compared her results with other evidence from the literature, and then reviewed her project and commented on how it could be strengthened or followed up.

(If you choose this style of research, you need to design it carefully, so as to avoid any ethical problems. Both groups of pupils deserve to be taught well, so you need to ensure that both approaches provide positive learning experiences.)

Case study 3 – William

William had a strong interest in recreational mathematics and wanted to investigate what would be the effect of a greater emphasis on puzzles and games in mathematics lessons. He set two very clear research questions:

- Does the use of recreational mathematics improve attitudes and motivation?
- Can recreational mathematics help to develop thinking skills that lead to higher attainment?

Having taught his classes for several weeks, and gained some knowledge about the abilities and the attitudes of the pupils in his classes, William began to teach his classes making regular use of mathematical puzzles. At the end of his teaching practice, he gave out a questionnaire that asked pupils about their attitudes to particular areas of mathematics.

At the end of his teaching practice, William wrote up his case study. He compared his observations with published studies, and tried to explain why in some cases, his findings were different from those reported elsewhere. His report focused on his two research questions, but he was able to make interesting observations about the effect of his changed teaching style on different groups of pupils.

FURTHER STUDY AND QUALIFICATIONS

At the end of your training your first priority will be settling in to your new job and making it a success. But you should also give some thought to your long-term career aims and aspirations. One way that you can enhance your professional expertise, and at the same time increase your chances of promotion within teaching, is to undertake professional development courses. Some of these courses, particularly those run by your local university, will provide credits towards a master's level qualification.

Your local university may also be a good place to meet other people who are interested in research into mathematical education. You may be able to make contact with someone engaged in a research project, and contribute to the project in some way. If you have a particular area of interest, then you may be able to obtain guidance about how to set up a project yourself. A lot of research consists of groups of teachers working together with academic staff from universities; teachers who are involved in research often report how much the project makes them reflect on and develop their own professional practice.

As you progress through your career, you should be looking to develop your curriculum vitae (CV). Your growing experience in school will provide you with the opportunity to broaden your CV in a whole range of ways. What can help you to stand out from other teachers is your evidence of additional study, and clearly the further that study has gone, the more impressive it is. Even if you do not have any higher degree qualifications, it is useful to be able to show you are working towards a master's degree, by listing the master's credits you have already attained.

Active membership of one of the professional associations also enhances your profile. Involvement in writing, in conferences or local associations demonstrates that you have an interest in mathematics beyond the day-to-day demands of the classroom. You show that you are interested in new ideas and in listening to other teachers discussing innovation.

CONCLUSION

Becoming a reflective teacher of mathematics is only the beginning. Once you have developed the skills of self-evaluation, and have become acquainted with all the different avenues available for staff development, you will continue to grow in your professional skills. In other words, you will continue to be a reflective teacher for the whole of your career, always looking for improvements, and always willing to try new and innovative approaches.

As a teacher of mathematics you will always face challenges, but you will find rewards in a wide range of ways, often in unexpected circumstances.

 Useful websites

Live links to these sites can be found on the companion website.

You will certainly want to visit the Ofsted website at some time during your training course. http://www.ofsted.gov.uk/ is the Ofsted website, containing links to school inspection reports, as well as information about the inspection process. Specific details about how inspectors make judgements can be found in the guidance on how to undertake inspections at http://www.ofsted.gov.uk/assets/Internet_Content/Shared_Content/IIFD/Files/schoolsFramework/usingTheEvaluationSchedule.pdf

The NCETM website (http://www.ncetm.org.uk/signin) needs you to register first. You will then gain access to a news section, together with a useful directory of regional and national professional development courses. In addition, there is a collection of free resources, including example lesson plans and interesting research articles. There are several links to other useful websites for mathematics teachers.

The Mathematical Association website is at http://www.m-a.org.uk/

The Association of teachers of Mathematics have a website at http://www.atm.org.uk/. A useful link within the site is the one that takes you to free resources; the direct link to this is http://www.atm.org.uk/free-resources/

Local authorities provide plenty of support online. It is impossible to list them all, so we give three examples of the materials available to you. For example, in Liverpool, the mathematics team have collected a range of easily accessible materials on the website at http://www.mathspool.liverpool.gov.uk/. Nottinghamshire have an index of useful mathematics links at http://www.nottinghamshire.gov.uk/home/learningandwork/cpd/cpd teaching/cpd-teaching-crd/nottinghamshirehandsonsupport-secondary-mathematics .htm. In Suffolk, a wide ranging website at http://www.suffolkmaths.co.uk/ gives links to training materials as well as teaching resources.

Details about the Career Entry and Development Profile are available online at http://www.tda.gov.uk/teachers/induction/cedp.aspx. The document itself and guidance for completing it are also available to download.

For further details about the induction year, the TDA website is the best place to look. The full link is http://www.tda.gov.uk/Recruit/becomingateacher/inductionyear.aspx

References

Chambers, P. (2007) 'Mathematics trainee teachers', in *Edge Hill Occasional Papers*, Autumn. Ormskirk: Edge Hill University.

National Foundation for Educational Research (NFER) (2006a) *Impact of Section 5 Inspections: Maintained Schools in England*. Online at the National Council for Educational Research website, http://www.nfer.ac.uk/research-areas/pims-data/summaries/ evaluation-of-the-impact-of-section-5.cfm (accessed 21 August 2007).

National Foundation for Educational Research (NFER) (2006b) *School Improvement: What Are Schools' Perceptions of Local Authority Support?* Online at the National Council for Educational Research website, http://www.nfer.ac.uk/publications/pdfs/downloadable/ ast06/annsurv06schoolimp.pdf (accessed 21 August 2007).

Office for Standards in Education (Ofsted) (2001) *Local Authority Support for School Improvement*. London: HMSO.

Office for Standards in Education (Ofsted) (2006a) *School Inspection: An Evaluation*. London: Office for Standards in Education.

Office for Standards in Education (Ofsted) (2006b) *Using the Evaluation Schedule: Guidance for Inspectors*. London: Office for Standards in Education.

Tanner, H. and Jones, S. (2000) *Becoming a Successful Teacher of Mathematics*. London: RoutledgeFalmer.

Training and Development Agency for Schools (TDA) (2007a) *Professional Standards for Teachers: Why Sit Still in your Career?* London: Training and Development Agency for Schools.

Training and Development Agency for Schools (TDA) (2007b) *Career Entry and Development Profile 2007/8*. London: Training and Development Agency for Schools.

INDEX

Added to a page number 't' denotes a table.